Living More with Less

●●●●●●●●●●●●●●●●●●●●●●●●●●

Doris Janzen Longacre
Introduction by Ronald J. Sider

HERALD
PRESS

Scottdale, Pennsylvania
Kitchener, Ontario

1980

Library of Congress Cataloging in Publication Data
Main entry under title:
Living more with less.
   Includes bibliographical references and index.
   1. Home economics. 2. Cost and standard of living.
3. Conduct of life. I. Longacre, Doris Janzen.
TX147.L58   640'.2   80-15461
ISBN 0-8361-1930-4 (pbk.)

Living More with Less

Copyright © 1980 by Herald Press, Scottdale, Pa. 15683
      Published simultaneously in Canada
      by Herald Press, Kitchener, Ont. N2G 4M5
Library of Congress Card Catalog Number: 80-15461
International Standard Book Number: 0-8361-1930-4
Design by Kenneth Hiebert
Printed in the United States of America

First printing, September 1980

Contents

Photographs of projects furnished
by contributors.

Photographs for chapter titles
in Part 2 by Kenneth Hiebert.

To Paul,
   whose gentle loving
helped bring
   hope to me
and life to this book

Introduction

●●●●●●●●●●●●●●●●●●●●●●●●●●

If you feel discouraged or alone in your pilgrimage toward simple living, if you have heard enough theory and want practical, concrete suggestions, if you are ready for challenge, read on. In this unique volume of personal testimonies woven together by superbly written, thought-provoking introductions, Doris Longacre offers an excellent combination of theory and practice.

At the heart of this exciting book are personal testimonies—scores of absorbing personal accounts of individuals and families struggling to be free from society's suffocating affluence. Each story is different. Each one captivates with its own unique magic.

In the past decade, many books, conferences, and declarations have vividly presented the need for a more simple way of living. Astonishing numbers of people have responded. What we have needed are good concrete models. This book fills that vacuum. Practical, workable models are here by the score. Nor are they theoretical models conceived by ivory-tower academicians. They are the personal testimonies of ordinary people all over the world who have begun the pilgrimage toward simplicity.

But, beware! Don't suppose that you should apply every one of the scores of illustrations presented here to your own life. The author is not saying that every serious Christian must imitate all (or 50.1%) of these models. She places vastly different illustrations side by side. She knows the story of an affluent family building a five-bedroom rather than a ten-bedroom house will help some people. The account of a new cave home will assist others. Find out where you are and let this book lead you into a joyful exploration of the next steps toward simplicity.

Approach this book as if it were an invitation to a treasure hunt rather than a summons to a final exam. Doris Longacre has no interest in legalism or works-righteousness. If you read each testimony as a standard by which to measure your life, you will misuse this book. And you may slide into depression! Instead, read it with the eager expectancy with which you begin a treasure hunt. The book is full of new ideas for you to discover. Hunting here for hints and suggestions to stimulate you and your family for the next steps in your pilgrimage will be a stimulating, challenging experience.

Writing an introduction for Doris Longacre's last book is a special privilege mixed, of course, with deep sadness. It was just a few short months ago that she sat with Arbutus and me at the U.S Consultation on Simple Lifestyle and asked us to help with this volume. Now she is gone—taken (prematurely it must seem from our human perspective) from her young children, her husband, and from all of us. Doris deeply affected the lives of hundreds of thousands of people around the world with her widely influential *More-with-Less Cookbook. Living More with Less* is her last gift to the church, the poor, and the Lord she served. May its powerful message stir us all to walk further along the path she carefully charted and joyfully trod.

Ronald J. Sider, Author
Rich Christians in an Age of Hunger

●●●●●●●●●●●●●●●●●●●●●●●●●●●

The Author

Doris Janzen Longacre, her husband, Paul, and daughters,
Cara and Marta, of Akron, Pennsylvania, are associated with
Mennonite Central Committee (MCC) and its worldwide
ministries "in the name of Christ."

Doris grew up in Elbing, Kansas, and Tucson, Arizona. She
attended Bethel College, North Newton, Kansas, and received
her BA in home economics from Goshen College, Goshen,
Indiana, in 1961. She also studied at Goshen Biblical Seminary
and Kansas State University.

She taught home economics at Hesston Academy and
College from 1961–63 and served along with her family in
MCC assignments in Vietnam from 1964–67 and in Indonesia
from 1971–72.

Doris was chairperson of the Akron Mennonite Church
from 1973–76, member of the Board of Overseers of Goshen
Biblical Seminary, Elkhart, Indiana, 1976–79, and a frequent
speaker and workshop leader at church conferences in Canada
and the United States.

In 1976 she compiled the *More-with-Less Cookbook,* which
has become a household item for persons wanting to cook more
responsibly in light of world food needs.

Doris's 39-month battle with cancer ended her life at 39
years.

Marta, Paul,
Cara, and Doris Longacre

Author's Preface

●●●●●●●●●●●●●●●●●●●●●●●●●

Journal Entry—January 10, 1979

This morning I want to begin writing the opening chapter of my book. . . .

Lord God, unless you write the book, I write in vain. Unless it's your message, why should we bother typing, editing, going through months of work and piles of paper—then publishing and selling?

This morning I plead for your Spirit in my thinking. I know I'm not writing the Bible, but still there must be inspiration. Unless you sit beside me—in me—at that typewriter, not much will happen. By now I know myself well enough to believe that.

God, I don't expect writing under your inspiration to be easy and fast and painless. My writing is always slow; it needs much revising. I'll do that. But Lord, please let it sing with your message, your glory, your beauty!

Journal Entry—January 15, 1979

God, help me. I feel a strong dependence on you from day to day now that I'm actually writing. To tell of the lives of your people around our world—your poor—it's such an enormous task. I don't know how to do it. How can I help unconvinced people see that their lives actually *do* affect the lives of the poor?

Another thing, God. Something in me rebels at reading and hearing more exploitation stories—more stories of suffering and repression. I want stories of hope, love, goodness. Perhaps you are showing me that somehow I don't really want to enter into the suffering of others. Forgive me. My own suffering has been sharp, but not caused by hard, wicked people and not *physically* severe, so I know only a little. Let me be willing. I can't write this book without being willing to enter in some way into the suffering of your people.

Journal Entry—September 14, 1979

God of the universe,
God of my person,
     today I come to you
     as a branch to the vine.

●●●●●●●●●●●●●●●●●●●●●●●●●●●

In fact I feel like one small
    and very droopy leaf.
You know from all the prayers
    of days past that this is another of my hard times.
I struggle today
    to cope with the task you've
    laid before me.
Your word says, "Unless the
    Lord builds the house . . ."
Does that mean,
    "Unless the Lord
    unravels my thinking,
    relaxes my muscles,
    restores my health,
    so that I can write the book"?
Perhaps it means,
    "Unless the Lord writes the book. . . ."
God of the universe,
God of my person,
    I am tired and afraid.
    So often afraid.
This morning I take my
    frayed bundle of faith
    and carry it to your door.
Unwrap it, fill it,
    rewrap and tighten it.
For today that means
    courage to forget the
    sleepless night just past,
    the tired back,
    tense chest and ribs,
    the uncertain stomach.
God of the lost sheep,
    come today and strengthen me
    for your work.
All Praise to You!
All Honor and Love, all Joy!

●●●●●●●●●●●●●●●●●●●●●●●●●●●

Journal Entry—October 6, 1979 (written in the Ephrata
Community Hospital)
Enough for now, I'm tired. But Lord, these too are days of
aliveness and I thank you for them. Keep my family in your
love. Keep my book on your timetable. Keep me patient.

Journal Entry—October 12, 1979
God, what do you want of me? I do not understand the
events into which I am plunged.
Third lung X-ray today—unchanged. Probably that
means no going home from the hospital tomorrow. And I'm
so near to finishing my book. If I could have just six weeks
of good health I could finish.
What is a virus, Lord? What is cancer? Only you know. So
I rest tonight in your peace.

Journal Entry—October 18, 1979
I confess to impatience, discouragement, and fear. Fear
that my lungs won't "open up" again. Fear that for weeks
and weeks I won't be able to work on my book.
Lord God, if it's not too much to ask, by your grace relax
these fears and give me daily small signs of hope, for I have
an impatient nature eager to be about your work.

Journal Entry—November 4, 1979 (written from Hershey
Medical Center)
I so much want to complete this book, one of the creative
works of my life. But weighed in the balance against more
time with Paul, Cara, and Marta, the book is like a dry
dandelion ready to blow. But I shouldn't have to make such
choices. If I get well enough to work on the book I will have
time with my family.

Doris died quietly, peaceably, and surrounded by family on
November 10, 1979, the manuscript not yet completed.
But the unfinished manuscript itself may be symbolic. The
task of living responsibly is never finished. In her preface to the
More-with-Less Cookbook Doris describes the search for more
responsible eating as a "kind of holy frustration." This holy
frustration for more-with-less living needs to continue in our
households, travel, recreation, and church life.

●●●●●●●●●●●●●●●●●●●●●●●●●●

The fact that others had to bring the book to completion is also symbolic. No one person is a final expert on the subject. We need help from each other. Doris had the primary inspiration and wrote Part One and all but the introductions to the chapters on transportation and church buildings. I finished these using her notes. Many others made this project a shared effort.

Approximately 500 people submitted material for this book, even though entries from only about 350 could be included.

Three persons made a special contribution to the book: Pat Hostetter Martin and Margaret Reimer helped to solicit and edit the entries; Gayle Gerber Koontz edited the text and helped Margaret and me shape the final manuscript.

Luis Correa, Jacob J. Enz, Tom Graff, Adeline Muller, Catherine Mumaw, Jean Rissler, Ron and Arbutus Sider, Peter Stucky, Perry and Elizabeth Yoder, and Don and Priscilla Ziegler read portions of the manuscript and offered suggestions, some of which have been incorporated into the final copy.

Bev Martin's competent typing and filing skills have helped immensely.

This book would not have been possible without the special cooperative arrangements between the author and Mennonite Central Committee. The office facilities, the inspiration and encouragement of the staff, and the particular help of William T. Snyder and Reg Toews were essential.

Usually the designer of a book receives only brief credit elsewhere. Ken Hiebert's role in this book and in the *More-with-Less Cookbook* merits more recognition than that. Working closely with the author from the book's inception, he insured creative integration of design and content.

Doris would have addressed a special thank you to her two daughters, Cara and Marta, who provided her with much joy, beauty, and inspiration.

The last paragraph of Doris's journal reflects a faith which continues to encourage our family and others in facing death—and life:

One more thing you say, Lord. "The eternal God is [my] . . . refuge, and underneath are the everlasting arms."

—*Paul Longacre*
Akron, Pennsylvania

13

More with less is not a
slogan—
it is a glimmer of hope
for disciples of Jesus
in an unjust world.
—J. Wilmer Heisey
  Elizabethtown, Pa.

Passing through a
barrio . . .
is no place for a person.
I feel as if the shacks are
holding their breath.
For an explosion?
Or to merely keep out
the smell?
—Shari Miller
  Tegucigalpa, Honduras

When someone steals a
man's clothes
  we call him a thief.
Should we not give the
same name
    to one who could
    clothe the naked
    and does not?
The bread in your
cupboard
    belongs to the hungry
    man;
the coat hanging unused
in your closet
    belongs to the man
    who needs it;
the shoes rotting in your
closet
    belong to the man
    who has no shoes;
the money which you
hoard up
    belongs to the poor.
—Basil the Great
  Bishop of Caesarea, c. 365

Consumers' Prayer

throwaway bottles
throwaway cans
throwaway friendships
throwaway fans

disposable diapers
disposable plates
disposable people
disposable wastes

instant puddings
instant rice
instant intimacy
instant ice

plastic dishes
plastic laces
plastic flowers
plastic faces

Lord of the living
transcending our lies
infuse us with meaning
recycle our lives
—Joyce M. Shutt
  Fairfield, Pa.
  Published in "The Mennonite"

It is not customary that
an intelligent person
clothes and cares for one part
of his body
and leaves the rest naked.
The intelligent person
is solicitous
for all his members.
Thus it should be
with those who are
the Lord's church and body.
All those born of God
are called into one body
and are prepared by love
to serve their neighbors.
—Menno Simons, 1552

Foreword

●●●●●●●●●●●●●●●●●●●●●●●●●●●

This is a book for people who know something is wrong with the way North Americans live and are ready to talk about change. This is a book about rediscovering what is good and true. This is a book about beauty, healing, and hope, a book about getting more, not less.

Volumes can be written on our unbelievable carelessness with God's gifts. We not only neglect the poor, for whom the gospel is to be good news—we exploit them. We nurture purses, professions, cars, and houses more than people. We relinquish freedom and personal productivity in favor of dull conformity. We spoil nature, the only home we have. We don't look beyond predictable, familiar voices for help. We fail to fortify each other in solid communities.

But if you do not already know all that, plus the fact that one fourth of our brothers and sisters in the world family are hungry, this book is not for you. Unless there is at least a whisper, and maybe a shout, within you against rich living, lay this aside.

Truth comes only to those who must have it, who want it badly enough. And gifts of healing come only to those willing to change. Jesus had his demands even for the blind and leprous. Go, wash in the Pool of Siloam. Show yourself to the priest. Sin no more. He had larger demands for the rich. Sell all and come.

There is hope for us
but no easy healing.
There is truth
but never without search.

There is beauty but only in the exercise of discipline and the control of waste. Our lives can be redeemed but only with lasting commitment to live under God's judgment and grace.

More with less, then, is no prepackaged way to "simplify your lifestyle." There is no fast, easy way. We can rehearse background facts, share experience, and distill standards to guide future decisions, as this book attempts to do. We can attend workshops and conferences, draw on still more experience, and collect a helpful library. But when we close the books and come home from the discussions, one voice still speaks in the silence. For Christians it is the call to obedience. Without answering that voice, and answering again and again, there is no new way to live. That much must be said from the beginning.

Styles and Standards

A book about lifestyles sounds more appealing than one about life standards. Style bears the stamp of the new, the distinctive, the fun. The word "lifestyle" itself is so new that dictionaries of the early seventies omit it altogether. Probably it's a word we began needing in the seventies because the way we lived changed so fast. We don't know yet if the word has staying power.

This book makes only limited use of "lifestyle." *Life standard* more aptly describes a way of life characterized by timeless values and commitments. I admit "standard" is rather lackluster. It doesn't have the zip and zing of "lifestyle," and has little to do with the latest models and fads, with chrome on cars or the color of bed sheets. Standard is a word that fits a way of life governed by more than fleeting taste. It is permanent and firm without being as tight as "rules."

Part One of this book discusses five life standards. These emerged from the materials which make up Part Two, materials submitted by many people struggling to live faithfully and simply.

In reality these standards cannot be easily separated. To number and analyze that by which we live does it some violence. Following and obeying Jesus Christ is never a list of responsibilities. It is perpetual response to the living God. Standards are divided and listed here only for ease in handling concepts. My hope is that after you absorb what's in this book the separate standards will melt together for you into a solid, integrated way of living.

More-with-Less Standards

Living by standards sounds like regulation, reminiscent of the third page of a private school catalog which spells out what you dare and dare not do if you want to remain on campus. But it need not mean holding to rigid rules which squeeze and pinch us.

More with less means that by using less we actually gain more for ourselves. The opening page of the *More-with-Less Cookbook* reads, "Put dismal thoughts aside . . . because this book is not about cutting back. This book is about living joyfully, richly, and creatively."[1] *Living More with Less* is built

on the same philosophy. So how does talk of the discipline of
living by standards really fit?

I can answer only this way. The trouble with simple living is
that, though it can be joyful, rich, and creative, it isn't simple.
Less of what? For more of what? And for whom? Every day
the average tradesperson or homekeeper makes a hundred
small decisions which, if you stop to think about what causes
what, become maddeningly complex. This book is
unapologetically about such small decisions. For example:

*Oh, not enough flour! I've got to take the car and run to the
store. No, I'll walk . . . I need the exercise . . . it's only a mile.
But I need the flour now. The bread must start rising or it won't
be done in time. I could buy the bread, but I do want to welcome
this family to our neighborhood with a nice meal . . . they seem
lonely . . . the rest of my meal is rather plain. I'll just grab my
purse and go before Ann gets home from kindergarten . . . oh,
there's hardly time!*

*Look, why am I always in a hurry? I've got to slow down, take
more time to think, see the clouds, listen to Ann . . . and
walking saves gasoline, energy. Everybody jumping into a car for
simple errands is one reason we get that statistic . . . what is it
. . . 6 percent of the world's population uses 40 percent of the
resources. That way of living makes other people poor.*

*But the flour. I need it. Now if the bike were here . . . but Bill
took it to work. What I really ought to have is another bicycle
just for my quick trips. But even good bikes cost plenty. The
flour! If my neighbor were home I could borrow it . . . but she
never has whole wheat anyway. We want to eat more whole
grains. . . . I've got to take the car. No way out.*

*Wait. Back up. I don't have to make bread today. That can
wait until I shop for the week . . . there's enough flour here for
that good muffin recipe. And, lucky me . . . I don't have to start
that until five o'clock. Ann and I can take a walk. . . .*

One tiny decision. Nothing that will change the world. But
that's the kind which form the building blocks of our lives. It's
the sort of decision on which we often falter if we slide
unthinkingly in the groove of our society. More-with-less
standards don't come naturally right now in North America.

Do justice. Cherish the natural order. Nurture people. These
and other standards must become second nature for Christians,
part of the heredity of our new birth.

Many decisions still will be hard. But strong standards
rooted in commitment to Christ offer hope for better choices.

The Testimonies

Part Two is a glimpse into the experiences of people trying to
live by standards of simplicity. The entries in this section invite
you to an old-fashioned testimony meeting. Christian response

in personal life to world poverty and hunger is the subject, with the voices in print instead of sound.

The voices you will hear come largely from the Anabaptist-Mennonite tradition. Notices asking for material were sent to church members through Mennonite and Brethren in Christ periodicals. This focus on Mennonites, one way of limiting the size of the "meeting," is not meant to imply that we have the answer to more-with-less living.

Testifying isn't easy. I sat in many testimony meetings as a child, and still occasionally hear our pastor call for words from the congregation. If I think I should speak, my palms still perspire and my knees tremble. Will people think my ideas foolish? Will they trust my experience? Is my life ever consistent enough that I dare open my mouth publicly? What I have to say is nothing new anyway!

These are the same feelings expressed by those who wrote (and sometimes refused to write!) for this book. Letters began in humble tones, often with some version of "undoubtedly you already have these ideas. They may not be usable anyway, but I'll share them just in case." Postscripts frequently read, "I know we haven't arrived" or "I know my living isn't really consistent." People everywhere confided that they *did* have ideas, but were afraid others might think them either proud or ridiculous. Some entries came only with firm promises from me that the book would clearly make this statement: no contributor believes his or her idea is right for every reader.

For help, let's look at what a testimony meeting tries to do. Such a meeting does not report how God always acts or how people always respond. It never assumes common experience—otherwise there would be no point at all in holding it! A testimony meeting expects that God gives unique skills and experiences to people and communities, and that sharing stories will strengthen everyone who hears. A testimony meeting believes in "many gifts, one Spirit." Accept in that framework what individuals offer through this book.

I believe the standards discussed here are all rooted in Scripture. That's why the list doesn't begin with "study the Bible." On the other hand, this book is not a thorough biblical study. Here the Bible is used as it traditionally has been used at testimony meetings—with familiarity and love, but with no attempt to look at all passages relevant to a subject. My writing and the entries from others lift up certain texts to show how they motivate action, connect with a story, or illuminate experience.

Note

1
Doris Janzen Longacre, *More-with-Less Cookbook* (Scottdale, Pa.: Herald Press, 1976), p. 12.

He who oppresses a poor man
insults his Maker,
but he who is kind to the needy
honors him.
—Proverbs 14:31

Rich and poor have this in common:
the Lord made them both.
—Proverbs 22:2, NEB

Do not lay up for yourselves
treasures on earth,
where moth and rust consume
and where thieves break in and steal,
but lay up for yourselves
treasure in heaven,
where neither moth nor rust consumes
and where thieves do not break in and steal.
For where your treasure is,
there
will your heart be also.
—Matthew 6:19–21

How blest are those of a gentle spirit;
they shall have the earth for their possession.
—Matthew 5:5, NEB

We trap God,
hang Him
in stained glass,
entrance Him
by organ music
and chorus

We bind Him
by ritual,
tickle Him
by prayers
and train Him
to become our pet.

And we freely
make Him
take off
our guilt
of exploiting
too much,

Of having
too much,
of wasting
too much,
of living
too comfortably
Once the desert God,
jealous
and wild;
now an amulet
on a charm
bracelet
—Yorifumi Yaguchi
  Sapporo, Japan

At a station in India

When I tried to eat,
suddenly
a small, dirty hand
came in front of me

and I saw the dark face
of a child
staring at me
with sunken eyes.

Embarrassed and even scared,
I put on his palm
a small piece of food and
quickly shut the window.

The train moved,
but his eyes kept
gazing at me—deeper
the more I pretended not seeing.

This of twenty years ago still
haunts me, and often
as I sit around the table
I feel his eyes gazing . . .
—Yorifumi Yaguchi
  Sapporo, Japan

Part 1
Living More with Less

	Do Justice
	Learn from the World Community
	Nurture People
	Cherish the Natural Order
	Nonconform Freely

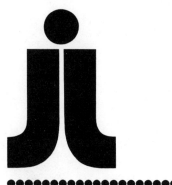

do justice

●●

Bertha Beachy, twenty years a missionary in East Africa,
makes this observation: "North Americans find it very hard to
believe that their wealthy ways of living affect poor people on
other continents. But in Africa, people are fully convinced that
North Americans and their actions strongly influence their
lives."

We're skilled at screening out and arguing away this
connection. We don't believe it, but the poor do. Marie Moyer,
a missionary in India, tells this story:

> In 1952 I was studying the Hindi language with my
> teacher, Panditji. From his philosophic mind, which
> probed the meaning of events and circumstances, I
> learned more than Hindi.
>
> I especially remember one lesson. It was
> Christmastime and as I awaited the arrival of Panditji,
> I quickly opened stacks of delightful cards,
> discarding the envelopes in the wastebasket. When
> Panditji entered the room, he sat down soberly and
> studied the situation. Then he solemnly scolded me
> in perfect English with these words, "The
> reverberation of this wasteful act will be felt around
> the world."
>
> Stunned, I asked, "What do you mean, Panditji?"
>
> "Those envelopes," he said, pointing to the
> wastebasket. "You could write on the inside of
> them."

Chagrined, I apologized and began taking them out of the basket. He carefully helped me, almost caressing each one. For every Hindi lesson he taught thereafter, I took notes on the back of an envelope. Our class also began sharing envelopes with his growing family, for he could not afford tablets for his children. Today I still carefully save paper in my home and office.

No Connection

A typical North American reaction to that story, however, is probably not to start saving paper. It's likely to be one of these two statements: "Okay, how? How does throwing out blank-on-one-side paper affect people on the other side of the globe? I don't see the connection." Or it may be, "What you say just makes me feel guilty. It's not good to raise all this guilt. We don't know what to do with it."

Let's look at the first reaction. I could now present pages of facts, statistics, and graphs to make a case for the link. This material would show, first, that North America actually imports a great many of the resources which underpin our way of life. And we import many of those resources at low prices from economically impoverished countries, while sending back ever higher-priced manufactured goods. Rich countries like Canada and the United States control the terms of those exchanges.

Second, we must talk about money, minerals, fuel, and human work hours wasted on the arms race, of which the United States is world leader and from which Canada also profits. Half the scientific researchers in the world work for the arms industry.[1] World military spending is now over one billion dollars a day, up more than 60 percent since 1960, even after allowing for inflation. Exports of weapons to low-income countries have quadrupled since 1960.[2]

Third, we must discuss how giant corporations, neither based in nor controlled by any one country, seize a kind of global power by using the land and labor of the poor to sell products to the rich. The human family is only beginning to understand this new power and to wonder how to deal with it. In an earlier time power rested largely with governments. If power was misused, people blamed the state and tried to change it. Governments still have power, but something new is at work which goes beyond the rule of the state. Economist John Kenneth Galbraith says:

When the modern corporation acquires power over markets, power in the community, power over the state, power over belief, it is a political instrument, different in form and degree but not in kind from the state itself.[3]

To really understand all this is to be awed and even terrified by the complexity of the connections. But we can never conclude that they don't exist! Part of the terror of the situation is that the connections are so tightly strung.

The reason all this is not thoroughly laid out here with statistics is that others have already done that work, and done it well. Two books published in the past decade are particularly helpful: *Rich Christians in an Age of Hunger*,[4] by Ronald J. Sider; and *Food First*,[5] by Frances Moore Lappé and Joseph Collins.

Sider addresses the question, How are we a part of sinful structures that contribute to world hunger? He analyzes our involvement in four areas: international trade, consumption of natural resources, food consumption and food imports, and profits to investments.[6] *Food First* outlines the need of poor nations to control access to their food resources. This book is rich in examples from specific countries and situations.

The witness of missionaries and service workers from many denominations about how our living patterns affect world hunger also fills church papers. These are our neighbors speaking, our fellow church members, our sons and daughters. Jim Bowman, an agricultural development worker, reports from Sumatra how that island is able to sell lumber but no plywood. Tariffs in Japan and other developed countries prevent underemployed Sumatrans from developing an industry they need. Christian journalist Dorothy Friesen writes from the Philippines how multinational food companies exploit impoverished laborers and take their land in order to market reasonably priced pineapple and bananas to affluent international customers, and bank huge profits at the same time.

Luis Correa, a Colombian Mennonite says,

"One good thing the United States could do would be to allow us to refine our petroleum.

They import our oil, refine it, then sell it back to us at an expensive price. So many times they exploit and then they leave. American enterprises have complete control over Colombian enterprises."[7]

Gordon Hunsberger, a retired Canadian farmer working in a Haitian agricultural development program, writes:

> The hard facts are that in order to raise significantly the standard of living of the many poor of the world it is necessary to lower the living standard of the rich. This means giving up some of the advantages the rich and

powerful have in favor of the poor. It means a kind of
political action and courage that has not yet been shown
among nations.[8]

Not Guilty

Refusing to accept a connection is one way to back off.
Believing it but refusing to accept guilt is another.

"Let's just be careful we don't raise too much guilt," says a
world hunger conference planner. "But you made us feel so
guilty about this coffee break," says the food committee
chairperson, passing out glazed doughnuts in the middle of the
meeting. "I guess we just go out of here feeling guilty,"
remarks the recreational vehicle manufacturer to his colleague
on his way out of the conference.

One thing is sure. How-to books on pop psychology of the
past fifteen years do not look fondly upon feeling guilty or
raising those feelings in anyone else. But what if you *are* guilty?

Is there no damage to the psyche of one who clearly
recognizes wrong in specific actions, but refuses to accept
responsibility? Can we squash down the guilt and blame it on
another? Statements like "This meeting, or this book, or that
person, or the poor of the world *make me feel guilty*" bear
careful scrutiny. From where comes the guilt? From those who
are poor? That's blaming the victim. From those who shared
the information? Or from us who live the way we do?

Imagine our current way of thinking superimposed on a
New Testament setting.

"Repent, you slippery snakes!" John the Baptist shouts. "Fill
the valleys and bring down the hills! How about a little more
equalization!"

"Don't make us feel guilty," responds the crowd. "Haven't
you heard that all of us need to feel okay?"

Instead the crowd asked, "What then shall we do?" And the
answer was clear. Repentance means to recognize and accept
guilt, to be forgiven, and then to change. John's answer could
hardly be more contemporary. "He who has two coats, let him
share with him who has none; and he who has food, let him do
likewise." Then on to the more complicated issues: Start doing
something about exploitation, respectable robbery, greed with
violence. Practice contentment.[9]

Certainly there are those who carry guilt out of its useful
function and into paralyzing complexes. But to live as most of
us do in North America, then to study world poverty and our
role in it, and to come away without seeing a need for
forgiveness and change—that is unthinkable.

Do justice must become the first standard for living by
which Christians make choices. Our knowledge of others'
needs and our guilt must resolve itself into a lasting

attentiveness. This means being mindful, conscious, aware, so
that never again can one make a decision about buying and
using without thinking of the poor. They lurk in the new-car
lot and behind the rack of fall outfits. They sit beside you in the
restaurant and wait for you in the voting booth.

This way of responding has a simplicity about it which
contrasts with the arguments usually called upon when
someone asks, "Does it do any good if I conserve?" Intricate
reasoning on the causes and solutions of world hunger has its
place. But there are times when the only answer is, "Because
they have little, I try to take less."

Remember the story of the Indian teacher who couldn't
watch his American student waste paper without honestly
exposing his feelings. The point is not only that a wasted
envelope reverberates around the world—or how in reality that
can happen. The point is that the student heard wasted
envelopes reverberate in the soul of her teacher who lacked
paper. And she could never be the same.

To make "do justice" a standard is to live by both reason
and compassion. The classic, universal truths of the Old and
New Testaments cut across our dodges and make escape
impossible:

> He has showed you, O man, what is good;
>> and what does the Lord require of you
> but to do justice, and to love kindness;
>> and to walk humbly with your God?
> Micah 6:8

> But if any one has the world's goods and sees his brother in
> need, yet closes his heart against him, how does God's love
> abide in him?
> 1 John 3:17

Simple Living Isn't Enough

I don't apologize for the seeming unimportance of individual
entries which make up this book. All of us should walk more,
save hot water, use less aluminum foil. These are small ideas,
small acts. But they offer a realistic place to start.

Doing justice, however, demands much more. The message
here is mainly one of first steps. This collection is about putting
our own houses in order. Yet in that process we invariably
move on to economic and political issues.

Actually, the two realms—conserving resources at home and
taking on economic and political issues—are as inseparable as
the yolk and white of a scrambled egg. It never works to say,
"I'll stop using paper towels and driving a big car, but I won't
take this world hunger thing past my own doorpost." Once an
egg yolk breaks into the white, there's no way to remove every
tiny gold fleck. Just so, once you walk into a supermarket or
pull up to a gas pump, you *are* part of the economic and
political sphere.

Certainly your influence is small. But whether you conserve or waste, it is real. *Many* people using or not using affects things in a *big* way. Gathering up the fragments of our waste— recycling, conserving, sharing—is a logical and authentic beginning. Such actions are the firstfruits of the harvest of justice. They are the promise of more to come.

The fact is that living by the standard "do justice" will draw us more deeply into economics and politics.

And for the sake of the poor and hungry, that's good. Solutions for their needs will come primarily through economic and political change.

But what does it mean to work for these large changes? One simple involvement is writing letters to lawmakers, even though the issues are complex. Since matters of justice and related legislation change with each community, country, and passing week, this book looks only at long-range goals. But the end of this chapter lists resources and organizations with a Christian perspective whose purpose is to keep citizens up-to-date on economic and political matters affecting the poor. These groups evaluate current legislation and suggest action.

What actions on the international economic and political scene are most needed to alleviate poverty and hunger? The following ideas come from papers prepared for this book by E. Wayne Nafziger, economist at Kansas State University, and Delton Franz, Mennonite Central Committee representative in Washington, D.C.

1.

Import-Export Agreements. Poor nations cannot resolve their people's need for improved income unless international export markets open for their products. Affluent countries should lower tariff barriers, especially those against manufactured and processed goods from poor countries.

2.

New International Economic Order. Poor countries must be given a stronger voice in international agencies which control the economic order. These include the International Bank for Reconstruction and Development, the International Monetary Fund, the General Agreements for Tariffs and Trade, and United Nations economic agencies. These agencies, especially the International Monetary Fund which sets rules for exchange rates and capital flow, are now dominated by rich countries.

3.

Corporate Farming. Cheap land and labor and low taxes now prompt North American-based corporations to operate massive farms in poor countries. This ties up land needed to produce nutritious crops for local use. The international system needs rules to govern multinational corporations to assure that poor countries benefit from their own resources.

4.

Global Unemployment. For many hungry people the primary problem is not food shortage but lack of income. The United Nations estimates 300 million people are already unemployed or underemployed. Urge more labor-intensive industry in developing countries, codes of conduct for multinational corporations including responsibility to pay fair wages, support of the United Nations International Labor Organization and its programs, and a challenge to repressive governments to allow workers to organize for just wages.

5.

Development Assistance and Grain Reserve. North America should make more creative efforts to design and support aid programs which meet the basic needs of poor countries. Current grants, loans, and agricultural assistance are not only minimal, but often support the interests of local elites or foreign donors. Aid should emphasize labor-intensive and appropriate technology, integrating women into development, and human rights reforms. North America should also lead in establishing a world grain reserve to meet emergency needs.

6.

No Enemies. We should not cut off economic ties with poor countries which remove themselves from the capitalist orbit.

7.

Arms Sales and Police Training. Through arms sales and credit arrangements, the United States and Canada supply developing countries more weapons than do all other countries combined. By selling tools for repression and offering police training to elitist military regimes, we help the rich who control land and food production to suppress the poor. Urge governments to stop arms sales to countries which deprive people of human rights and economic development opportunities.

8.

Farm Policy. Work for revised North American farm policies which will safeguard small family farms, assure equitable returns, and reduce "bigness" with its dependency on agribusiness corporations for costly petrochemicals and farm equipment.

Entries in Part Two which reflect concern for doing justice are marked with the symbol 𝕛𝕝

Helpful Organizations
Bread for the World
32 Union Square East, New York, N.Y. 10003
Telephone 212–260–7000
GATT-*Fly*
11 Madison Ave., Toronto, Ont., Canada M5R 2S2
Telephone 416–921–4615
Interreligious Taskforce on U.S. Food Policy
110 Maryland Ave., N.E., Washington, D.C. 20002
Telephone 800–424–7292
NETWORK: *A Catholic Social Justice Lobby*
806 Rhode Island Ave., N.E., Washington, D.C. 20018
Telephone 202–526–4070

Notes

1
From a speech delivered by Henk Koosen,
Netherlands, at the Mennonite World Conference,
Wichita, Kan., July 28, 1978.

2
Ruth Leger Sivard, *World Military and Social
Expenditures* (Leesburg, Va.: WMSE
Publications, 1978), p. 6.

3
John Kenneth Galbraith, "Power and the Useful
Economist," *American Economic Review* (March
1973), p. 6.

4
Ronald J. Sider, *Rich Christians in an Age of
Hunger* (Downers Grove, Ill.: InterVarsity Press,
1977).

5
Frances Moore Lappé and Joseph Collins, *Food
First: Beyond the Myth of Scarcity* (New York:
Houghton Mifflin, 1977).

6
Sider, p. 139.

7
Interview conducted by Linda Shelly at the
Mennonite World Conference, Wichita, Kan.,
August 1978.

8
Gordon Hunsberger, *Women's Missionary and
Service Commission Voice* (July 1976), p. 9.

9
Luke 3:7–14.

learn from the
world community

If you as a North American travel to an economically poor country such as Haiti or Bangladesh, your first reaction is likely to be shock. You have heard of poverty, and seen it in pictures. But to find yourself face to face with hungry people jars your soul with feelings for which you are unprepared.

After a time, shock gives way to ideas for development projects typically conducted by church agencies. These usually promote better education, nutrition, agriculture, sanitation, family planning, small business investments, and, increasingly, a concern that people receive just access to resources. These are the problems we believe need attention, though of course we are always in danger of misreading needs and running ahead or to the side of those actually involved.

These reactions are certainly warranted. God help us when poverty no longer shakes us into action. But how rarely we realize that persons from other countries often go through a similar thought process when living with us!

What if we asked them for help with our problems? What if the flow of development assistance became two-way? It's exciting to dream about the possibilities. As a beginning, the United States Department of Agriculture could invite a thousand Chinese advisers to show the School Lunch Program how to prepare vegetables!

"We think we know it all, the poor peasants know nothing,

and we are going to go and tell them what to do," says Romeo
Maione, of the Canadian International Development Agency.
"Many of the world's poor survived for thousands of years
with none of our technology. That feat takes wisdom worth
learning about."[1]

For we, of course, have problems too. No one wants to hear
the whole sordid list again, but it begins with materialism,
violence in streets and homes, family breakdown, drug and
alcohol abuse, automobile accidents, poor diet and
degenerative diseases, waste of material resources, pollution,
and nuclear proliferation. What if we became as concerned
with our *over*development or *mal*development as we are with
the *under*development of poor nations? Would they have
anything to say? Could they help?

Consider this imaginary list of development projects for
North America, suggested by the comments of Mennonite
Central Committee Exchange Visitors who have lived and
worked in North America for a year and by other international
guests. I include European and Japanese opinion. Although
their countries might also be considered overdeveloped, they
offer an especially helpful resource, since they manage a high
standard of living on half or less the food and energy consumed
per person in North America.

Project One: Building an energy-efficient public transportation
network among small towns and cities.
   Both the United States and Canada are automobile
   countries. It's quite inconvenient for people who do not have
   their own.—**Mari Nagao, Japan**
   The large and comfortable cars impress me. People waste
   lots of energy by using them. They don't like to go ten
   steps—they always need their cars. They have large cars,
   although only one person uses them. Some older couples
   have two big cars.—**Barbara Walz, West Germany**
   Children in high school here go by car—sometimes even
   their own car! Almost everybody in Holland who goes to
   school or college goes by bike or motorcycle. Schools don't
   have parking space for cars.—**Antina Bennink, Netherlands**

Project Two: Learning to cook simple, nutritious meals. This
would include conserving meat and fats, and accepting more
fruits and vegetables, fewer sweets, and less waste.
   In the Netherlands you don't see so many people who are
   all out of proportion.—**Alle Hoekema, Netherlands**
   Americans have too much good food. If they open their eyes
   they will realize how many people lack food and that some
   starve. I cannot understand it when I sit beside someone in
   church here and he gives twenty-five cents to the offering.
   Terrible! I know he earns forty dollars a day and I know he
   has too much good food.—**Leonard Triyono, Indonesia**

Americans eat lots of cookies. There is always a can with sweet things nearby—you only have to reach out and put it in your mouth. From the Austrians, Americans could learn to use more "full food" [opposite of "empty calories"] such as whole wheat, raw fruits, and vegetables.—**Sylvia Furgler, Austria**

During our three years overseas, we were impressed with the thrift of Koreans. They balanced their diet without much spending. For example, in summer they tied carrot, radish, and onion tops (which we discard) into small bunches, hung them under the eaves to dry, then stored them. In winter these were finely chopped and added to the daily soup for flavor and nourishment. They suffered few dietary diseases and had good teeth.—**Gladys and Walter Rutt, Mississippi**

Children don't like vegetables? No, I never heard of that in my country!—**Taiwanese nutrition student, Kansas State University**

On the tables in North America you see more than four kinds of food.—**Elias Acosta, Dominican Republic**

Project Three: Using few kitchen appliances. This includes energy-saving skills in cooking such as cutting food in small pieces and cooking only a brief time, stacking kettles on a single heat source, cooking only once a day.

Most Americans don't live very simply. The money they waste by buying a dishwasher can better be sent to developing countries where people perish with hunger. The use of dishwashers and other electric things is much lower in Holland.—**Ellen Orthmann, Netherlands**

To cook we use firewood or gas which are more economical than electricity. We prepare everything before we fire the stove to cook.—**Guillermo Abanco, Philippines**

We think Americans could live without appliances like dishwashers, electric knives, and can openers. In Paraguay we don't use as much fuel partly because we don't have so much equipment. When I was in Indiana during an unusually cold winter we were told to cut back on fuel. Our family couldn't find anywhere to cut! But some of our neighbors were able to cut back 20 percent. Why don't they do it all the time?—**Anni Weichselberger, Paraguay**

Project Four: Living without disposables, setting up community systems for repair and recycling, reducing waste.

America is a wasteful society. In every store you see disposable things. People want everything to go fast, so after using things once, they throw them away.—**Jusef Sumadi, Indonesia**

People in North America don't care to repair things once they are out of order. There are few repair shops. I cannot

imagine how many TVs and refrigerators are put into junk
which are repairable.—**Guillermo Abanco, Philippines**

Project Five: Planting home and community gardens.
Chi Sau, our domestic helper in Vietnam, lived in a two-
room cardboard and plywood home she shared with a family
of eight. Her wages covered only their rice and salt.
Wherever we lived, she requested use of the flower beds for
planting vegetables.
   Back in Canada, we remember Chi Sau and others in her
situation. We try to cut out overconsuming, have a large
garden, and accept produce as payment for farm labor.
—**Claire Ewert, Drake, Saskatchewan**
American communities are beautiful. But instead of growing
vegetables or fruits, the people prefer grass and spend money
taking care of it.—**Guillermo Abanco, Philippines**
In Germany urban apartment dwellers like ourselves can
rent garden plots situated on the outskirts of cities. For
thirty years we enjoyed our plot. We often spent afternoons
and evenings there. During summer the children and I began
our hike to the garden immediately after sunrise. We took
our food along and sat under a small canopy if it rained. In
some areas gardeners are permitted to sell produce from
these plots in the stores.—**Mary Woelke, West Germany**

Project Six: Valuing family ties and friendship above making
money.
   In the cities everything travels so fast that we can hardly
find people who value cooperation, love, and understanding.
They just value their time for money, money, money. The
poor dream of having wealth like the rich, and thus there are
many robberies and other sorts of crimes.—**Leonard
Triyono, Indonesia**
North Americans have to work more in order to buy things.
For that reason they spend less time with their families,
thinking that to be comfortable is more important for the
family than to give them love and time together.—**Inez
Morales de Rake, Bolivia**
One thing I hope never changes in my country as it becomes
more modern is the way families live together. I feel terrible
when I see how your old people are treated.—**Sammy
Sacapano, Philippines**
When people have fewer possessions it is easier for them to
be satisfied with what they do have—each other, for
instance.—**Ellen Orthmann, Netherlands**
The Koreans, with whom we lived for three years, had time
to meet with God every morning at five o'clock for a period
of prayer.—**Walter and Gladys Rutt, Mississippi**

Project Seven: Building simpler, less expensive facilities for
churches.
> People in North America have more facilities for everything
than one can imagine. How can they spend so much
knowing there are people even in their own country who
need these things?—**Luis Correa, Colombia**
> Christians in North America seem to be members of the
good class of society. In France it's not like here. There are
more poor people in my church.—**Maryline Filleur, France**
> When we first walked into a North American church, my
friend from Indonesia said, "The cost of this carpet alone
would build a beautiful church in Indonesia."—**Sammy
Sacapano, Philippines**
> People in North America are rich and wear fine clothes, even
Christians. Clothes are so expensive in my country that I
wear only used clothes, and even those are expensive. I
suggest rich church groups come visit Latin America and let
our church be in charge of the tour. We can show them what
they need to see to understand.—**Pastor from Latin America**

It isn't hard to hear us North American realists responding
to the idea of development projects carried on *here* by *them*.
We know why it wouldn't work. Let imagination carry you
through the discussion:
*First of all, they would have to understand that these things
just aren't economically feasible here. Repairing everything.
Buses between small towns. Our system doesn't operate that
way! Probably those people weren't here very long and don't
really understand us. Anyway, it's not the sort of thing our
government promotes. Besides, many of the things they do just
aren't part of our culture. You can't get people to change so
easily. And they don't know our language—they can't begin to
speak it without an accent. Nobody would listen to them. No,
we'd better figure out our own problems in our own way.*

We don't want to accept advice from outside, especially from
people so different from ourselves. I, too, believe their ideas
can't be imposed directly on us.

But can we not realize that these are exactly the same
adjustments we ask people of other countries and cultures to
make when we go to them? All the above arguments against
development work they might carry on *here* are simply
reversals of the problems our missionaries and service workers
contend with daily over there. The poor are also pretty sure
some new seeds and irrigation methods aren't economically
feasible, and sometimes they're right! We subject our hearers to
faltering attempts at their language, or even expect them to
learn ours. And although we're becoming more sensitive, we
still introduce ideas foreign to other cultures. A few ideas take,
many do not. Overall, we have to be satisfied with small gains.

But still we believe in Christ's mandate to go and tell and
share.

Today Christian churches are solidly rooted in most
economically poor countries. Our responsibility to share and
tell doesn't necessarily diminish, but something new is added—
the responsibility to accept and listen. If we will, we can call it
a privilege, an opportunity to grow. Now we have a mirror to
hold to ourselves. We have loving brothers and sisters around
the world ready to wipe the fog from that mirror and tell us
how they see our lives in light of God's kingdom.

To listen is more than good worldwide church politics. It's
more than interesting cross-cultural exchange.

The best reason
for listening to
and learning from
the poor
is that this is one way
God is revealed to us.

As the conference of Latin American Catholic bishops affirmed
in 1979, "The testimony of a poor church can evangelize the
rich."

The Apostle James' well-known treatise on the relationship
of rich and poor can be summarized with these central words,
"Listen, my beloved brethren. Has not God chosen those who
are poor in the world to be rich in faith and heirs of the
kingdom which he has promised to those who love him?"
(James 2:5).

Look carefully at that paragraph in James. There's no way
"poor" can be spiritualized. The Apostle Paul also repeatedly
emphasizes the strength of weakness: "God chose what is
foolish in the world to shame the wise, God chose what is weak
in the world to shame the strong" (1 Corinthians 1:27). In
Jesus' parable of the rich man and Lazarus, even the rich man
finally decides Lazarus would be the best possible missionary to
his affluent brothers, although by the time he figured that out it
was too late. Like us, the rich man had no ears for Lazarus
while he lived; it took the next world to clarify his thinking. If
we cannot learn from the poor, why should we claim to follow
one born in a barn and executed with thieves?

We have far to go in bringing reverse development to North
America, but it has already begun. At the 1978 Mennonite
World Conference in Wichita, Kansas, a Spanish-speaking
Bible study group left the following notes:

Someone from Latin America said they appreciated
Mennonite Central Committee workers not just for the work

they did, but also because their presence gave the local church
and community a chance to teach some North Americans
about simple living and issues of justice. They felt these
workers then went back home willing and better able to live
responsibly with a world perspective. The group felt that a
voluntary service unit made up of people from poorer world
areas and North Americans committed to a simple life and a
just society could make an impact if placed in a rich
Mennonite community.

Entries in Part Two which show people learning from the
world community are symbolized with an **⌐**

Note

1
Speech given by Romeo Maione at the Mennonite
Central Committee Annual Meeting in Kitchener,
Ont., January 1978.

nurture people

●●●

In the hard decisions of living, to choose that which *nurtures
people* is another guiding standard.

Nurturing is feeding, but it is more than feeding. In the
musical words of invitation that open Isaiah 55, the writer
begins by offering food and drink.

"Ho, every one who thirsts,
  come to the waters;
and he who has no money,
  come, buy and eat!"

The call is to come to a bountifully stocked grocery store—
but then the twist! *The store has no cash register.* The food is
free. Now Isaiah poses his real question: "Why do you spend
your money for that which is not bread, and your labor for that
which does not satisfy?" "Eat what is good," he says, "that
your *soul* may live" (Isaiah 55:2, 3, emphasis added). Then
follows a glorious vision of what can be—living by covenant
and love, with peace, and culminating in redemption of the
natural order. Nurturing includes all actions which bring
others to this full life and growth in the kingdom of God.

A Kentucky farmer and writer, Wendell Berry, says that to
understand our own time and predicament we can view
ourselves as divided between exploitation and nurture. He
describes a division not only between but also within persons.
Here is how Berry explains it:

> The standard of the exploiter is efficiency; the
> standard of the nurturer is care. The exploiter's goal
> is money, profit; the nurturer's goal is health—his
> land's health, his own, his family's, his community's,
> his country's. . . . The exploiter wishes to earn as
> much as possible by as little work as possible; the
> nurturer expects, certainly, to have a decent living
> from his work, but his characteristic wish is to work
> *as well* as possible. The competence of the exploiter
> is in organization; that of the nurturer is in order. . . .
> The exploiter typically serves an institution or
> organization; the nurturer serves land, household,
> community, place. The exploiter thinks in terms of
> numbers, quantities, "hard facts"; the nurturer in
> terms of character, condition, quality, kind. . . . The
> exploitive always involves the abuse or the
> perversion of nurture.[1]

To make choices which nurture each other, we must always be asking the question: What do we want for ourselves and the persons we love? That's hard enough to answer. But then comes another question: Is what we *say* we want borne out by our choices? For example, in the last chapter Inez Morales de Rake from Bolivia says Americans think comfort is more important than time for family fellowship. Few people Inez learned to know in her North American visit would say that. But actions define their values more clearly than words.

Work and Getting Out of It

One common trap in our society leads people to make choices which at first seem to nurture people but in the end erode human productivity. This is the trap of buying more and more labor-saving devices.

Work-saving inventions can be good for people. My mother shudders every time she sees an old-fashioned washboard refinished and turned into a wall hanging. She remembers her bleeding fingers as she struggled at age fourteen to finish the laundry piled up by eight brothers. She thanked God for Maytag.

In an earlier time, to sweat and labor to stay alive was the only option, except for a few of the elite. This is how life orders itself still for most people in poor countries.

What we forget today is that while labor-saving devices are not all bad, neither is labor. The danger now in North America is that too many labor-saving devices will atrophy our ability to respond resourcefully to the environment. Without electricity people no longer know how to warm a room, cook a meal, or keep themselves happy through an evening at home. Without an engine they have no way to raise food or to travel.

Genuine need to respond to the environment brings out creative response in people. The Creator fashioned us in his image—therefore, to be fully human we also must create. Our moral and physical senses should always be at work in a situation to tell us what we need and what to do about it. But when every possible need is satisfied before we even have a chance to perceive and respond to it, creativity and resourcefulness can't flourish.

We become victims of the great disease of technological society— meaninglessness.

This disease is not caused by bacteria, virus, or vitamin deficiency. It's caused by having nothing important to do.

Besides damaging the human spirit, unquestioning dependence on machines is bad for the human body. One of the big jokes of the century is the way we North Americans have to step out of our comfortable cars and run to stay alive. Henry Fairlie, essayist for the *Washington Post,* analyzes it like this:

> **The American people may be the first to make a complete dissociation between living and leisure, regarding it as wrong to have to make any physical effort in order to live, but quite right to compensate by straining themselves in exercise. I am guilty myself by using an electric typewriter . . . but at least I chop my own vegetables. . . . [Chopping] is concentrated physical effort, it is a skill, it is always thoroughly enjoyable, and I can probably chop a leaf vegetable very fine as quickly as any. If I left this to an electrical gadget, I would have to take my fingers jogging.[2]**

Another way in which labor-saving devices defy nurture is that they can be offered as imitation love. A husband gives a food processor for his wife's birthday instead of regularly helping her cook. She gives him a cordless weed trimmer to clean the lawn's edge instead of joining him outdoors with a grass clipper or hoe. Together they offer bedroom television sets to their children instead of hikes or the opportunity to talk. They can choose to cook, garden, and relax with others and nature, or substitute machines. Which choice nurtures people?

"But we haven't got time," is the certain cry. True, the choice is ambiguous. A dishwasher may mean a family can spend time reading aloud or helping a neighbor garden. And a strong desire to do everything "by hand" may mean that a person has less time to spend with a child or grandparent. Observation tells me, however, that those with many machines are not less harried. A machine itself must be nurtured— selected, worked for, oiled, kept clean, repaired, and stored, not

to mention filling out and mailing its ID card—or warranty!
Labor-saving devices soon become labor-making devices.

Some families, especially those where the adults are called by
vocation or necessity to work outside the home, are exploring
other alternatives. Rather than buying more machines, some
hire people who need or want work to help with household
tasks. Neighbors and church members trade labor and goods.
Others deliberately choose to work part time or to arrange for
one adult to work at home to free the household to nurture
others. We often forget that laughing, crying people can
redeem by nurture the otherwise menial job.

Nurture, Contentment, and Health

After two years as a volunteer in Nepal, Willard Unruh of
Newton, Kansas, visited his hometown and wrote these words:

Just about everyone is busy. I began wondering if Western
society is overstimulated. We see a good play on Friday
night that moves us deeply. Before we have a chance to
digest it, there's a sports event on Saturday night, a probing
sermon on Sunday morning. We get the same glassy feeling
one has from driving too long a stretch at one time.[3]

As medicine for the problem Unruh describes, meditation
groups and silent retreats are popping up in every community.
This treatment will help, if getting to these events doesn't cause
more stress than it cures. But we should also look for
prevention.

How do we nurture each other with choices that offer more
calm, quiet, and time to reflect on and integrate life? Nurturing
people surely involves a commitment to reduce stress.

Medical experts
now estimate
that 80 percent
of diseases
are directly linked
to frantic living.

We have the options of going and doing and being. Our
heavy energy investment provides the ever-ready car and
airplane. Our generation doesn't have to milk the cows or keep
the hearth fire burning or stay home to cook for Grandpa. We
can run. But accepting these options without control is
destructive.

It sounds too simple, even for a book on simple living. But
when we are more content to stay at home, to think and to
pray, we are better able to nurture each other.

Part of nurture is good health care. With medical costs

soaring, what more-with-less standards should we observe?
Seven rules which couldn't be cheaper to implement are getting
increasing attention in preventive health care. Dr. Nedra
Belloc studied the relationship between living patterns and life
expectancy. She centered on these habits:
—Three meals a day, avoiding snacks
—Breakfast every day
—Moderate exercise two or three times a week
—Seven or eight hours of sleep at night
—No smoking
—Moderate weight
—No alcohol, or only in moderation

Belloc found that a 45-year-old man with six or seven of
these habits could expect to live eleven years longer than one
with only two or three.[4] A study by Belloc and Dr. Lester
Breslow indicated that a man who had six or seven of these
habits was as healthy as a man *thirty years younger* who had
only one or two. The significance of this finding jumps into
focus when you consider that between 1900 and 1970, life
expectancy for white forty-year-old men increased by only *half
a year,* despite all medical advances of that period.[5]

In other words, doctors and pills don't work the big
miracles. It's the way we live that counts.

Nurture and Security

Recall again Inez Morales de Rake's observation that
earning money is not necessarily good nurture for those we
love. But in our world, money is security. And surely those
who love their families will want to provide security.

For many people security is the life insurance policy, the
prepaid college education, the expanding business, the
comfortable retirement plan. All these are choices that seem to
nurture. Yet too often these choices mean second jobs, late
working hours, frequent long-distance travel, and no one at
home when children come from school. When does time spent
nurturing children to be strong and responsible become the
better part—better even than an assured higher education?
Might time used to build family and community ties offer more
security than life insurance? Finally, how can people dependent
on money for security be nurtured to depend on God? Do they
need God at all?

Hear some African insight into security:

A pastor from Zaire visited North America. After we
traveled together several days visiting homes and churches, he
announced to me, "We'll get to heaven before you. In fact, you
might not get there at all!"

"What on earth do you mean?" I asked.

"You have everything you could ever need," replied the
Zairean. "Why should you go to heaven?"—Fremont Regier,
Kansas

If you are strong inside, you will survive. If you have beautiful cars, clothes, and houses but are empty inside, when the crunch comes you will cave in.—Motlalepula June Chabaku, South Africa

One of the most pervasive things we learned from Africans is dependence on God. No day, the safety of no journey, is taken for granted. Life is in God's hands. The Ashanti tribe expresses it with the phrase "Except God—but for God—" The Efik people put it in their common everyday greetings: "May you live to see another day." "Thank God, you have seen another day."

If one has such an awareness of God's care, life and all within it is a gift. Then it is easy to live out more with less.

We Westerners think we deserve a comfortable life—not riches, perhaps, but certainly a decent house, an education for our children, enough to eat, new clothing every year. We attribute such comforts not to God, the Maker and Giver, but think in terms of my job, my salary, my family, my money, my needs. Whereas the African personality thinks, "But for God. . . ." —Delores Friesen, Accra, Ghana

Entries in Part Two which report choices made to nurture people are symbolized with **P**

Notes

1
Wendell Berry, *The Unsettling of America: Culture and Agriculture* (New York: Avon Books, 1978), pp. 7–8.

2
Henry Fairlie, "America's Real Energy Crisis," *The Washington Post* (June 24, 1979), p. G8.

3
Mennonite Central Committee News Service, December 1, 1978.

4
Donald M. Vickery, *Life Plan for Your Health* (Reading, Mass.: Addison-Wesley Publishing Co., 1978), p. 23.

5
Ibid.

cherish the natural order

When I was a child, farm home walls in our Kansas community were decorated mainly with calendar pictures provided by the co-op or grain elevator. Summer-month pages usually treated us to nature scenes of pristine beauty. Purple-blue mountains, always snowcapped, towered behind cool reflecting lakes framed with pine trees.

My father, prairie grime trickling down his neck from a hot morning at the thresher, would stand in the even hotter kitchen at noon, look at that calendar, and contemplate that somewhere there was land created so beautiful that its only purpose was to be viewed. It must have been at such times that he planned our family vacations.

When work slacked off, regular August trips took us to every national park in the West. In our 1950 Pontiac we took every mountain pass on the maps, peering through the windshield for signs announcing a scenic view ahead. For this we had come! Later I loved looking at the color slides Daddy carefully snapped at those stops. Sometimes he captured mountains, lakes, and pine trees in perfect composition—just like the calendars! A few slides did show our somewhat rumpled family in the foreground gazing off into the view. But my favorites were always pure nature, empty of people.

People in the Pictures

Today people still hope to preserve those untouched places,

those scenic resources which remind us what nature is like
before humans take over. Conservation societies now print no-
people pictures in their fund-raising brochures. Maybe this will
indeed aid the battle against aluminum can litter and service
station signs towering into the clouds. We badly need
untracked wilderness as a checkpoint from which civilization is
taking us. Mostly we need it to give us the humbling experience
of leaving something alone.[1]

But the still bigger task is to put people successfully into our
nature pictures. Not just dreamy-eyed lovers strolling a lonely
beach. Not three hikers with backpacks on a mountain trail, or
sunny-haired children gathering wildflowers. We need nature
pictures that can include without being ruined what we
honestly need in order to live—farms, factories, roads, homes,
places to live and work and relax. Right now we seem to know
instinctively that the way we do these things often spoils the
scene.

We destroy instead of accommodate because, strangely, we
see ourselves pitted in battle against nature. An oil company
commercial cries, "Nature is tough, but we are tougher." An
international materials systems company advertises like this:

Progress
has become a matter
of doing what nature never intended.

Doing it with materials nature never dreamed of.

Man wants to touch the moon and farm the sea.

Man
wants a world of highers and deepers,
hotters and colders,
strongers,
lighters,
fasters,

And nature hands him some wood, some rock, and some
ores.

But tomorrow is beyond the limits of these.

However poetic, this is nothing less than a war whoop
against nature. This attitude has characterized the
development of North America ever since European settlers
first came and displaced native peoples. By contrast, the
Indians harmonized their lives with earth's restrictions.

Sioux Chief Luther Standing Bear says Indians never
thought of nature as wild or a wilderness to be tamed. Earth
was bountiful and surrounded its people with blessings. "When
the very animals of the forest began fleeing from his [the white
man's] approach, then it was that for us the 'Wild West'
began."[2]

Again, those apparently too poor or powerless to know
anything become our teachers. The Wintu Indians of
California, more out of respect than thrift, burned only dead
wood for fuel and used every portion of a hunted animal's
carcass. Says an old Wintu woman:
> The white people never cared
> for land or deer or bear.
> When we Indians kill meat,
> we eat it all up.
> When we dig roots
> we make little holes.
> When we build houses,
> we make little holes. . . .
> We shake down acorns and pine nuts.
> We don't chop down the trees. . . .
> But they chop it down and cut it up.
> The spirit of the land hates them.
> They blast out trees
> and stir it up to its depths. . . .
> Everywhere the white man has touched it
> [the land], it is sore.[3]

A Peace Treaty with Nature
Humankind's most violent acts against the environment took
place in the past two hundred years. Today we have the means
to make our home totally uninhabitable. One standard for
living for modern Christians must be to cherish again the
natural order. Even if our environment were not in present
danger, simply obeying what the Bible says about our
relationship to the earth requires such care.

The following ideas on people and nature are mainly from
Willard Swartley's study, "Biblical Sources of Stewardship."[4]

First, Scripture clearly states that because God created
everything, God is owner of all. "The earth is the Lord's and
the fulness thereof, the world and those who dwell therein"
(Psalm 24:1). In the church we talk about stewardship of land
and possessions. It must be clear that, according to the Bible,
this never means judicious use of what is *ours*. Faithful care of
what actually belongs to God is the only biblical perspective.

Second, the truth that we are created in God's image has
bearing on our relationship to the earth. We are to care for the
natural order as God cares for it. In the biblical Hebrew "to
till" means to serve the land. But Genesis 3 and 4 records that
humankind's first and lasting sin is refusal to *be* God's image.

Instead of
representing God's rule,
we choose to be like God.

We act not as caretakers, but as owners. We usurp the right to exploit and waste. With shameless greed for profit we proceed in pushing the limits, doing what nature never intended.

This Old Testament creation-theology must be seen in the context of God's covenant with Israel. That God owns the land was fundamental. "The land shall not be sold in perpetuity, for the land is mine; for you are strangers and sojourners with me. And in all the country you possess, you shall grant a redemption of the land" (Leviticus 25:23–24). In the covenant, this divine claim was the basis for sabbatical and jubilee years to assure that land would be well cared for and that privilege for its use could never center in the hands of a few wealthy people. In the context of such radical social legislation we can understand Isaiah's indignation at those who "join house to house, who add field to field" (Isaiah 5:8) and Amos's golden text of the prophetic ethic, "Let justice roll down like waters, and righteousness like an ever-flowing stream" (Amos 5:24).

Swartley shows how the Old Testament vision of justice and righteousness finds fulfillment in Jesus' teachings and actions. The poor inherit God's kingdom, the blind see, the lame walk, prisoners go free. The image lost at the fall is restored through Christ. The study concludes:

> For those who have ears to hear, biblical teaching speaks to the contemporary issues of world hunger, rich nations vis-a-vis poor nations, and the ecological crisis. God created mankind to be a steward of the earth's essential resources . . . to represent *God's* ownership in the world, to exert dominion in justice, and to enjoy the world's wealth by accepting it as a common possession of all humanity. Herein does love for God and for the neighbor find perfect expression.[5]

Modern and Organic

If we accept the demands of living in God's image, we will cherish the natural order. Grabbing and exploiting will give way to sharing. We can learn much about doing this by looking back at the life patterns of North American natives before Europeans arrived on this continent. We can observe indigenous systems around the world in which private ownership bows to the communal good. Grandparents raised here fifty years ago can also help.

Earlier, human ways conformed to nature because nature was in control; humans lacked the power to act otherwise. Only if they accommodated did they survive. Although this is ultimately true for us also, today, judgment on failure to accommodate is not quite so immediate.

Today we own the machines for full-scale plunder of our environment. *Craftsmen of Necessity,* a photographic essay on indigenous peoples responding to their environment, says,

"Machine technology drove a steel wedge between man and his home."[6]

For our future we need a modern "organic technology." We need a blend between the peasant's ecological skill and our contemporary knowledge of what is possible. The answer in housing is likely not a tepee or log house, but a small, sturdily built, comfortable structure heated by the sun. The answer to the litter problem is not an end to ketchup or grape juice sold in glass bottles, but standard sizes that must be returned and will be refilled by any company. The answer to lung-choking smog in cities is not moving everybody to the countryside, but strong restrictions on private cars and adequate public systems for moving around. We need not give up manufacturing, but we must make ethical choices between factory pollution and human health.

Finding these blends means that we consciously choose to fit the way we live to the environment, not trying to reshape the environment to our whims. Sometimes this will cost more initially than the old system of using up, throwing away, and destroying. Certainly it will take more imagination. Above all, cherishing the natural order requires a willingness to live in God's image and live peacefully with the earth.

Waiting for the Big Answer

Right now, depletion of energy sources is one of our biggest environmental headaches.

On a plane trip I took several years ago, I sat next to an amiable young man from Canton, Ohio. Somehow he seemed different from the usual three-piece-suit crowd who sip cocktails and study profit-loss sheets.

This man pulled out pictures of his family with whom he was eager to be reunited. He explained his business and asked me about my work. But when I told him I was returning from a church conference where I spoke about conserving food and energy, his smile became indulgent.

"That's really nice of you," he said. "I know we could all do better. But you know, science is going to get us out of this energy problem somehow. When you think about the things we didn't know thirty years ago! I believe that by the year 2,000 some new innovation we've never even dreamed of will be our main source of energy!"

In the half hour before we landed, my scariest questions on where we will be if that doesn't happen never dented his optimism. He was a cheerful example of an outlook described by former United States Secretary of the Interior Stewart Udall:

We all lived through such statements as "there are no problems, only solutions." "Today's science fiction is tomorrow's reality." Or the one the week we landed on the moon. "This proves we can do whatever we want to do. . . ." Most people in the country are still wearing those eyeglasses from the 50s and 60s. They are getting up in the morning, waiting to pick up the newspaper to find that someone in a laboratory has discovered a substitute for petroleum. We are living in a fool's paradise. . . . We are unwilling to act to save ourselves or to protect some kind of future for our children.[7]

My airplane seatmate has company everywhere, for doomsday books on the energy crisis make tiresome reading. It's hard to put them down with a smile. And for those who don't worry about violent consequences, there actually may be temporary solutions in sight. If the Middle East won't sell us the oil we want at a price we can pay, we can try taking it by military force. We also can build and are building nuclear power systems to help meet our wasteful habits, although we still don't know how to dispose of unimaginably dangerous radioactive by-products.

Although we can scrape together the energy to continue, our waste steals from other countries which cannot pay high prices for fuel to meet even the barest human needs. Luann Habegger Martin writes from Accra, Ghana:

The real energy crisis for the poor in developing countries is the growing scarcity of firewood. About 90 percent of the people in these countries depend primarily on firewood to cook their food and in colder climates to provide some warmth. Due to deforestation, women are walking farther and farther to get enough firewood to cook their family's meals. If we North Americans had to go to such efforts to get our fuel and water, I'm sure we would use these resources more judiciously.

First and Second Questions
Of any course of action, Christians must never ask first, "Is it scientifically possible?" and "Can we pay for it?" When asked first, those are conformed-to-the-world questions. Inquiry tends to stop right there.

"Does it nurture people?" and "Does it protect our environment?" are the conformed-to-God's-image questions. If the answers are yes, the other questions also need to be researched. But the order in which we ask them shows who and what we serve.

So far, our best information still points to two sources of additional energy which are safe and abundant. The first is the energy we now waste. The second is solar power.

A Worldwatch Institute paper called *Energy: The Case for Conservation* says that in 1975 the United States wasted more fossil fuel than two thirds of the world's population used.[8] If Canada's population were larger, they wouldn't be far behind. Consider these statements which Worldwatch carefully documents:

—More than half of the current U.S. energy budget is wasted.

—For the next quarter century the United States could meet all its new energy needs simply by improving efficiency of existing uses.

—Conservation could relieve us of pressure to use dangerous energy sources before exploring other alternatives, reduce our vulnerability in foreign affairs, and improve our balance of payments position.

—A dollar invested in wise energy conservation makes more net energy available than a dollar invested in developing new energy resources.

—Energy conservation could lead to more exercise, better diets, less pollution, and other indirect benefits to human health.[9]

Where can you find a stronger testimony for more with less? We needn't wait longer for the big answer. The miracle can begin if we put our wills to learning judicious ways of heating, cooling, and transportation.

Solar energy, which includes wind, falling water, methane and alcohol production, and direct sunlight, is the other safe, abundant resource. In North America, solar technologies are only beginning to develop and are still somewhat costly. We lag behind other countries where fossil fuels are more expensive. But hopeful signs are everywhere.

More than 2,000,000 Japanese and 30,000 Australian households now rely on solar water heaters. A fifth of Israeli households use solar-heated hot water.[10]

Already in North America most communities have a house or two on which rooftop solar collectors announce new ways to control indoor climate. Some of these innovations are not as expensive as we've been led to believe. When you consider lifetime costs and energy security, solar investment is attractive.

For anyone building a new house, some of the sun's benefit is available even without collectors, pumps, pipes, and storage tanks. All that is required is a row of large, south-facing windows under overhanging eaves. The eaves let in low winter sun and shade out high summer sun. Heavy curtains to draw across the double-paned windows on winter nights, and deciduous trees that shade the house in summer give additional protection.[11]

The noticeable difference between such a house and one designed without regard to the sun is the fuel bill. As Paul T. Yoder of La Junta, Colorado, said in his entry for this book,

"The most underutilized resource to aid in simple living is our own heads."

Within this book's size and scope there isn't space for helpful how-to information on solar technology. Books and pamphlets devoted solely to those innovations are rapidly appearing in bookstores and libraries.

When people most affected by a problem work toward solving it, they gain self-respect and learn to understand the bigger issues of their society. They have control over their future. Right now most North Americans are powerless when it comes to acquiring their energy supply. Conservation and solar power hold hope for greater freedom.

Entries that show people cherishing nature and conserving its gifts are marked with a ℭ

Notes

1
Wendell Berry, *The Unsettling of America: Culture and Agriculture* (New York: Avon Books, 1978), p. 30.

2
T. C. McLuhan, comp., *Touch the Earth* (New York: Pocket Books, 1972), p. 45.

3
Ibid., p. 15.

4
Mary Evelyn Jegen and Bruce U. Manno, eds., *The Earth Is the Lord's* (New York: Paulist Press, 1978), pp. 22–43.

5
Ibid., p. 41.

6
Christopher Williams, *Craftsmen of Necessity* (New York: Vintage Books, 1974), p. 3.

7
Stewart Udall, "A Time of Challenge," *Journal of Current Social Issues* (Fall 1978), p. 30.

8
Denis Hayes, *Energy: The Case for Conservation,* Worldwatch Paper 4 (Washington, D.C.: Worldwatch Institute, 1976), p. 7. Available from Worldwatch, 1776 Massachusetts Ave., N.W., Washington, D.C. 20036.

9
Ibid., summarized.

10
Bruce Stokes, *Local Responses to Global Problems: A Key to Meeting Basic Human Needs,* Worldwatch Paper 17 (Washington, D.C.: Worldwatch Institute, 1978), p. 45.

11
John Prenis, ed., *Energy Book 1: Natural Sources and Backyard Applications* (Philadelphia: Running Press, 1975), p. 94.

nonconform freely

●●●

Willard Swartley, seminary professor of New Testament, writes, "If it hasn't already done so, the church in the 1980s must recognize that it lives in a pagan society; it must seek for values and norms not shared by society. In short, it will either recover the Christian doctrine of nonconformity or cease to have any authentic Christian voice."[1]

"Don't let the world around you squeeze you into its mold," writes Paul to the Romans, "but let God remold your minds from within."[2]

But nonconforming is a complicated endeavor. The subject is loaded with touchy two-sided questions. Words such as easy and hard, liberty and law, freedom and slavery, independence and submission volley back and forth like ping-pong balls through New Testament discussions. Jesus, who warned that the gate to life is small, the road narrow, and those who find it few, also said, "My yoke is easy and my burden is light." When early Christian leaders had to respond to problems faced by new congregations, the epistle writers wrestled further with apparently conflicting principles.

"Always speak and act as men who are to be judged under a law of freedom," says James. "Live as free men, not however as though your freedom were there to provide a screen for wrongdoing, but as slaves in God's service," adds Peter. After a long discussion of all sorts of immorality, including greed, Paul states, "All things are lawful for me, but I will not be enslaved by anything."[3]

Striking a Balance

How can Christians committed to simplicity keep their balance? Mennonites have long seen a link between faithfulness and nonconformity, but everyone knows that sometimes we failed to balance this emphasis with freedom. We quoted, "Be not conformed to the world," to the point where our children wanted nothing more than freedom *from* nonconformity. Clothing practices provide a good example. For some Mennonite youth of years past, to follow a fashion magazine's rather than an elder's advice on clothing looked like the road to true independence. This bid for liberty went on mainly in restrictive rural communities. But at the same time, the children of affluent suburbanites who could wear what they pleased also rebelled. For them *fashion's* dictatorship was the enemy. These young people amused real farmers, who now often prefer two-piece khaki outfits, by showing up in town with bib overalls. The balancing act isn't easy to perform.

Clearly there is more than one way to relinquish freedom. Those who grew up floundering for direction and discipline may be the first to sign up under a new legalism. North American Christendom, including the now powerful evangelical wing, offers good examples with its blind personality cults and models of education in which all answers are either right or wrong.

On the other hand, those who were denied choices in their youth by poverty or rules seem particularly susceptible later to the pulls of respectability, security, and the good life. Many simply grew up when "Can we afford what we need?" was the legitimate question, and aren't able to reverse their thinking to "Do we need what we can afford?"

Anne Harder, Edmonton, Alberta, writes:

It is doubtful that children of immigrant parents can live a simplified life. Our parents were insecure in this new land with a new language and way of life during economically depressed times. Their insecurities became ours. We wanted to shed poverty and all that goes with it. We grew up making-do, making-over, doing without. We learned economical management that served us well and is our identification, but our aim was to escape these simplicities. Plainly, we did not believe in them.

Today we need be always on the alert not to become carried away with the "bigger and better" slogans of our society. We have the example of Christ and a higher purpose for our earthly life.

To live a simplified life you must believe in it. The young

must be taught to appreciate the freedom of not being
enslaved to material things.

Slavery in the Free World

There is another side of the freedom-slavery paradox. North
Americans seem to have almost unlimited political, economic,
and personal freedom. We live in the "free world." In fact
North Americans believe they lead the way to liberty for
everyone else. Yet we submit daily to brainwashing by
commercial interests that must be equal to, if not more
powerful than, the political posters and slogans of totalitarian
governments.

One American who recently visited the People's Republic of
China said that at first he wondered how people could tolerate
the constant barrage of slogans on walls and radio telling
everybody what to think. Then he realized that his own society
reels under nonstop messages just as inane.

We can't get away from advertising. Our children's values
are programmed through television commercials just as surely
as they would be if they chanted political lines in nursery
school. Advertising covers billboards and buses. It claims most
of the space in our newspapers and has taken over our personal
mail. It infiltrates educational materials used in public schools.
The home economics curricula which I studied and taught
were constantly fueled with free educational materials,
complete with brand names, from companies selling vacuum
cleaners, dessert mixes, and dress patterns. While she attended
public school third grade our child brought home page after
page of fill-in-the-blank sheets from a unit on economics. All
carried at the bottom the name and mark of a large fast-food
chain.

In a panel discussion at the 1978 Mennonite World
Conference, participants questioned a pastor from Latin
America about how he carried on church activities and
evangelism under such a repressive system.

"Frankly, I feel
the affluence
of Christian people
in North America
is a more serious threat
to the church here
than political repression
is to ours,"
came his piercing reply.

At the same meeting Bishop Festo Kivengere, who escaped a tyrannical regime in Uganda, said, "Technology and material things can never liberate you. They have a tendency to squeeze you into their own image."

Surprised by Freedom

From nonconformity's paradox we can distill at least this much: Simplicity is a narrow road of self-discipline, but the alternative—money and materialism—is only another master. With marvelous elements of surprise and mystery, disciplined simplicity offers freedom.

The Upside-Down Kingdom, a book by sociologist Donald B. Kraybill, is really all about nonconformity. It's a biblical study showing how everything about God's new kingdom is reversed from what society expects. The chapter on economics is called "Luxurious Poverty." Kraybill says Jesus never said material things are evil in themselves, but rather warned that they threaten our freedom.[4] In this context, simplicity is not restriction, sacrifice, or denial. It is emancipation. We are back to more with less.

E. F. Schumacher, author of *Small Is Beautiful,* describes the journey of people learning to live with less:

Many of them had a better time than they ever had in their lives because they were discovering the new freedom— the less you need, the freer you become. They discovered and kept discovering that they were carrying far too much baggage and so they dropped pieces right and left, all the way, and the more they dropped, the happier they became . . . and when they thought they had dropped nearly everything, they discovered that they were still needing and using and wasting more than the great majority of mankind.[5]

Mennonite communities in Kansas remember the witness of Andrew and Viola Shelly, more-with-less prophets long before simple living was a popular subject. This family consistently culled excess baggage. Their daughter Linda emphasizes liberation:

My parents always made it clear that we were living simply by choice rather than necessity. They gave the money we did not spend on ourselves to help others.

As children we became involved by contributing our money to family Bible Society projects and CROP drives. We learned to know missionaries in family devotions. My parents stressed the biblical importance of stewardship. It wasn't until I began filling out forms for college that I realized my parents were giving away over 20 percent of an income that was already below the median national level.

Knowing that we were keeping expenses low for a cause made it all the more challenging and fun to go to garage sales to buy clothes and games or to learn to sew and make useful items at home. It actually felt liberating—we were free from the spending patterns dictated by the availability of money.

The Narrow Road

More with less means choosing limitations. Few of us, however, can live alone by new standards. Taking the narrow way is too risky. As the preacher in Ecclesiastes puts it:

Two are better than one; they receive a good reward for their toil, because, if one falls, the other can help his companion up again. . . . And, if two lie side by side, they keep each other warm. . . . If a man is alone, an assailant may overpower him, but two can resist; and a cord of three strands is not quickly snapped.[6]

An old German painting of the biblical narrow and broad roads pictures the narrow way as a steep stony path leading off into the woods. Fearful crevices and wild animals lurk around the bend. *Pilgrim's Progress* comes to mind. Perhaps in our time a more appropriate visual image is a car moving the wrong way down a freeway during rush hour!

In either case, one needs help.

If you head
into unfamiliar woods,
you had better find
companions first;
if you want to buck traffic,
organize a convoy.
To nonconform freely,
we must strengthen
each other.

"If I were a super strong, determined, stubborn, disciplined, organized person I could singlehandedly overthrow a lifetime of captivity to the North American consumer culture," writes Jim Stentzel from the Sojourners Fellowship, Washington, D.C. "But I'm one who makes New Year's resolutions that last about a week. I buy into the televised good life even as I profess my belief in higher things. I am a creature of the Fall whose appetite has moved far beyond mere apples. I need help when it comes to more responsible use of God-given resources."

Elsie Dyck, who spent three years in voluntary service away from home after living thirty-two years in one city, emphasizes how hard it is to keep a resolution to live more simply upon

returning home: "Whether we will now be able to keep a
simple lifestyle with all the pressure to conform to dishwashers,
big cars, cottages, cleaning ladies, fancy homes, and pools
remains to be seen. You do get a feeling of not being in the
same league with your friends."

When the first signals of a new king and new kingdom came
to Mary, Jesus' mother, she sought out Elizabeth for
confirmation and courage. Jesus himself gathered a core of
disciples and sent them out two by two to spread the good
news. Believers from the young churches of Acts clustered for
mutual support throughout the Mediterranean world and
beyond. From then until now the practice of *church,* or
congregation, and of *Christian community* has never ceased.
God is building his kingdom with people whose relationships
are being redeemed and who are thus stronger together than
any of them ever could be separately.

Lonely Freedom
In the past Christians needed each other to lock arms against
the crowd. But today when we try to live obediently in the
midst of affluence, new forces tug at us—mobility and personal
independence. The fact that we feel so free to move from place
to place makes it more important than ever that we check our
sources of support.

In a fast-moving society relationships are seldom permanent.
When asked to comment on American life as she observed it
during her visit, a Palestinian Christian said, "When *we* work
with someone for awhile, our bond with that person runs very
deep and the friendship is seldom broken; but you seem to
make and break relationships so quickly."

This characteristic of our society has implications for
Christians who know they must support each other. Most of us
move every two or three years. There may be no one with
whom we work or worship who knows our grandmother's
name, our father's values, or the community expectations
which shaped us. Consequently no one feels well enough
informed or responsible to hold us to specific life standards.

No one feels obligated
to catch us if we fall.
We've traded the restrictions
of tightly laced
communities
for a lonely freedom.

Moving to a new town often provides financial advancement; people follow a better-paying job, a bigger house, access to shopping malls and recreational sites. But do such moves offer the wealth found in Bandhumunda, a rural Indian village? Biology professor Dwight Platt lived there several months and describes what he saw:

The first impression of most Americans is that Bandhumunda is primitive and poverty-stricken.

I lived in the home of a weaver and often sat on the earthen front porch watching villagers prepare for the night. Small earthen huts with thatched roofs clustered together surrounded by cultivated fields. A mother watered the squash vine climbing the roof of her house. Dust clouds raised by the village cattle billowed up against the setting sun. I moved aside as the weaver's cows climbed to the porch, entered the front door, and moved through the living room to the cowshed at the rear.

Here was no carpeting to spoil—just earthen floor swept very clean. No wallpaper either—but artistic paintings done by women in the home decorated some of the mud walls. My host's father lived in the family home but no longer worked on the loom—instead he wrote poetry.

Indian village life provides social interaction in the strength and intimacy of families with several generations; in sharing resources such as borrowing coals from a neighbor to start a fire without the price of a match; in the cooperation of village men hauling earth to repair the dam for a village pond; in the weekly market with opportunity to meet friends from neighboring villages; in all-night monthly dances with seasonal symbolism.

The Indian village is not utopia. There are angry disputes and power struggles. But there is strong community identification. I found life rich despite poverty.

Compare this with the isolation of a father-mother-two-children family in a new suburban location. They have a shag carpet, a family room, three bathrooms, and a microwave oven. But one spouse and the children have no contact with the other spouse's workplace. Grandparents, cousins, and high school friends were left behind two moves earlier.

In such settings, a parent at home all day with small children may suffer acutely. Responses include child abuse and addiction to TV, antidepressants, alcohol, and shopping. All things considered, a mother who spends the morning at the mall buying something new for herself, the house, or the children is taking the safest temporary "high" available.

Both parents working full time is the usual way out. This becomes necessary to provide for the high cost of material comforts and may alleviate loneliness for the adults. But it can

be a poor solution for young children if they have no
permanent relationships with other caring adults. In a mobile
society, children also battle loneliness. If the marriage itself
cracks and breaks under the strain, their problems multiply.

Where Is Help?

Finding a nice church with warm handshakes and well-
planned programs is not enough.

Friendships developed in many churches will provide tennis
partners and dinner invitations, but not the level of support
needed for living the standards here discussed. Even small
groups within churches easily falter. Most of these are fine at
carrying in meals after you have surgery but are less ready to
caution you about buying too big a car. Money and how we get
and spend it remains the single great privacy from which few
dare lift the cover. It's the area in which our individualism
sprouts most persistently.

Entries in Part Two indicate that God's Spirit shows the way
in many directions—all the way from finding a budget partner
to full economic sharing in intentional communities. These are
signs of hope.

Intentional Christian communities give the problem most
attention. Building a common life as a solution to personal
greed is an old and well-tested practice. Although such groups
formed here and there all through church history, and not only
in the Catholic monastic setting, most contemporary
Christians looked askance at their new growth spurt in the
fifties and sixties. People watched and clucked their tongues
and waited for these experiments to fall apart.

Today intentional communities have proved themselves. Just
as with more traditional congregations, some did not last. But
many others are solid, viable, and well beyond their early
growing pains. Simply applying the wisdom of Gamaliel (Acts
5:38–39)[7] means we must now thank God for their prophetic
presence among us.

Most members of Christian intentional communities
probably do not see "strengthening each other for simple
living" as their goal, however. Their vision of being the body of
Christ envelops a great deal more than sharing money, living
space, cars, and washing machines. Jim Stentzel, quoted earlier
in this chapter, says, "Simple living is not our goal. Simple
living is merely a means by which we can free ourselves and
our resources for service to others in a world gone awry."

Not all Christians who take simpler living seriously will
choose an intentional community for support. I know persons
who, although they would humbly shy away from claiming
success in living by more-with-less standards, have actually
governed their lives this way for decades. They've done it in
one-family homes, at ordinary jobs, with personal bank
accounts, and while attending middle-class churches. If most of

us lived as they do—like songbirds in a flock of crows—I wouldn't bother compiling this book.

One such friend wrote:

For many years we tried to make choices with needs, rather than what-everybody-else-has, as our criteria. Now that simple living has become popular, I hear a lot of talk about support groups being necessary to assume a lifestyle of this sort. But it seems to me that there is no scriptural justification for needing to have consensus before acting in ways consistent with kingdom-building principles. None of the prophets waited for others to agree before they set out to proclaim by their actions what God had spoken to them. When Jesus called his disciples he didn't say, "When we get our group together we'll decide what we ought to do."

Her warning, which is valid only in light of the fact that she has long lived obediently, adds balance to our perspective. With mercy, God speaks through close-knit groups and through prophets who stand alone. God is unlikely to be limited to a single model.

Ronald J. Sider, author of *Rich Christians in an Age of Hunger,* belongs to a noncommunal church but one which provides strong challenges on economic questions and is located in a low-income city setting. He says there are few good suburban models for simple living. Sider hints at the beginning of our task by saying:

I think what has to happen is that a small group of people in a church must covenant together and be accountable to each other for their economic discipleship. In our church we have small groups that regularly take up our family budgets, discuss them in the light of biblical priorities and kingdom values.[8]

Testimonies about freedom and self-discipline and which show how people strengthen each other for nonconformity are marked with the symbol *ϐ*

Notes

1
Willard Swartley, "Mennonite Higher Education Facing the 1980s," *Gospel Herald* (September 26, 1978), p. 726.

2
Romans 12:2 (Phillips).

3
James 2:12 (NEB); 1 Peter 2:16 (NEB); 1 Corinthians 6:12.

4
Donald B. Kraybill, *The Upside-Down Kingdom* (Scottdale, Pa.: Herald Press, 1978), pp. 113–122.

5
E. F. Schumacher, "Taking the Scare Out of Scarcity," *Psychology Today* (September 1977), p. 16.

6

Ecclesiastes 4:9–12 (NEB).

7

"For if this plan or this undertaking is of men, it
will fail; but if it is of God, you will not be able to
overthrow them. You might even be found
opposing God!"

8

Ronald J. Sider, "Prophet to a Rich Church,"
Eternity (April 1979), p. 19.

●●●

*In the following
series of photographs
from Third World
countries,
significant values
are expressed
which may be missing
from our lives.*

*A second look
for these aspects
is revealing.*

Look again!

In this family
weaving business
in North Jordan . . .

. . . the father
is a visible example
to his children

Look again

... children learn
survival skills
and do not
require entertainment

... younger children
learn from older ones

... use of hands
keeps a sane balance
between physical
and mental
activity

... nonrenewable
energy requirements
are nonexistent

... materials used
are produced
locally

Look

again

MCC Photo

A home environment
in Chad uses local,
naturally replenished
materials
for building . . .

. . . reduces utensils
to a few important ones
which give a
sense of unity
to each home
and to the community

. . . uses sunlight
as a natural
disinfectant

. . . provides an
unpolluted, restorative
environment

. . . preserves a oneness
with the
natural order

UNICEF Photo by Bernard Pierre Wolff

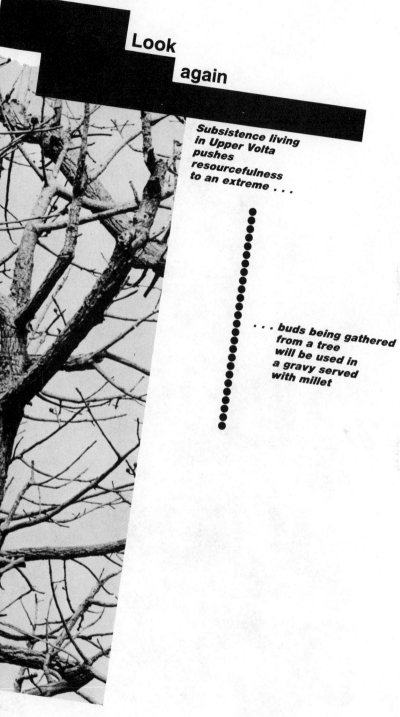

Look
again

**Subsistence living
in Upper Volta
pushes
resourcefulness
to an extreme . . .**

**. . . buds being gathered
from a tree
will be used in
a gravy served
with millet**

MCC Photo

●●●●●●●●●●●●
*Pooling scarce
resources in
Bangladesh
also produces
unforgettable,
spontaneous
experiences among
people.*
●●●●●●●●●●●●

Look again

*Take long walks in
stormy weather
or through deep snows
in the fields and woods,
if you would keep your
spirits up.
Deal with brute nature.
Be cold and hungry and
weary.
—Thoreau*

*In the religious
community,
sin can take a very high
polish.
—Truman Brunk
  Akron, Pa.*

*And why are you anxious
about clothing?
Consider the lilies of the field,
how they grow;
they neither toil nor spin;
    yet I tell you,
    even Solomon in all his glory
    was not arrayed
    like one of these.
—Matthew 6:28–29*

*The fallow ground of the poor
yields much food,
but it is swept away
through injustice.
—Proverbs 13:23*

*Stand by the roads,
and look,
and ask for the ancient paths,
where the good way is;
and walk in it.
—Jeremiah 6:16*

*It is better to eat soup
with someone you love
than steak
with someone you hate.
—Proverbs 15:17, LB*

*No one can be a slave
to two masters;
he will hate one
and despise the other.
You cannot serve
both God and money.
—Matthew 6:24 TEV*

Part 2
Living Testimonies

1. Money
2. Clothes
3. Homes
4. Homekeeping
5. Transportation and Travel
6. Celebrations
7. Recreation
8. Meetinghouses
9. Eating Together
10. Strengthening Each Other

In this section the standards codes are placed next to practices which effectively demonstrate their use. (See page 21.)

*You are not making a gift
of your possessions
    to the poor man.
You are handing over to
him
    what is his.*
*—St. Ambrose
    Bishop of Milan, c. 380*

*There are two ways to
be rich:
1. Acquire great wealth.
2. Acquire few needs.
—Source Unknown*

*Enter by the narrow gate;
for the gate is wide and the way is easy,
that leads to destruction,
and those who enter by it
are many.
For the gate is narrow
and the way is hard,
that leads to life,
and those who find it are few.*
—Matthew 7:13–14

Money is sharper than a sword.
—Ashanti Proverb

*The fruit of wisdom is peace,
and the fruit of riches is fatigue.*
—Oriental Proverb

*Riches are like water in the house
whose channels are obstructed;
if it finds no exit
it drowns the owner.*
—Oriental Proverb

*Critical
of the rich
Sympathetic
toward the poor
Comfortable
with being in the middle*

*Then
blocks of burned-out buildings
dirty streets in all directions
men and women without work
and children with no future
took the blinders from my eyes*

*Being in the middle
is rich
and Jesus said
a camel goes through the eye of a needle
easier
than a rich person enters the kingdom.*
*—Lynette Meck
    Bronx, N.Y.*

1.
money

●●

Our society has clear rules about handling money.

My friend told this story from a supermarket checkout line. Just ahead of her, a woman in a long black cape dress and bonnet began writing a check as her groceries were tallied. In our eastern Pennsylvania town, clothing clearly marked her as a member of one of the plain Mennonite groups.

"Do you have a check-cashing card for this store?" asked the clerk.

"No, I don't."

"What about a credit card?"

"Sorry, no."

"A driver's license, then! You have to have some identification! What *do* you have?"

The clerk's tone became rude. She eyed the string of waiting carts, gave an exaggerated sigh, and buzzed the manager.

The plain woman's lowered head and bonnet almost hid a rising pink blush. But then a few nearby shoppers heard her soft voice.

"I don't have any of those things. I just have trust."

With a glance at face and garb, the manager initialed her check. The woman took her bags in arm and was gone. Now the clerk rolled her eyes to the ceiling in mock horror.

"Some people have got their nerve!" She snapped it out to the customer line-up, then played again the cash register's

staccato music for canned soup, cornflakes, and cash.
Those who do justice
learn from the world community
nurture people
cherish the natural order
nonconform freely
will also do the improbable with money.
People who follow Christ have that sort of example. He
overturned the money-changers' tables and spilled their cash
boxes. He suggested loaning money to those with poor credit
ratings. He sent out missionaries without allowances and told
his disciples to look in a fish's mouth for coins to pay a tax. In
churches today such actions would be termed unlawful,
disrespectful of others' property, or at least embarrassing and
impractical. People would say, "It's a bad witness."

Are we really asked to be so foolhardy? To be certain,
testimonies in this chapter aren't very radical. No one denies
the convenience of identification for cashing checks or refuses
to use banks at all. None go so far as Henry David Thoreau,
who would have found no use for the pocket calculator. He
wrote,

> "An honest man
> had hardly need count
> more than his ten fingers,
> or in extreme cases
> he may add his ten toes,
> and lump the rest.
> Keep your accounts
> on your thumbnail."[1]

But those who provided these entries are ready to redefine and
limit the power of money in their lives.

Money: A Basic Biblical Issue

Earlier I described this book as a testimony meeting, not a
thoroughgoing biblical study. The end of this chapter lists
books which give the subject of money in the Bible the serious
attention it deserves. No one who proposes to live by biblical
standards can ignore such study. According to Lutheran pastor
and writer Wallace Fisher, Jesus spoke five times as much
about money and earthly possessions as about prayer.[2] And the
rest of the Bible is far from silent on the subject.

Begin with Old Testament law and its provision for limiting
private acquisition, its condemnation of charging interest.
Today scholars investigate with fresh interest the Jubilee

concept, designed to redistribute wealth periodically to the
poor. As a witness that Israel failed to live by this system, we
have the prophetic critique of exploiting the poor.

Then come Jesus' startling stories of the new kingdom. Why
do so many begin with "There was a rich man" or "There was
a poor man"? A master teacher, Jesus leaves the meaning of his
stories slightly elusive. Thus their reality, their universal and
timeless truths, still needle us: What connection is there
between the fool who builds more barns and the faithful
servant who wisely invests his talents? Which am I?

Finally we have the early church's example of divestment,
communal ownership, sharing, and care for the poor. And
everywhere the warnings. Money has power, wealth is
addictive. Be careful, be on your guard.

Time Is Not Money

We'll never exhaust Bible study on the subject of money;
there's too much material and too many possibilities for
creatively applying it to our own time.

Nevertheless, a thorough search would prove at least one
thing: most of the maxims by which North Americans handle
money aren't found in the Bible, not even in Proverbs.
Although Solomon's undoing can be traced partly to "another
day, another dollar," it wasn't he who said it aloud!

One of our most pervasive notions is that time is money.
That, most assuredly, is not in the Bible. Indeed, as far as I
have been able to determine, the idea is found in no language
except English nor in any culture outside North America. One
recurrent observation that the stream of returning missionaries
and service workers who visit the Mennonite Central
Committee offices make is that in many other places people are
rich in time. Time is *not* equated with material gain. Time is a
free gift. Time comes from God, the Source of Life.

Kosuke Koyama, an Asian theologian, describes God as the
one who "went so slow that he became nailed down in his
search of man."[3] He is still not sure but what the holy must be
approached on foot, not on a motorcycle.

Here Koyama describes what happens when free time
changes to time as money:

Time [in Asia] was traditionally experienced as being as
unlimited as a loving mother's milk is unlimited to her baby.
Time was generously given. It was not sold as pork chops are
sold. . . . Time was cyclical, that is to say, calm and level-
headed. . . . It was communal.

Now, this has been changed without any consultation with
us! . . . Time is now located in the export-import
companies, motorcycle manufacturers, stores and shops.
. . . It is now private business property. Once it was shared,
now it is monopolized. Time does not heal us now. Time
wounds us.[4]

What can all this mean for living more with less and managing money? One of the following contributors tells of choosing part-time work, with its resulting freedom to participate in action for peace. Another says, "We deliberately choose for Gladys not to be employed full time so that our household work can be done in ways that save money and energy and to slow our pace of living."

While these entries reflect joy, it is significant that they describe the lives of women. The North American church will have progressed much further in learning that time is not money when more men discover how to unchain themselves. Signs of hope come from physicians and others who deliberately limit their hours and incomes.

More Than Thrift

When I began compiling the *More-with-Less Cookbook,* a letter from the heart of one rural Mennonite community urged: "So often when one of the women's magazines runs an article on economy cooking, it ends up being more expensive than the way we've already been doing things. Now what we want in this new cookbook is something truly low-cost." The last three words were triply underlined!

One side of me dearly loved that letter. I, too, scoff at so-called money-saving recipes which assume olives and packaged biscuit mix. But my other side trembled in fear. Why had I imagined that I could write an economy cookbook for these old-time experts, these grown-up refugee children and Depression brides? On every visit to my mother-in-law's kitchen she showed me, the home economist, another way to pinch the nickel!

Today I still grapple with the paradoxes that envelop thrift and simple living. On the one hand, pure frugality is a rare bird, an endangered species in our waste-crazed society. Few people still know how to make soup with leftovers, set a neat patch, or squeeze the last smidgen of hand soap onto a new bar. Who still cares for the skill of coming to a week's end with an empty garbage pail and extra dollars in the purse? Someday when all the grandparents born before World War II are gone, they'll begin teaching courses on thrift in high schools.

But living more with less is more than thrift. Partly, it's putting what you save to some good use for others. Might we change the familiar proverb to "A penny saved is a penny given"? But even with that, we dare not be satisfied.

Now and then,
living more with less
means paying more money.
It may mean

buying better quality—
leaving behind
repetitive purchases
of discount house junk
for one expensive,
well-made,
thoughtfully designed tool
that will last.

Increasingly it means asking questions such as: Where did this
come from? Who benefited and who got hurt in its production?
Ought I to be gloating over its cheap price, or not buying it at
all?

Spending money by alternative standards also means asking:
Where will I make my purchase? Shall I spend my money at
our town's little sandwich shop where I can still ask for cheese
on whole-wheat, or at the zingy new franchise with its limited
options prepackaged in styrofoam? Should I stop at a hardware
store reopened in a downtown area struggling for survival or at
the massive new mall carved from a cow pasture? Can I meet
my need from the limited selection of a mom and pop clothing
store where they know my name but where I may have to wait
while they order and alter? Or must I see at once fifty suits in
my size to come away satisfied? And will I still drive fifteen
miles to save $2.98 at a sale?

There's more! Are my shopping habits so erratic, so tied to a
moment's whim that I pay stores to stay open every night of
the week plus Sunday? And are shopping centers, with no
sound of bird or sight of tree, my favorite recreational sites?
Said one older man, "My sister is now retired on a good
pension, and though she has no particular need to buy,
shopping has become her favorite sport. Busloads of retired
people spend one day after the next at various shopping
centers. They call it malling."

Admittedly, decisions about where to buy get tough. We
juggle trade-offs. We find some choices adequate, some good,
only a few that are perfect. But here's a principle to remember:
Even if prices run a bit higher, it's worth considering the small
and local. Buying at a place to which you can walk or bike
saves gas. And given transportation savings, you might spend
no more for slightly higher-priced items. Any product raised,
manufactured, and sold in its own locale saves everyone's
energy supply. And the friendship you make with a druggist or
woodworker humanizes your community and might wrest
away from outside control decisions you could be making
yourself.

Money—The Big Secret

You and he belong to the same body of Christ in this town. Today you sit together in the pew, sharing a hymnbook: "Take my life and let it be consecrated, Lord, to thee."

This morning your hands met in greeting and while passing the offering plate and communion tray. You're on the same committee and in the same weekly prayer group. Your families often call a short-notice picnic. You offer casseroles when they're sick and they feed your dog when you go on vacation. You phoned them first when your last baby was born and they you when their grandmother died. Last year you even spent Christmas Eve together. Best friends. And in the Lord.

But still, you keep The Secret.

And now the fourth verse, he on tenor, you on bass: "Take my silver and my gold, not a mite would I withhold."

Heart-stopping words, those! Words which now and again you notice a few honest people refuse to sing. But there's one comfort. As well as you know this friend and others, because of The Secret you'll never challenge each other on whether or not you meant it. You're both safe.

Money. How much does each have and what do they do with it? We have our stewardship drives and our poster thermometers for special projects. But seldom does anyone divulge to a sister or brother in the church the specific information needed to receive counsel in handling what 1 Timothy 6:10 calls "the root of all evils." The scarcity of testimonies which express freedom between Christians in guiding each other on money's use suggests hard tasks ahead for the church. Here are a few such tasks:

1. Encourage specific discussion within small groups or between brothers and sisters in the church on how people are earning and using their money. This does not mean waving one's budget before a whole congregation. It does mean confessing openly that we need each other's help.

2. Develop local voluntary service structures using the resources of households with extra time or too much money. Suppose business flourishes, or both spouses work at high-paying professions. Suppose prayerful scrutiny with other Christians affirms the basic worth of such professional services, but the monthly income is much more than the household needs. What opportunities can congregations and larger church structures offer for those who choose to commit such money, time, and talent to God's kingdom, yet who do not want to uproot their families or leave satisfying jobs?

3. Expand our understanding that money is not the only old-age security. With spiraling inflation, we can't batten down all the hatches anyway. Attention to cultivating family, church, and community relationships may do more to assure a joyous old age than tenuous financial investments.

4. Investigate more carefully how we earn money and where

it's invested. Can a Christian conscientiously write the advertising script for resource-consuming gadgets? Manufacture low-nutrition snack foods? Or promote the burgeoning jewelry, cosmetic, and fashion industry? When does a Christian back off from enterprises which threaten the natural environment?

Investment is more than an individual problem. During the Vietnam War many church institutions withdrew their investments from military defense. Is it now time to do the same with banks and corporations involved in exploiting the agricultural and mineral resources of poor countries?

David Augsburger in *A Risk Worth Taking* offers this final warning:

Money. 200 proof. Taken straight or mixed with many lovely things, it's the most intoxicating substance known to man. . . .

To one affluence addict Jesus said, "Kick the habit, cold turkey; then come and follow Me."

But he went away sad, for he was hooked.[5]

Books to aid biblical study on money:

Batey, Richard. *Jesus and the Poor.* New York: Harper and Row, 1972.

Birch, Bruce C., and Rasmussen, Larry L. *The Predicament of the Prosperous.* Philadelphia: Westminster Press, 1978. A message of judgment and hope showing how various biblical teachings speak to affluent Christians.

Kauffman, Milo. *Stewards of God.* Scottdale, Pa.: Herald Press, 1975.

Kreider, Carl. *The Christian Entrepreneur.* Scottdale, Pa.: Herald Press, 1980.

Sider, Ronald J. *Rich Christians in An Age of Hunger: A Biblical Study.* Downers Grove, Ill.: InterVarsity Press, 1977.

Notes

1
Henry David Thoreau, *Thoreau on Man and Nature,* comp. Arthur G. Volkman (Mt. Vernon, N.Y.: Peter Pauper Press, 1960), p. 27.

2
Wallace E. Fisher, *A New Climate for Stewardship* (Nashville: Abingdon, 1976), p. 23.

3
Kosuke Koyama, *50 Meditations* (Maryknoll, N.Y.: Orbis Books, 1979), p. 9.

4
Kosuke Koyama, *No Handle on the Cross* (Maryknoll, N.Y.: Orbis Books, 1977), p. 19.

5
David Augsburger, *A Risk Worth Taking* (Chicago: Moody Press, 1973), p. 32.

●●●●●●●●●●●●●●●●●●●●●●●●●●●●

Time or Money

You can either save time or money, seldom both. Fast living is   ℮
expensive living. When we're in a hurry we buy convenience
food from the most accessible store. Because we don't want to
take the time to prepare meals at home, we eat in restaurants.
To arrive somewhere moments earlier, we drive too fast
endangering lives and using more gasoline and tire tread than
necessary. Because we don't have or take time to repair them,
we throw away our socks or sweaters when the first holes
appear. We buy what we want when we want it.

Maybe if we learned to slow down we could catch up with
ourselves. In our family we often wait to get something until
we can find it on sale or at a thrift shop. We deliberately choose
for Gladys not to be employed full time so that our household
work can be done in ways that save money and energy and
slow our pace of living.
—*Gladys and Edgar Stoesz*
  Akron, Pa.

In September my youngest child started first grade. I could   ₱
now go back to the office as a marriage and family counselor.
But if I did that it would put our family in a higher tax bracket.
I wouldn't have time for those special projects and I couldn't
develop those relationships with friends that I feel I should.

My husband and I decided that resuming my profession is
not the answer now. Maybe it never will be. Being active in the
Peace and Social Concerns Committee, teaching an adult
Sunday school class, and participating in congregational
committees are opportunities for me to relate to and help
others. I know God is aware of my education and needs. As I
make myself available to him, he uses me to honor him.
—*Donella Clemens*
  Souderton, Pa.

For several years now I've been working part time, this after
two decades of full-time employment plus church-related
assignments.

Filling the time gaps is mostly joy and creative challenge. I
have time for reflection and listening to the inner voice of God,
especially concerning the meaning of being a peacemaker.
—*Hedy Sawadsky*
  Elkhart, Ind.

Ever since we returned from an agriculture and nutrition   ⌊
project in Bangladesh three years ago, my husband and I have
tried to consume less of the world's goods and be more faithful
to Christ's call to share and minister to the poor and hungry.
Our biggest struggle is trying to decide what our standard of

living is to be. How much money do we need? We farm one-half to two-thirds of the land which economists claim a grain farmer's family needs in order to live comfortably. By simplifying we hope we won't need to expand.

Not having money doesn't mean that I'm not materialistic. I admit that there are times when I wish we had more money to pay off the farm faster. Then in ten or fifteen years we'd be free of debt. But we do have time right now for volunteer projects. We decided that if we don't start immediately doing what we feel is important we never will do it.

—Ramona Smith Moore
North Manchester, Ind.

●●●●●●●●●●●●●●●●●●●●●●●●●●

Skills Are to Use

During our years in the Philippines, Jose, one of my students, regularly visited us in the village to cut my hair. That was one of the most pleasant amenities of belonging to the community.

After that, going to a barbershop lost its appeal. Haircutting could be done at home. First my wife and then the children each had a hand in it. I don't think I'm known for my hairstyle, so I doubt that many realize I've robbed the barber profession of a generation of haircutting income.

Rather than count all the money we've saved since 1947 I delight in the dividend of simply staying at home, sitting on a stool with my eyes shut, newspaper spread on the floor, and either Velma, Paul, Nancy, or Mary Jane snipping away. That beats the coziest barbershop I've ever entered.

—J. Wilmer Heisey
Elizabethtown, Pa.

Members of our group felt clearly that we shouldn't charge the market rate for our carpentry work. We decided to let the employer on each job set the price. Our biggest task is to help people feel at ease doing this.

We're much more comfortable working for those who can't pay regular carpenters' wages like the elderly and those on lower incomes. Since we are doing work in solar heating, we're hoping that the poor might be among the first in our area to have solar additions on homes.

—New Covenant Fellowship
Athens, Ohio

Instead of sending our children to nursery school, we formed a play group. While the children played together one morning a week, mothers rotated supervision responsibilities.

We all gained precious time with our growing children, transmitting our values to them while spending less money. We

watched them mature in group situations and enjoyed being a
part of the progress.
—*Grace Wolfgang*
  Sellersville, Pa.

I encourage friends who are out of work to tackle new kinds of
jobs. When a friend put in an extra window in my house I
benefited by not having to wait months for a contractor. I also
enjoyed our lunches and afternoon teas together. Meanwhile
he was earning money, widening his work possibility by
learning to do something new, and setting up his own work
schedule.
—*Gathie Falk*
  Vancouver, B.C.

●●●●●●●●●●●●●●●●●●●●●●●●●●●

Remember Micah

Foreign-owned companies which grow fruit for export are a
distinguishing characteristic of the Southern Philippines. In
Honduras, Costa Rica, and Ecuador, the same companies—
Castle and Cooke (Dole), United Fruit (Chiquita), and Del
Monte—supply North America with fruit.

Here, Castle and Cooke use 7,000 hectares (17,297 acres) of
prime land to grow bananas, mostly for export to Japan. Local
contractors hire workers who labor from 6:00 A.M. till
sundown or later. Maximum salary is $1.50 per day. Many
times medical benefits and sometimes salaries are not paid.
Tuberculosis, malnutrition, and skin diseases are endemic.
Rashes and sores frequently result from the liberal use of
chemicals throughout the growing and delivery process.

Last year a corporate executive of Castle and Cooke earned
about 500 times as much as a plantation worker. This disparity
will almost inevitably lead to violence unless it is corrected
soon.

It is impossible to justify the use of all this good land for the
export of fruit to an overfed part of the world when more than
75 percent of the children here suffer from some form of
malnutrition.

I can't forget the lines that Micah penned so many years ago:
"How terrible it will be for those who lie awake and plan
evil! When morning comes, as soon as they have the chance,
they do the evil they planned. When they want fields, they
seize them; when they want houses, they take them. No
man's family or property is safe" (Micah 2:1–2, TEV).
—*Gene Stoltzfus*
  Davao, Philippines

Love Does Not Wrong a Neighbor

In July 1978 we discovered that the account of our church was with the Bank of America. This bank's financial support of companies producing napalm for the Vietnam War had left us with a bitter taste. In recent months we'd read of students protesting its huge loans to the government of South Africa. At our request, Mennonite Central Committee's Peace Section in Washington, D.C., sent us pertinent newspaper clippings and pamphlets.

During a Sunday school discussion it became clear that loans to the government of South Africa or to American businesses there were strengthening apartheid policies. We were shocked to think that our bank account was interlinked with the suffering of black people a continent away. At the next church council meeting we unanimously passed a resolution to withdraw the church's account from the Bank of America. Five families in the church have decided to withdraw their personal accounts, too. We're still in the process because of the difficulty in locating a bank without ties to South Africa loans. All five major California banks—Bank of America, Wells Fargo, Crocker, Security Pacific, and United California Bank—are involved.

We have written Clergy and Laity Concerned in New York, a Christian group organized to oppose social injustices, to help us identify an alternate bank. They will also be sending us letter forms to give our banks upon withdrawal of our accounts so that our reason for this action will be clear.
—*Jo Ellen Johnsen*
—*Donald G. and
Barbara King*
—*Floyd and Evelyn
Lichti*
—*Mabel and Alvin
Saltzman*
—*Mary Drawbond*
—*Bob and Ruth Schrock*
—*John Miller*
—*Tim and Carolyn Lichti*
—*Anna Clem
Upland, California*

Too much of our lives is bound up in systems that are unjust. Here are some things I do:
1. I try to consider the country and the corporation that controls the products I buy.
2. I buy locally grown or manufactured items whenever possible.
3. I preserve vegetables from my own garden for winter use.
4. I try to maintain awareness of economic and trade practices between my country and developing countries using

Mennonite Central Committee's *Washington Newsletter* and
Bread for the World publications as guides. I write letters to
Congress when legislation is pending that affects these
relationships.
5. I remember Gandhi's saying: "He who has more than he
   needs is a thief" by contributing to agencies which focus on
   justice and equality.
—*LaVonne Platt*
Newton, Kan.

Some Chilean members of our food co-op in Winnipeg called
attention to the apples the co-op was distributing. We had
assumed the apples were from the orchards in British
Columbia or Ontario and were surprised to see they came from
Chile. The Chileans felt we should not support the economy of
a country where many were held in prison without trial and
hundreds were declared missing. They themselves had left for
their own safety. Since that incident I read labels more
carefully and ask store managers when necessary to find where
items are produced.
—*Joan Gerig*
Gaborone, Botswana

Every time you buy coffee or bananas or another imported
product from which workers do not get adequate
compensation, put a self-imposed excise tax in a jar. At the end
of every month, send that amount to an agency that is
concerned about alleviating world hunger.
—*Perry Yoder*
North Newton, Kan.

I never get used to the long shelves of pet foods in American
stores. Recently I read that it takes up more shelf space than
even breakfast foods and that Americans spend $2.5 billion a
year on it—enough to feed one third of the world's hungry! I
am unprepared for this devotion to animals.

There are multitudes of reasons for having pets. But I find
myself haunted by the hungry look of Africa as well as
America. In some cases it is hunger for food but other times it
is a cry for a human touch. Can we take the risk of lavishing
our food, time, and love on fellow humans? This is more
rigorous but is the way to life and wholeness.
—*Bertha Beachy*
Salunga, Pa.

●●●●●●●●●●●●●●●●●●●●●●●●●●●●

Where Shall I Buy?

Euclid Food Club began as an effort of Sojourners Fellowship
to feed our own forty-five members economically by buying in
bulk. Soon friends and other members of our parish began to

ask if they could join us. It felt good to share. When our
community moved to the inner city, it made sense to include
our geographic neighbors.

For those of us who buy about three-fourths of our food
here, the saving is about 30 percent. Prices are wholesale plus
10 percent—an experimental figure we chose to cover expenses
and spoilage. The membership fee is twenty-five cents. Those
who participate in the club's work schedule receive a 5 percent
discount. Besides financial savings the club gives us greater
control over the quality and purity of our food.
—*Ann Carr*
Washington, D.C.

Nearly everything we bought in India was grown and
processed locally.

Near my Kansas home people produce wheat, chickens,
beef, pork, eggs, milk, honey, and many kinds of fruits and
vegetables. Yet the only way to buy locally produced food is to
go directly to the producer—our grocery stores handle only
produce trucked in from their warehouse miles away. When I
buy from producers it costs me more in both time and money.
It doesn't make sense to me to buy chicken from Arkansas
when ten miles away a farmer raises chickens to send to
Nebraska.
—*LaVonne Platt*
Newton, Kan.

As a matter of principle I patronize mom and pop stores rather
than large chain department stores or supermarkets. I find that
locally owned and operated stores are more likely to have the
items I need. Somehow I find myself wanting gloves in May or
skewers for shish kebab in February.

How often have I wanted to stand in the middle of a
suburban department store and shout: "Help! Help! Will
someone help me!" Clerks might come running, but I know
their answers would be: "I'm sorry. Everything we have is out.
We don't stock that item in spring—only in fall."

So I go back to the small locally owned store where a clerk
who still believes in friendly service will go to the attic
stockroom and find just what I want. The price is usually not
much higher and, as a bonus, I get better quality which means
fewer shopping trips in the future.
—*Paul Longacre*
Akron, Pa.

Both our backgrounds are frugal; my husband is Scottish, and
I, Mennonite. So while shopping for apartment furniture we
used classified ads to find secondhand articles.

It takes time to read ads, locate addresses, examine articles,
and perhaps bargain with the seller. But the bonuses, besides
low price, are meeting interesting people and often finding a

history behind the furniture: our dining table was brought over by Danish immigrants and our piano had been in the family of a female police sergeant for twenty-five years.
—*Mary Johnston*
  Calgary, Alta.

●●●●●●●●●●●●●●●●●●●●●●●●●●●●

Middle Class Means Rich

Being personally acquainted with people living on the poverty level provides a tremendous balance against the strong "You owe it to yourself" and "You deserve it" philosophies so ever present in North America.

Once in Vietnam a missionary family recently returned from furlough praised the Lord for his generosity in providing a new air conditioner and friends who had outfitted them in better clothing than they would ever have bought themselves. A Vietnamese co-worker, listening in, wondered why the Lord was barely providing enough food for his table or money to educate his children!
—*Mary Martin*
  Allentown, Pa.

For about two years I managed the Re-Uzit Shop at New Holland, Pennsylvania.

One purpose for the shop is to sell new and used donated items of good quality with all proceeds being forwarded to Mennonite Central Committee's worldwide relief and service program. The shop also sells hand-crafted articles from economically depressed areas, in this way enabling many to earn a living.

Becoming better acquainted with needy people at home and abroad was an important part of my involvement at the shop. It's good for me to realize that as a world citizen I am rich. It helps me to share my time and talents in building the kingdom of God.
—*Phyllis Toews*
  Akron, Pa.

●●●●●●●●●●●●●●●●●●●●●●●●●●●●

A Small Investment Yields Big Returns

People with lower incomes are less able to take advantage of tax breaks. They pay a higher percentage of their income in state tax than do people who are more affluent.

A Baptist friend of mine from Kentucky gathered information and wrote an editorial for the state's leading newspaper proposing that state income tax be figured simply by taking a certain percentage of the federal tax. Most people would be able to compute their state tax on two lines!

Not only would this simplify filing state income tax returns, but it would distribute the tax burden much more fairly. He showed that a typical family of four with an income of $15,000 under the old system pays $440 in state income tax, while under the new system they would pay $233. Most families with an income of $40,000 or less would benefit from the change, while a family with an income of $100,000 would have to pay $850 more, about half of which could be deducted from federal income taxes.

Supporters of the proposal took advantage of its political popularity by injecting the issue into the state's gubernatorial campaign.

The new governor does support the plan. Hearings held before the Joint Appropriations and Revenue Committee reported out a bill containing the essential features of the original proposal. Every indication suggests that it will soon become law. If it does, low-and-moderate-income families will save hundreds of dollars. A relatively small investment of time and energy will result in greater justice.
—*Ted Koontz*
  Everett, Mass.

●●●●●●●●●●●●●●●●●●●●●●●●●●●●

They Take Their Own Medicine

When I set up my own medical office recently, these are some ideas I used that have been successful for me:

1. Instead of elaborate dictating equipment I use a good quality standard cassette recorder with a hand-held microphone which has an on-off switch. The cost is about one third of a standard dictation machine.
2. I hired employees whose philosophy and work standards are similar to my own. This has resulted in a big saving of emotional stress.
3. Whenever possible I ask patients to send in their own insurance claims. This saves on administrative cost for my office and educates the patient as to the cost of medical services.
—*Paul T. Yoder*
  La Junta, Colo.

A Danish doctor here in Zambia is conservative in his use of pain relievers. He contends that a little pain builds character! He's joking when he says he wants to specialize in substandard medicine but serious about wanting to make efficient uses of medication where supplies are not plentiful or even available at times.
—*Esther D. Spurrier*
  Choma, Zambia

I am a family physician in a group medical practice of seven
partners. Each of us regularly schedules time to be with our
families, assured that our patients are receiving attention as
needed. Every sixth year each of us has the opportunity to take
a sabbatical.

We've determined to give the best possible medical care to
our community and to make this equally available to all.
Because of our interest in the poor we assisted in starting a
neighborhood health center in Lancaster. One of our
physicians worked there full time for two years. Two of us are
involved as Lancaster County prision physicians. Our staff
includes three counselors who deal more intensely with
psychological, social, family, and other problems.

When billing patients we include a pink slip which gives
clients the options to pay only a percentage of the bill as they
can afford it. We're willing to cancel the rest if they discuss it
with us.

We feel that to accomplish our goals and maintain a unified
group we, as physicians, need to be committed to the way of
Christ. One reason for our success in staying together with
minimal problems for over five years is a commitment to sit
down for an hour every Monday and Friday and talk over our
feelings, disappointments, and patient problems.
—*Herbert Myers*
Rheems, Pa.

●●●●●●●●●●●●●●●●●●●●●●●●●●●

Freedom to Live with Less

We prefer to live on a lower income rather than help pay for
war. We feel this is one way of speaking to the government
about our opposition to the armaments race.

While I was teaching at a Christian high school, I had my
salary reduced to $1,200 a year so that my tax deductions
would be less. Now that Mark is the only wage-earner in our
family, he has chosen to do janitorial work in order to keep our
earnings lower.

Resisting war tax payments is probably more difficult than
objecting to physical participation in war. Because we believe
Jesus' teaching concerning peace we will continue even though
immediate success isn't obvious.

We realize that since we're not self-employed, we're really
only taking halfway measures at tax resistance: some tax
money is withheld by the institution where Mark works.
Eventually he hopes to be self-employed. The important thing
for us now is that we're speaking out.

One of the most exciting freedoms that Jesus Christ has
given us is not to have to earn a lot to keep up with a high

living standard. We're finding that it's possible to live happily on a low income.
—*Marty Kelley*
Rothsville, Pa.

It was not an easy decision to accept a voluntary service assignment in Germantown. We're rural Iowans and the assignment put us in the middle of a large city, far from family and friends. A question loomed before us and was reinforced by others in the church: Is it sensible for thirty-year-olds with a family and school debts to enter voluntary service?

Now that we're here, we're surprised at how small an issue finances are. Pressures decreased as options of middle-class living were reduced. Many in this city subsist on far less than we do, even though we are below median-income level.

The money we earn is completely divorced from our experience, skills, and education. We increasingly believe that pegging human worth to monetary reward is a major social problem. Working toward solving it is biblically and ethically sound and essential to reducing tragic human injustices.
—*Weldon and Marg Nisly*
Philadelphia, Pa.

Our two sons are both preparing for Christian service at Eastern Mennonite College. We're convinced this is for us, despite the tuition cost of nearly $5,000 a year. My husband is a high school teacher so our salary is not large. Here's how we manage.

Both boys take summer jobs and hold work study jobs while at school. We share our money with them as much as we can and have borrowed some from our local bank. We drive low-priced cars, live in a very modest house with low taxes, and buy only used furniture. We often have guests but we keep in mind that good fellowship is more important than expensive food. As we've committed this matter to the Lord, he's been faithful in helping us.
—*Esther J. Yoder*
Hartville, Ohio

I am a lawyer in the poorest county in New York state. I often take cases where clients can pay little or nothing. I try to gain expertise in areas like public assistance and Social Security, normally ignored by attorneys. I volunteer time to the local Office for the Aging and other agencies assisting the disadvantaged. Since the Bible speaks clearly about cases concerning widows and orphans, I try to give them special consideration. I also reject cases that could produce large fees but conflict with my standards and convictions. Whenever possible I try to explain my actions in terms of my personal faith.

God gave me a desire to open a legal aid clinic for needy people in our area. Since my income has doubled each year I've been in the practice, I hope to be able to support my family working part time at the law firm and giving the balance of my time to the clinic. I'll work in the practice only enough to meet our basic living needs.
—*David T. Pullen*
Houghton, N.Y.

●●●●●●●●●●●●●●●●●●●●●●●●●●●●

Budgeting and Sharing

I have the bad habit of impulse buying. Recently I took a hard look at my buying pattern and did the following:
1. I accounted, penny for penny, for an entire month's salary. I was amazed at the amount I'd frittered away on trivia.
2. My future husband and I tested our compatibility by showing each other our budgets. When I realized I didn't trust him to decide what he needed for himself, I wondered how I could trust myself.
3. I decided that having lived with an Amish family and in Costa Rica proved that I could do without a television, blender, electric blanket, expensive stereo system, curling iron, and the shower massage.
4. I read 1 John 3:17.
5. I invited a friend to be my budget partner. We consult with each other regarding the necessity, practicality, and economics of any purchase not in the regular budget.
—*Marti Stockdale*
Canton, Ohio

To me, scriptural simplicity means using all I have, whether much or little, whether material, spiritual, or intellectual, in such a way that it is available to help others.

We've tried to do as much as we could with as little as possible. Since Aaron had been teaching on a low-salary scale, his half-time employment during graduate school required no major adjustments. We've never needed all the money we had so it was a delight to be able to help several young friends through school.

We all like doing things rather than being spectators. One person's interest is enough to get us all to participate. We outfitted the six of us for backpacking by shopping at sales and making simple things. The cost was less than most shops charge for a single outfit. We enjoy free public lakes, parks, and concerts. Our four boys all took free music lessons at school. They bought and repaired old instruments, learning skills as they did so.

We like to contribute to hunger programs but are somewhat

frustrated by suggestions to cut out a luxury in order to do it.
The luxuries are usually things we don't buy.
—*Ruth Martin*
Ephrata, Pa.

When we became old enough for Social Security, we decided to
volunteer our services to Mennonite Central Committee and let
the payments help to cover our living expenses instead of
building a bank account.

We were thinking of an American assignment but MCC
asked us to go to Korea. Even though our Social Security
money could be sent to us, we would be ineligible for it if we
worked more than seven days a month. Since this was
unsatisfactory, Social Security people offered to give power of
attorney papers to a bank or trust company to collect and place
the checks on our account. We authorized a friend to draw on
that account and send the money to MCC.

During our three years in Korea our Social Security
payments covered two-thirds of our total expenses.
—*Walter and Gladys Rutt*
Gulfport, Miss.

We were in Voluntary Service for a year and experienced living
on a food budget of forty dollars per month per person. We
decided to maintain that budget when we completed our term
of service. Since we now have more money, we decided to
symbolically feed another person by sending a contribution of
forty dollars per month to Mennonite Central Committee for a
food-related project.
—*Perry and Liz Yoder*
North Newton, Kan.

1. We reject all credit cards except one which we use primarily
   when we travel, especially for unexpected expenses.
2. We buy only when we have sufficient cash to pay for
   purchases.
3. We don't shop for the sake of shopping. We go to the store
   only as needs arise.
4. We refuse to invest money in the stock market. A high
   percentage of companies manufacture products of which we
   don't approve. Our cash investments are in the program of
   the Mennonite Church. In this way the larger church can be
   expanded at less cost than would be necessary if money
   were borrowed from banking firms at high rates of interest.
—*John and Kathy Hostetler*
Akron, Pa.

During our service assignment in Labish Village, a
disadvantaged community near Salem, Oregon, we learned
something new about generosity. It is not limited by income! In
fact, it sometimes seems to be inversely related.

Again and again our poor neighbors surprised us with their generosity. After working long days picking fruit and vegetables in the fields, families would bring boxes of their pickings to share with us even though their earnings were determined by the amounts they picked.
—*Warren and Connie Hoffman*
  Bloomfield, N.M.

●●●●●●●●●●●●●●●●●●●●●●●●●●●

Lending and Borrowing

I helped to supervise a toy lending library for disadvantaged children as part of our Bible study group's community outreach project. We inherited truckloads of toys when another library closed, and rented space in a community building.
  Parents and children discovered the learning value of a variety of good, educational toys which they could check out to take home.
—*Grace Dickerson*
  Washington, D.C.

A few years ago our Mennonite Fellowship members each listed items we had to share with others and skills we had to teach or use for others. Items ranged from household appliances to car repair tools. Skills included crocheting, knitting, typing, bicycle repair, and car maintenance. Now each summer there is a rush on my pressure cannner. It's an expensive item, needed only a few weeks each year. With a little planning we all have time to use it.
—*Ruth Guengerich*
  Ann Arbor, Mich.

●●●●●●●●●●●●●●●●●●●●●●●●●●●

Trading and Bartering

When I went to enroll my daughter in nursery school I debated whether to send her two mornings, which we could afford, or stretch our budget to three mornings. Talking to the director I found that the staff was concerned that the children eat nutritious food. I wondered about the possibility of exchanging two loaves of my whole wheat bread for a morning of school. I was afraid he would laugh at this but instead the director immediately agreed and kept commenting on what a good idea it was. Now if I could only barter for seminary tuition!
—*Jan Abramsen*
  Allentown, Pa.

A friend and I arranged a barter of skills. Her family wanted me to paint a family dairy operation sign. Since her mother and grandmother are avid quilters and a quilt appealed to me more than cash, we decided to negotiate a talent swap.

Now the star patch quilt keeps me toasty warm and is cause for many "oohs" and "aahs." Pleasant Ridge Farm hung out its shingle and the dairy business continues to flourish.
—*Jim King*
Akron, Pa.

I swap professional services for services my patients may have to offer. I once exchanged three medical office visits for the custom framing services of a graduation certificate.
—*Paul T. Yoder*
La Junta, Colo.

We have a small farm with a poultry operation. Recently a friend asked for some manure for his plot of ground. He has wood which we need for our fireplace, so we traded. This saved us both money, gave us the opportunity to work together, and helped develop a beautiful and sharing friendship.
—*Keith Lehman*
Akron, Pa.

Our thirteen-year-old daughter was interested in taking a sign language course. I realized that in addition to the expense of the course, I'd be spending those twenty hours waiting in the car—or browsing in a nearby shopping center!

The agency was helpful in developing an interesting and profitable arrangement. I agreed to do volunteer work in their office each week during Ann's class time as payment for the class fee.

Besides saving money and using time constructively, I gained insight into the needs and problems of the hearing-impaired. And I developed an interest I can share with my daughter.
—*Barbara Weaver*
New Holland, Pa.

My aunt wanted to buy a picture frame from me. We agreed that preparing several meals for my elderly father while I take a leave of absence would be equal to the price of the frame. Both of us were happy.
—*Edna G. Detweiler*
Sellersville, Pa.

**Ways to Get What You Need
with Little or No Money:**

●●●●●●●●●●●●●●●●●●●●●●●●●●●

Gardening

Our church is sponsoring garden projects for low-income and   ℰ
elderly residents of three large housing complexes. One
afternoon we removed tires, cement slabs, pieces of pavement,
sheet metal, and other trash from a one-acre tract which we'd
leased for one dollar a year. Then we hauled in a few tons of
elephant manure from the local zoo and thirty tons of sewage
sludge from the city. After discing we seeded the plot with oats
and crimson clover as a cover crop for the winter.

   In spring we'll divide the tracts into plots. A local
Community Action Program will make seeds, plants, and
fertilizer available. Some of us from the church plan to spend
some time hoeing and weeding with the gardeners.
—*John Hofer*
   Susan Corsaro
   Knoxville, Tenn.

To assure early lettuce for our table and to avoid its high cost   ℰ
in the store at that time of year, I use a wood frame covered
with plastic. This protects the tender lettuce from winds, ice,
and snow or from rabbits and birds who also like early greens.
I plant the seeds as early as the soil can be tilled, water
generously, and place the cover over the seedbed making sure
dirt is packed around the frame. Periodically I see if watering is
necessary, then return the cover and seal the edges.
—*Hilda Janzen*
   North Newton, Kan.

Sharing the Surplus

Two years ago the Food and Hunger Concerns Committee of   ♓
Souderton, Pennsylvania, wanted to help the church focus on
local needs. Since many Mennonites grow their own vegetables
and have an overabundant harvest, the idea of sharing the
surplus emerged.

   The goals we outlined were:
1. To supply fresh vegetables at an affordable price to low-
   income families in cities.
2. To eliminate waste of produce.
3. To use the money from this project to support nutrition
   programs sponsored by Mennonite Central Committee in
   other areas.

   The Pennsylvania Agriculture Extension Service helped us
determine market locations and obtain permits. Community
center directors and a social worker showed us areas which

housed predominantly low-income Spanish-speaking, black, and elderly people. The community centers distributed printed flyers in Spanish and English to advertise the project.

Someone was at the Souderton Thrift Shop each collection day to package the produce in bags. As soon as the truck arrived at the selling locations, people gathered to buy. We displayed all prices on a chart. These varied with the supply but were kept at a minimum.

Because some vegetables were new to city buyers, we printed recipes for these in Spanish and English and distributed them. Shoppers could also taste samples of prepared dishes. Agriculture Extension Service charts and personnel explained the nutritional value of the vegetables.

A special blessing of this project was the joy buyers experienced when they discovered that *they* were contributing to help the hungry in other countries. These people had always been too much in need themselves to help others.
—*Donella Clemens*
Souderton, Pa.

Weeds

Gardeners, spare those weeds! Some of them are good cost-free eating! Our family enjoys purslane as a salad ingredient and lamb's quarters as a creamed vegetable or in soups. Dandelion blossoms dipped in a light batter and fried are delicious and dandelion leaves may be served as a raw or cooked green.
—*Evelyn Krehbiel*
Bluffton, Ohio

Modern-Day Gleaning

We've learned to salvage what our society throws away. We find much wasted food in the big garbage dumpsters behind grocery stores. Winter is an excellent time for scavenging because low temperatures help to preserve the produce.

Some of the things we've found are fifty pounds of popcorn, fifteen pounds of walnuts, as well as grapes, melons, potatoes, yogurt, cheese, milk, cookies, celery, peppers, lettuce, cabbage, cucumbers, tomatoes, plastic wrap, tape, and plastic containers. We've found exotic things like guava, pomegranate, avocados, and honeydew melons! Once we discovered bushels of oranges, apples, and grapefruit.

Often the food we find is excellent. Many stores throw out an entire bag when one item is spoiled. Others throw out fruit and dairy products when they are outdated. Since we're used to cleaning garden produce, we find it easy to sort, clean up, and cut out bad spots from the produce we salvage.
—*New Covenant Fellowship*
Athens, Ohio

Since coming to Idaho we haven't bought potatoes. We pick up
a year's supply in the neighbor's field—gleaning what is left
after the potato harvester has done its job.
—*Erna Bartel*
  Aberdeen, Idaho

Since my husband has a business in drywall he is aware of new
building sites. Plenty of scrap lumber around these areas is
thrown away. Builders said any piece under a meter (three feet)
may be picked up by the public. This is perfect wood for the
fireplace or wood burner. For us, it's probably the cheapest fuel
available anywhere.
—*Leona Biggs*
  Salem, Ore.

Four times a year we have what is called a *Sperrmuell Tag*
(extra trash day). On this day sidewalks are piled high with
everything people no longer want, from kitchen sinks to living
room sofas! Anyone may help himself to whatever is there. At
night special garbage trucks come to clear away what is left.
  Most of our household furnishings have been acquired in
exactly this way. We find the old furniture particularly
attractive. It is often made of solid wood which requires only a
little polishing or stain. We used the wood from old fashioned
beds to make lovely and sturdy bunkbeds for our children as
well as shelves and bookcases.
—*Margaret Sawatsky*
  Neuwied, West Germany

Professional Services

If you live near a major city, chances are it has a dental school.
Although fees vary, they are only 20 to 50 percent of the usual
private practice fee of the same service.
—*J. R. Eshleman*
  Midlothian, Va.

I am the director of Legal Aid Manitoba, a program to assist
persons who, when left to their own means, cannot retain the
services of a lawyer. Even though an applicant's gross income
exceeds the eligibility guidelines, he or she may obtain legal aid
by agreeing to contribute to part of the cost.
  Legal advice is available through the Lawyer Referral
Service which is run by law societies or bar associations
throughout most of the United States and Canada. Both the
Lawyer Referral Service and legal aid offices might be used for
obtaining initial advice on a matter and for getting second
opinions at little or no cost.
—*Norman Larsen*
  Winnipeg, Man.

Landscaping

I like to use native wild flowers and grasses in landscaping. Doing this requires changes in esthetic attitudes since these plants will not usually stay green throughout the growing season. When my buffalo grass lawn turns brown during a hot dry period, is it bad or is it a sign of a successful biological adaptation? Wild flowers are often smaller and less dramatic than garden flowers. But is bigger always better? Isn't the dainty heath aster in the corner of my wild flower garden just as pretty as larger cultivated asters?

Here are advantages of my native plantings:

1. They're adapted to the soils and climate and will survive and grow without fertilizer, irrigation, or protection from pests.
2. They add diversity which will probably contribute to the environmental stability.
3. They provide food and other requirements for native animals, including beneficial insects and birds.
4. An established prairie requires mowing only once or twice a season.

—Dwight Platt
Newton, Kan.

●●●●●●●●●●●●●●●●●●●●●●●●●●●●

We can be poor because of the things we have. In debt and committed to the hilt, living from one paycheck to the next means a person has no room to wiggle!
—William T. Snyder
Akron, Pa.

I suppose in North America it is against the law, but here we resterilize disposable syringes hundreds of times to use and reuse without signs of harm.
—John R. Schmidt
Asuncion, Paraguay

We've been vegetarians for quite some time, so we don't need to stand in front of the meat counter pinching our pennies.
—Katie Myers
Dacca, Bangladesh

We accept only one outside responsibility per year, usually church-related. This gives us more time with our family.
—Marcia Yoder
Goshen, Ind.

Shop in cities! You help to preserve the city and save the farmland where the big shopping malls keep springing up.
—Erma Wenger
Musoma, Tanzania

Strawberries along the fence or walk, rhubarb and mint tea plants on the north side of a building, two or three pepper plants in the flower bed, and half a dozen tomato plants staked in a sunny spot make for plenty of good eating.
—Sarah E. Campbell
Dayton, Va.

Fremont always drinks his tea without sugar, remembering those who work unjustly for our abundance. Little acts of worship and sacrifice are a beginning.
—Sara Regier
North Newton, Kan.

A man is rich in proportion to the number of things which he can afford to let alone.
—Thoreau

People always say simple living takes too much time. Actually it's like typing. At first it's slow but the better you become at it, the faster it goes. When you get good at it, it saves you lots of time.
—Andrew Shelly
  Newton, Kan.

Jesus says one will leave family for the kingdom— a radical statement in his society. North Americans leave their families for anything, especially money.
—Urbane Peachey
  Ephrata, Pa.

I do not subscribe to any popular women's magazines. When well over half of a magazine is devoted to advertising, it is not worth its price.
—Pat Hostetter Martin
  Phoenixville, Pa.

Mennonite churches are growing in the Third World. Those which are not growing are in Europe and America. One thing which hinders growth in Europe and America is affluence. We pray that you may grow, and we pray that this crippling aspect may not be the case in other places.
—Million Belete
  Nairobi, Kenya

The minimum responsibility for any Christian in the area of finances is that he share economic secrets with his brothers and sisters.
—Art Gish, Author of
  Beyond the Rat Race

While pursuing our careers, Weldon and I want to have as much time as possible for our children and the church. We've reached out into our community for helpers to ease the workload at home. Our family gains immensely from this help and these friendly associations. At the same time, our helpers gain an essential income.
—Rebecca Kreider Pries
  Cambridge, Mass.

2.   *clothes*

●●●

We wear clothes to keep us comfortable in varying temperatures and to provide the degree of modesty a culture expects. There you have the basics.

After that we branch out to protection—the construction worker's hard hat and steel-toed shoes; convenience pockets for a pen, hammer, or stethoscope; and visual interest—a striped scarf or embroidered apron. All are legitimate. But enter plenty of buying power, technology which takes the toiling and spinning out of clothing production, and a modern fashion industry for which a spokesperson said, "It is our job to make women [add men and children!] unhappy with what they have." The result? Five-foot closets, seen as necessities in every singly inhabited bedroom. These replace the hooks on the wall and an occasional wooden wardrobe which, one hundred years back, served large families.

The result is also a lively thrift shop movement in support of church agencies and other good causes. I support these shops. Any attempt to recycle instead of buying new is a foot on the brake instead of the accelerator. But we must realize that communities which can stock one thrift shop after another are rich, wasteful communities. In many parts of the world a thrift shop movement is unthinkable. To organize a thrift shop or buy there is blessed, but to live so that you have little to donate is an equally high calling.

Priscilla Garrett from Elkhart, Indiana, writes:
When we lived in Guatemala, a fourteen-year-old Kekchi boy named Amiliano worked for us. My husband had some shirts he couldn't wear anymore, and I wanted to get rid of them. I offered one to Amiliano, but he said, "No, thank you. I have two shirts, and I don't want more. With two, I wash one while I wear the other. If I had a third one, it would just mildew."

Beyond saving money, reasons why dressing simply helps the hungry and poor are not always obvious. Does owning fewer clothes save land for food production, conserve energy, and free the poor? Why not just enjoy the excitement of a new fabric, a new cut for the season? After all, clothing in North America is relatively cheap. (In many countries a new outfit costs not a day's wages, but a month's.) And there are always sales. Fashion changes so quickly that stores must move leftovers out every season to make way for the new, to the clever shopper's advantage. One morning when a fellow staff person in our office returned from a conference on world hunger and lifestyle I asked him, "Well, how is it in the churches? What are Mennonites thinking?" His answer: "Mennonites are still able to justify buying on sale!"

Actually, clothing connects with several standards of more with less:

Do Justice. Why are we able to afford so much? Not only because production is efficient, but also because the mass production of cloth and clothing has long been the dull, repetitive factory work of poor people paid low wages. Art Gish, author of *Beyond the Rat Race,* says we should wear our clothes as long as possible and sew our own just to make as little as possible of this depressing work necessary.[1]

Today much of the inexpensive clothing on North America's discount house and bargain basement racks comes from the sweatshops of Korea, Hong Kong, Taiwan, the Philippines, or Singapore. Young women, especially, provide cheap labor, often standing to work at monotonous tasks ten or more hours a day, six days a week. In part, this makes possible the "Asian economic miracle" these countries exemplify. Becky Cantwell, reporting on a visit to an Asian export-oriented industry, describes adolescent and teenage girls waiting to be interviewed for jobs at one factory as "bubbly, giggly, and carefree" while regular workers had a "wilted, broken quality." Often the daughters of struggling small farmers, these girls are sent into town to supplement their parents' meager incomes.[2] Their lives bring to mind the Industrial Revolution's nineteenth-century offenses—long working hours, low wages, and inadequate child-labor laws.

At least they have jobs, we reason. At least they eat. And how can we know if it helps for us to buy more of this clothing

or less? Although the lines that connect them with us are
tangled, I believe Christians can never justify closets bulging
with the products of another's exploitation.

Nurture People. The work of creatively restoring a garment
to full use enriches the sewer along with the wearer. Many
older people have developed mending into a careful art which
they report enjoying more than sewing new clothes. My
mother-in-law is such a mending expert. She can recover the
most baffling rips with know-how and firm stitches. She often
works on the spot when a problem occurs to keep clothing in
circulation and avoid the discouragement of a large mending
pile.

Several people sent in advice on what to do with new and
good used fabric pieces. These activities fall in the category of
crafts, and are quite time-consuming. But certain times in life
allow such enjoyable projects. I pieced two quilts one peaceful
winter when I was home with children already out of diapers
but not yet in school. For many people, retirement years are
the right time for putting to attractive use an extended family's
fabric scraps.

Protect Nature and Conserve Energy. Although the
percentage of energy used to produce textiles is low (2.4
percent of the 1974 energy expenditure of U.S. industry), fabric
production does deplete resources. Cotton is about twice as
energy-efficient to produce as synthetics derived from
petroleum and natural gas, including energy inputs for raising
the cotton.[3] Wool is even more energy-efficient than cotton.
While synthetics are long-wearing and require no cropland for
production, they are produced from nonrenewable resources
and are not biodegradable. When I visit a thrift shop, I sense
by the number of waiting rackfuls that nobody really knows
how to get rid of five-year-old polyester doubleknit dresses!

Twenty-one percent of the energy used in North America goes for changing our indoor temperature.

Therefore the most important consideration connecting
clothing choice and energy conservation is whether garments
keep us cool in summer and warm in winter. Synthetics may
come off well in climates which face no extremes. But they give
free steam baths in hot weather, and are cold and clammy in
winter. To be comfortable in them you need the new concept in
heating and cooling—"climate control." The smooth, glass

rod-like fibers of synthetic fabrics do not absorb perspiration or
allow skin to ventilate as does crinkly cotton fiber. By the time
our children were three or four they pulled cotton play shirts
from their drawers, refusing anything "itchy" of nylon or
polyester.

Synthetics cannot match wool for winter warmth. Wool is a
scaly, stretchy fiber abounding with microscopic air spaces for
trapping body heat. Although it is harder to clean than most
fibers, wool has an amazing capacity to shed dirt and wrinkles,
and needs less care than most fibers. Balance the money spent
for occasionally dry cleaning wool against the cash and energy
bill for the frequent washing and drying required by "easy-
care" fabrics.

Wool is long-wearing and biodegradable. If you don't like
the rough texture of some wools next to your skin, try it over a
layer of cotton for winter comfort. Layering can also reduce
cleaning costs. For centuries wool has been raised on the rocky
hills of marginal terrain and requires the barest energy input to
produce.

Fabric decisions do not need to be cast solely in terms of a
natural-versus-synthetic fibers debate. Technology also
provides us with combination fabrics. Washable, wrinkle-free
materials that are mostly cotton or wool may be the most
energy-efficient and inexpensive in the long run.

Nonconform with Freedom. For most people energy use in
choosing clothing is scarcely a consideration. Style is what
counts.

Certain Mennonite groups have had a long history of
rejecting changing styles. Doctrines of nonconformity and
simplicity were carefully articulated in clothing practice.

As early as 1525 Johannes Kessler wrote concerning the
Swiss Brethren: "They shun costly clothing, and despise
expensive food and drink, clothe themselves with coarse cloth,
[and] cover their heads with broad felt hats. Their entire
manner of life is completely humble."[4]

Yet most scholars believe that contemporary Mennonites'
spiritual forebears, the sixteenth-century Anabaptists of the
Netherlands, Switzerland, and South Germany, had no
prescribed dress codes. They wore conventional clothing of the
common classes from which most of them came. Melvin
Gingerich in *Mennonite Attire Through Four Centuries*
suggests that legalism developed much later. As the modern
world encroached upon the borders of Mennonite communities
in various countries to which they migrated, old customs and
styles were frozen to maintain social cohesion.[5]

What was significant in Anabaptist clothing practice is not
what they advocated but what they rejected. Menno Simons'
writings explode with disdain for religious leaders who mark
this position with ostentatious finery while neglecting the poor.

A typical passage cries out against "the greatest and highest
esteemed preachers of our day, men whose names have become
famous." Notwithstanding the "accursed, ungodly splendor of
their houses . . . the vain and fancy ornaments, chains, rings,
silks, and satin of their women and children . . . they are
called the evangelical theologians." "Alack and alas,"
concludes Menno, "of the comfortable and carnal gospel!"[6]

The Amish, one contemporary religious group descended
from sixteenth-century Anabaptists, stopped the clock of style
centuries ago. Their clothing expresses obedience to the
Ordnung, or rules of the congregation, and to the suppression
of *Hochmut,* or pride.[7] *Hochmut* is a term formerly used in the
Kansas Mennonite, congregation in which I grew up. *Hochmut*
meant any way in which you tried to put yourself above other
people, and carried the connotation of stuffiness, putting on
airs, the upturned nose. *Hochmut* was a balloon waiting for a
pin.

Where is *Hochmut* in the clothing practices of North
American churches today? Does it lie in not being able to wear
the same dress or suit three Sundays in a row? In buying
jewelry to complement each outfit? In the flashy matched attire
of Christian musical entertainers? In the firm tradition that
nylon stockings and neckties must go to church even in hot
weather, thus necessitating air-conditioning? In the subtle
desire to be respected as Christians? Even in thinking that only
those who wear jeans to church live simply?

Rules are no answer. *Living more* with less suggests freedom
from legalism, recognizing that it comes in more than one
form. Requiring so many pleats in the head covering or "jeans
only" is one form. Being enslaved to the new and fashionable is
another. Entries for this chapter exemplify these principles:
1. Dress for comfort according to the weather. Failure to do so
   means energy waste in heating and cooling.
2. Buy or make good quality clothing of timeless, classic cut.
   Wear clothing until it wears out, mending carefully and
   creatively to keep a neat appearance.
3. Recycle unused clothing for further wear or alternate use,
   being willing to be the recipient as well as the donor.
4. Express your personality through dress but do not regularly
   allow clothing to become an answer to boredom or a
   substitute for inner resources of self-assurance. Respect
   your sexuality and that of others with modest, becoming
   clothes.
5. If you wear a certain type of clothing to fit in, be aware of
   that and evaluate how it squares with the message of
   Christ's kingdom in a world of poverty.
6. Heavy investment of time, money, or concern with what
   you wear is always a danger signal. Remember Jesus' words,

"Do not be anxious about . . . what you shall put on. For life is more than food, and the body more than clothing" (Luke 12:22–23).

Notes

1
Arthur G. Gish, *Beyond the Rat Race* (Scottdale, Pa.: Herald Press, 1973), p. 31.

2
Becky Cantwell, "Asians Struggle for Rights," *CALC REPORT* (New York: Clergy and Laity Concerned, September 1978), p. 5.

3
Sara L. Butler, "Textiles and Energy," *Journal of Home Economics* (May 1978), pp. 44–45.

4
"Dress," *Mennonite Encyclopedia,* Vol. 2 (Scottdale, Pa.: Herald Press, 1956), p. 101.

5
Melvin Gingerich, *Mennonite Attire Through Four Centuries* (Breinigsville, Pa.: The Pennsylvania German Society, 1970), p. 13.

6
Menno Simons, *The Complete Writings of Menno Simons,* trans. Leonard Verduin, ed. John Christian Wenger (Scottdale, Pa.: Herald Press, 1956), p. 737. Menno wrote in the Netherlands in the mid-1500s.

7
From the film script of *The Amish: A People of Preservation,* by John Ruth. Available from Encyclopedia Britannica Educational Library, 425 North Michigan Ave., Chicago, Ill. 60611.

••••••••••••••••••••••••••••

Asking and Giving • While living in Calcutta I was daily aware of the disparity between rich and poor. One day a mother came to our apartment to tell me that her daughter would be working in the mountains during the winter and needed a pair of warm slacks. "Could she have a pair of yours?" she asked.

I knew I could not explain that I had only two pairs—a bare minimum in North America. She would think that absurd. Were the Bible passages to be taken literally?

After deciding which pair of slacks to give, I added the matching top as well. I'm embarrassed to admit now that I never missed that outfit. The remaining pair of slacks saw me through two winters.
—*Herta Janzen*
London, Ont.

A Streamlined Wardrobe • When we last lived in Israel, an Arab woman made for me a long black-with-red embroidered *tobe*—the traditional dress of the village women. I decided that, having made the investment, I should really use the dress here at home. Long, loose, machine-washable and dryable, opaque, comfortable, and modest, this is my shopping-school-church-wedding-funeral-dress! This summer, for the first time in over three years, I bought a dress of conventional make to wear on hottest days. I wore it once or twice, both times uncomfortably, and quickly changed back into my *tobe*.

This gesture will surely not be taken up by many women. Most will not have the opportunity to get such a dress. But several people told me that because of it they were inspired to streamline their wardrobes drastically. Maybe sometimes it takes a far-out idea to help us move just a little closer toward a life of "more and less"—more investment in the life of the kingdom and less preoccupation with what we shall eat and what we shall drink and how we shall be clothed.
—*Miriam Lind*
Goshen, Ind.

Keeping Cool • May is the middle of the hot season in India. One morning the temperature soared and wind blew hotly across the plains as I ventured out with a newly arrived American friend to the police station for the necessary check-in.

Wearing a sari, I slid easily behind the wheel of my little car. My friend, bare-legged and wearing a knee-length, sleeveless dress, joined me on the front seat.

"Wow, this seat is hot!" she exclaimed. We stretched a matting under her. "Everything we touch is hot these days," I said. "I hope I can park under a tree at the office. Inside there will be fans and maybe a *cus cus*"(a mat made of special roots hung at an open door or window and kept wet so that the breeze is cooled as it enters the room).

As we approached the office, we saw the *cus cus* and heard the whirring fans. The chief of police welcomed us. "Have chairs," he said. "This is a hot day. May I order tea for you?" Since I was a foreign resident and had to make periodic visits to this office, we were well acquainted.

We conducted our business in English but as we finished, the policeman spoke to me in Hindi. "You are appropriately dressed for this hot weather. A sari gives you protection. She should wear one, too," he said, indicating my friend.

Driving home, I mentioned the policeman's concern. I explained how I spread my sari *pallu* over the chair arms, and how the length of my skirt protected me from the hot seat. The flowing gauze-like cloth dampened by perspiration also served as an air conditioner.

Understanding why Indians find more rather than less clothing comfortable in hot weather, my friend was quick to accept this custom for herself.
—*Marie M. Moyer*
  Telford, Pa.

Converted to a Blanket ● The Lesotho winter gets icy cold with snow and bitter winds in mountain areas. To keep warm, people here use blankets as clothing. Traditionally, these were animal skins, but now colorful wool blankets are the style. They are simply slung around the shoulders and fastened with a large safety pin, at the shoulder by men or at the sternum by women. Even though I have a coat, I'm totally converted to a blanket for a variety of reasons.
1. One size fits all: width is adjusted by overlapping at the front; length is determined by folding under at the top.
2. It lasts a lifetime: no need constantly to buy new coats for growing children nor worry about fashion. Here a woman usually receives a new blanket as a wedding present from her husband.
3. All-season use: on cool summer evenings the blanket can be worn over light clothing, in the dead of winter the same blanket fits over layers of sweaters.
4. Great freedom of movement: in a blanket one isn't restricted or mummified. If worn properly it does not get in the way of hand actions.
5. Comfort: the wearer can snuggle up in it, obtaining not only physical but also psychological warmth.
—*Rebecca Dyck*
  Roma, Lesotho

●●●●●●●●●●●●●●●●●●●●●●●●●●

Gray Hair and Liberation

ℓ Like the ad says, I was "too young to look old." At age twenty-five I found my gray hair depressing, but going to Zambia for a teaching assignment meant good-bye to my hairdresser.

Coloring my hair was not only impossible there, it was totally unnecessary! As I became interested in my new environment and acquainted with the reality of living in a less wealthy country, I saw aging and health care in a new perspective. Average life expectancy in Zambia is thirty-eight years. I realized I had been acculturated to believe that hair color was important to the quality of life! This new awareness brought on my personal version of liberation.
—Barbara Weaver
New Holand, Pa.

I. After spending five years in the tropics I got out of the habit of wearing either shoes or nylon hose. But when pleasant fall weather in Pennsylvania turned into a ferocious winter I realized sandals would no longer do. I bought a pair of sturdy, all-purpose leather shoes that would last a long time.
As for nylon hose, I couldn't bring myself to wear them again. They seemed silly. They don't keep my legs or feet warm; they are expensive and impractical. For the same price I can buy a good pair of warm knee socks which outlast the nylons by at least a year. I wear slacks or long skirts, whichever seems more appropriate.
—Pat Hostetter Martin
Phoenixville, Pa.

●●●●●●●●●●●●●●●●●●●●●●●●●●

I. **Style and Men** ● The minute we begin talking about style and fashion our attention usually goes to women. I'd like to direct these thoughts to men.

What is the dress code in the office in which you work? Who sets it? Why? What is the criteria for establishing standards for dress? Sometimes in the middle of introductions I look at a man's clothing for an obvious clue to his vocation. Surely this pompous assumption is made from stereotypes I tuck away in my file of values.

Don't most of us have preconceptions about those who wear jeans to church or sport three-piece suits for preaching on television? These may be extremes; however, I'm convinced that few of us escape the influence of style. From where else do we receive the annual prompting to gather a new wardrobe during year-end sales?

My clothes shouldn't make a difference in how I present myself to others. Wearing coats and ties may be appropriate for

some. For myself a sweater and corduroy trousers provide comfort and a neat appearance in my church-related office job.
—*Charlie Lord*
Akron, Pa.

Jeans and a Suit ● A year ago I was standing in a

reception line with about a hundred foreign ambassadors waiting to congratulate the president and prime minister of Laos on the second anniversary of the People's Democratic Republic.

Suddenly I had a shocking realization: I was the only male in the room not wearing a suit or tuxedo, even though my allowance as a Mennonite Central Committee volunteer was higher than the salary of the Lao president. When my turn came to greet him, Mr. Souphanouvong expressed polite appreciation for MCC's efforts in Laos. Yet I couldn't help wondering if my attire seemed appropriate to an Asian for whom clothing was an important symbol.

Growing up in the 1960s, blue jeans had virtually become my uniform. Through high school, college, and graduate school I had an old worn pair for everyday use and a newer pair for dressier occasions. I tried to dress simply but neatly. I accumulated as few clothes as possible, only buying new items after old ones wore out.

Following my return to the United States this spring, I took a job in Washington, D.C., to be a voice for Vietnamese and Laotian people who face hardship resulting from decades of war and natural calamities. I bought my very first suit. After six months of practice I have even learned to put on a tie. My experience at the Laos anniversary celebration taught me not to make clothing a barrier to relationships.
—*Murray Hiebert*
Washington, D.C.

Receiving from Others ● Our friends and relatives readily

recognize our entire family as grateful recipients of used clothing. I average one major purchase a year, but growing children need clothes more often. We constantly marvel that clothing from friends is exactly what we need and coordinates well.

I used to frequent sales but reduced prices tempted me to buy more than we really needed. Now I pray before I shop to prevent impulse buying. I recognize God's direction in helping me find what I need quickly and economically.

Receiving from others has helped us build relationships and change our values. We give less thought to external appearance, of ourselves and others. We feel we relate more easily to needy families and individuals whose friendship we try to cultivate.
—*LaVerna Klippenstein*
Winnipeg, Man.

One Woman's Guidelines ● In public school I dressed as a plain Mennonite girl. Sometimes I felt self-conscious about my appearance. This distracted me just as much as if I'd been proud of my looks.

Dressing comfortably frees me to meet people and new situations without being preoccupied with my clothing. To avoid spending lots of money or energy on this, I developed the following guidelines for myself:

1. I either sew or buy clothes on sale. Even elementary sewing skills save money if one makes simple skirts or dresses. I buy more complicated items such as blouses and jackets.
2. I try to choose clothes with classic lines that are in style for several seasons. This way I'm not tempted to discard clothes just because they're outdated.
3. I have one basic color for fall and winter and another for spring and summer so that I can mix and match and avoid the need for a variety of coordinating shoes or purses.
4. A month or so before a change in season, I gather together all items left from previous years and spread them on my bed. I make sure I have appropriate clothes for work, outdoor activities, meetings, and church. Usually I need only a few new items. I know exactly what I need and am rarely tempted to buy impulsively.
5. At the end of each season I look ahead and buy on sale only items I'm certain will be needed.

—*Joanna Reesor-McDowell*
Unionville, Ont.

Sharing Used Clothing ● After sharing children's clothes informally for a period of time, our Sunday school class set up a systematic way of exchanging them. Money and hours are saved and the clothing gets full use.

Twice a year, everyone brings clothing that is no longer needed to someone's home. We sort and spread them out. After each of us finds what we can use we sort for the next exchange or send the rest to a thrift shop.

—*Lois Beck*
West Liberty, Ohio

Adult Hand-Me-Downs and Bargains ● Hand-me-downs are common among youngsters. But why not translate this tradition into adulthood? People living in close proximity or community can intentionally recycle clothing. We find it a caring act.

We also discovered that with patience and perseverance bargains can be truly fantastic at secondhand stores. We shop with a specific list at discount centers which sell factory seconds. A sense of adventure makes less money buy more.

—*Karin Michaelson*
Washington, D.C.

Outfitting a Newborn • Baby showers are overdone. It   **P**
seems as if people think the fancier a baby can be dressed, the
better!

Fifty years ago when I was a young mother, people didn't
give many presents for a new baby. I wonder if mothers today
don't miss a great blessing by not sewing their own baby
clothes. During the hours in which I made outfits for my
babies, I enjoyed a special time of prayer. I used scraps left
from other sewing. I decorated with lace and embroidery.
Admiring the tiny wardrobe I made, my husband and I were
drawn closer together.
—*Helene Janzen*
  Elbing, Kan.

●●●●●●●●●●●●●●●●●●●●●●●●●●●●

Cut Home Sewing Costs

Sewing clothes can save money but sometimes homemade   **C**
garments end up being as expensive as those purchased. Here is
how I cut down the cost of home-sewn garments.
1. I revived grandmother's button jar, collecting buttons from
   discarded clothing and leftovers on button cards. Sometimes
   secondhand stores have buttons. Children have fun pouring
   them out on a large baking pan and sorting them.
2. I save good zippers from otherwise worn-out garments.
3. I reuse patterns, some from secondhand stores or garage
   sales. Public libraries and churches often have pattern
   exchanges.
—*Janice A. Kreider*
  Vancouver, B.C.

I purchase good, used clothing at thrift shops to cut down for
smaller-sized garments. Each of our girls was heading into her
teens before she owned a store-bought coat. No one knew the
difference unless I told them.
—*Linda Richert*
  New Waverly, Tex.

Our lifestyle in Zambia had no place for a sewing machine so I   **L**
reconciled myself to living several years without the creative
expression of sewing.

As our children grew and ready-made clothing was not
always available, I discovered that Zambian women were
dressing their families with garments sewn by hand. In a rare
burst of insight, I realized I also was capable of developing this
skill!

I learned the basics: stitching a fine, neat, strong seam. For
this I had many willing teachers and enjoyed the company of
new friends as we worked. They shared with each other and
with me various methods of sewing without patterns—a

fantastic creative experience! The bright geometrics and cotton prints, themselves so attractive and intricate, demanded simple styling. This meant no more zippers, buttons, or interfacings, and significantly fewer commercial patterns!

I continue these creative expressions since returning home and find joy in sharing ideas and discussing techniques with friends and neighbors.
—*Barbara Weaver*
New Holland, Pa.

●●●●●●●●●●●●●●●●●●●●●●●●●●

How-To:

Piece a Comforter from Jeans ●
After our university days we had lots of old jeans that could no longer be worn but still included good sections of denim. In a magazine I saw a crazy quilt made from old jeans. I decided this was a perfect way to provide a warm coverlet for our four-year-old's bed!

The resulting comforter is much warmer than I expected. Along with an insulated blanket, it gives sufficient warmth for sleeping in our unheated upstairs. However, it's rather heavy to launder.

● Materials Needed:
   —worn-out jeans
   —brightly colored calico
   —an old sheet
   —quilted fabric for backing

● Directions:
   1. Cut one large jean patch at a time, any shape, using as much of the fabric as possible.
   2. Immediately begin sewing patches by matching onto the sheet, starting at the corners. Leave pockets, belt loops, snaps, and leather labels on to add interest. (Matt found the pockets a good place to hide his treasures!)
   3. Any place where patches don't quite fit, fill in with calico.
   4. When patching is complete, knot on a backing of quilted fabric. Make backing a little larger all around than the quilted top.
   5. Finish edges by folding backing over blue jean top, turning under, and sewing in place. The comforter is reversible.

—*Nancy Fisher*
Eureka, Ill.

Whip Up a One-Piece Shirt • While it cannot be termed
national dress, variations of this shirt are worn throughout
urban Africa. Tailors quickly whip up these shirts of Katangi
print to enhance the design of the fabric. When using striped
fabrics, they follow the line of color for the few seams needed.
Creative designs are often machine-embroidered around the
neck opening. The finished product is a cool, loose-fitting
garment. In cold weather a knit pullover may be worn
underneath.
• Materials Needed:
—2m of 90cm-115cm fabric (2 yds. of 36"–45") with selvage
  edges
—bias tape
• Directions:

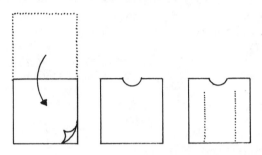

1. Fold fabric in half, one end over the other, right side out.
   (Fig. 1)
2. Cut slight arc for neck opening, in the center ⅓ section of
   the fold. Trim with bias tape. (Fig. 2)
3. Sew two seams, about 18cm (7") from the top. (Fig. 3)
4. Hem or fringe bottom edge.
Variations:

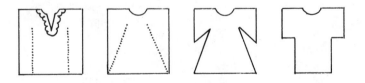

1. A slit or V-neck front opening seems to suit some
   patterns nicely.
2. Sleeves are sometimes sewn diagonally from the bottom
   corners, creating a butterfly effect.
3. Turn fabric inside out, sew seams for sleeves and cut
   away extra fabric. Turn right side out to wear.
4. To make a dress use about 2.8m (3 yds.) of fabric. A
   floor-length robe requires about 3.6m (4 yds.).

—Norma Johnson
Akron, Pa.

Make Rubber Tire Sandals ● I needed shoes. At the same time, a pair of old leather shoes and an old rubber tire needed regeneration. Adding some eager muscle for stitching and cutting and about two hours of time, I made myself a pair of sandals.

I've had this snugly fitting, comfortable, air-conditioned pair of shoes for about four years and have walked many miles over surfaces worse than those in a Ford pickup commercial. They still don't shown any wear.

● Materials Needed:
 —an old car tire
 —leather from old belts, shoes, boots, or mitts
 —#140 (or heavier) waxed nylon thread from shoe-repair shop, hobby shop, or hardware store
 —a buckle
 —a sharp knife (such as an electrician's knife)
 —a large needle
 —a pair of pliers
 Optional:
 —copper split rivets
 —leather punch
● Directions:

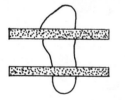 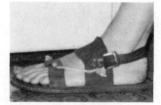

1. With the knife, carve two soles from the rubber tire.
2. Sew two leather straps across the top of each sole using pliers to help ease the needle through the rubber. These may be reinforced by punching holes through leather and rubber, inserting rivets, and securing them snugly with pliers. (Fig. 1) Stitching and/or riveting between the treads of the tire not only makes the work easier, but creates a stronger sandal since thread and rivet are indented from surface.
3. Cut three leather spacers to fill in the rest of the sole. (Fig. 2)
4. Cut two leather soles. Sew and/or rivet the soles and spacers over the base.
5. Loop the straps to fit the foot, sewing or riveting in place. These can be adjusted later when leather stretches.
6. Cut a heel strap that will go over and across both inside foot straps and around the heel. Attach securely. Sew the buckle to the outside strap near the ankle. Adjust to fit.

—Peter Sprunger-Froese
Saskatoon, Sask.

Sew a Wrap-Around or Flared Skirt ● Clothing patterns
in Zambia are hard to get and very expensive so naturally we
were quite excited to receive this set of instructions which can
be used to make a wrap-around or flared skirt of any size.

For either pattern we avoid plaids and stripes but find that a
fabric with a large design is ideal since we don't spoil it by
cutting it up. The flared skirt is a half-circle with a back seam.

● Materials Needed:
—firmly-woven fabric (twice as long as wide)
   2.3m of 115cm fabric (2½ yds. of 45″) for adult size
   1.8m of 90cm fabric (2 yds. of 36″) for child size
—thread
—18cm (7″) skirt zipper for flared skirt
—a fastener or button for flared skirt
—seam binding (optional)
● Directions:

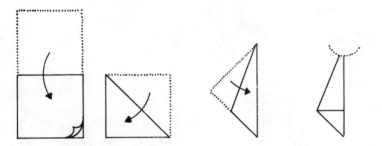

1. Fold fabric in half to make a double square. (Fig. 1)
2. Fold one corner over to make a triangle of four
   thicknesses. (Fig. 2)
3. Fold one of the short sides of the triangle so that it falls
   alongside the long edge resulting in 8 thicknesses. (Fig. 3)
4. Measure your waistline.
   For flared skirt: Add about 2cm (1″) for seam allowance
   and divide by 8. Example:
   75cm waist
   $75 + 2 = 77 \div 8 = 9.6$cm
   29″ waist
   $29 + 1 = 30 \div 8 = 3¾$″
   For wrap-around skirt: Add 38 cm (15″) and divide by 8.
   Example: $75 + 38 = 113 \div 8 = 14$ cm $(29 + 15 = 44 \div 8$
   $= 5½$″).
5. Measure across the top of the triangle and cut an arc to
   equal the final answer. (Fig. 4)
6. Measure skirt length, making allowance for hem. Cut the
   bottom in a gradual arc equidistant from the waist edge.
   (Fig. 5)
7. For flared skirt: Sew up back seam and insert zipper. For
   wrap-around skirt: Hemstitch or topstitch sides.

8. Cut waistband from remaining fabric and sew to waist
edge. For wrap-around: Make the waistband at least
twice as long as waist for tying. Sew a large perpendicular
buttonhole on the waistband approximately 36 cm (14")
from one side of the skirt, through which the belt may be
drawn.
9. Hem.
Pockets may be made with scraps.
—*Liz Hunsberger*
Kathy Fast
Lusaka, Zambia

Create an Afghan from Scraps • I find that afghans are
appropriate for gifts and relief sales. This is a good way to use
scraps from my grandchildren's sewing projects.
• Materials Needed:
—fabric scraps
—crochet hook
—yarn
• Directions:
1. Sort scraps according to harmonizing colors.
2. Cut pieces 20 x 30cm (8" x 12") in size.
3. With a crochet hook, make the buttonhole stitch around
raw edges.
4. Crochet or sew blocks together. Most of my afghans have
6½ blocks in each strip and are six strips wide. By
staggering the blocks the way brick is laid, the four
corners need not be joined precisely. Harmonize colors
and blend plaids, stripes, and prints with plain colors. If
materials ravel it may be necessary to machine zigzag
around the edges before crocheting.
—*Clara Hooley*
Goshen, Ind.

●●●●●●●●●●●●●●●●●●●●●●●●●●●

Rags to Rugs

℮   Rug-braiding is a good way to use discarded clothing. I find
myself hooked on this craft! The excitement of seeing the result
makes me lose all consciousness of time.
First I rip and wash the garments: worn woolen coats are
especially good. After tearing the fabric into 8cm (3 in.) strips I
sew them together on the bias and wind them into hanks.
I plan a color scheme ranging from light to dark, repeating
this pattern several times. Taking three strands I secure them
by pinning them to a pad on a chair back. I braid these, making
sure each strand is folded flat. After braiding enough to make
several rows, I unpin the strands and begin the lacing process.
Working on the floor or using a table, I lace and braid

alternately so that the rug lies flat. Sometimes I lace the thread through two folds in the outer braid when going around the ends of the rug to give extra fullness. When the rug is big enough, I taper the strips and sew them to the side.

Because this is a heavy rug, I lace back to the center again, catching any folds I skipped the first time. This guarantees a durable, reversible, and artistic product.

Length of center row determines proportions of the rug. A 30-centimeter (1-foot) center row yields a rug 30 centimeters (1 foot) longer than wide, such as 90cm x 120 cm (3 ft. x 4 ft.)
—*Areta G. Lehman*
  Goshen, Ind.

In our community, carpet weavers will buy balls of rags to make into rag rugs. Strips of fabric must be sewn together by hand or machine, giving some thought as to how colors will be mixed when the rug is finished. The kind of fabric used will determine how well the rug will wear. Cut heavier cloth into 2.5cm (1 inch) widths and lighter cotton fabrics into 5–8cm (2–3 inch) strips. The material should roll tightly to the thickness of a pencil. Overlap the ends of the fabric strips and sew them together. Roll strips into a ball and find a carpet weaver.
—*Anna Mary Brubacher*
  Kitchener, Ont.
—*Fern Shantz*
  Baden, Ont.

●●●●●●●●●●●●●●●●●●●●●●●●●●●

Be wary of all enterprises that require new clothes, and not rather a new wearer of clothes. If there is not a new man, how can the new clothes be made to fit? If you have any enterprise before you, try it in your old clothes.
—*Thoreau*

Babies are wonderful and fun, but expensive. I've found that using cloth diapers instead of disposables saves about $700 a year, even counting laundry costs.
—*Connie Buller*
  Blair, Neb.

Zairean women wear tops made of strips of cloth sewn together—a very simple patchwork. They also sew strips together to make the long cloths they wrap around for skirts.
—*Retha Baer*
  Kinshasa, Zaire

At eighty years of age, my mother still had the slip she wore for her wedding in the "everyday" drawer. Tucks around the skirt to accommodate shorter styles and lots of neat patching with old soft fabrics kept it useful.
—*Marnetta Brilhart*
  Scottdale, Pa.

Whenever our family gets together for a reunion, we all bring usable clothing to trade. Some dresses have made the rounds for over fifteen years! We have bargain hunting fun and the thrill of sharing.
—Betty J. Rosentrater
  Nappanee, Ind.

I've been a preacher all my life. My wife buys all my suits and she gets them at used clothing stores. She loves me so much she splurged once and spent $7.50.
—Andrew Shelly
  Newton, Kan.

A special place to dress simply is in church. At our Friends' Meeting in Chapel Hill, North Carolina, most people come to worship dressed in the same casual clothes they wear at home on a weekend.
—Susan Reimer
  Durham, N.C.

To determine how much clothing we need, I calculate how many changes of apparel are necessary between washdays. That helps me set a limit.
—Marlene Kropf
  Portland, Ore.

When children's slacks become too short for another season or have worn-out knees, I make shorts using some of the leg fabric to trim a blouse with a decorative symbol or pocket. Once I overheard my daughter tell her friends, "My mommie sewed a heart on because she loves me."
—Ruth S. Weaver
  Reading, Pa.

A used light bulb helps to make a smooth job of darning heels and toes of socks. If you don't have yarn to match the sock, use a bright contrast. Our children like it.
—Erma Wenger
  Musoma, Tanzania

Our sons pour warm fat drippings along the soles and leather stitching on their work shoes. This helps prevent cracking. Hardened fat can be used for shoe polish. It preserves the leather and repels water.
—Rhoda King
  Cochranville, Pa.

Both my grandmothers were well-known quilt makers. One also made rugs. Not one scrap was wasted. If you don't have time for this, take scraps to a thrift shop where they can be sold for craft purposes.
—Martha K. Kauffman
  Atglen, Pa.

I buy only black socks. They match every color, they do not soil easily, new pairs can be formed if mates are lost, and it eliminates one hard decision each morning.
—Vernon R. Wiebe
  Hillsboro, Kan.

Mother often made gingham aprons. She put pockets on both sides and made all seams flat. When someone came unexpectedly, she quickly reversed her apron to the cleaner side.
—Martha K. Kauffman
  Atglen, Pa.

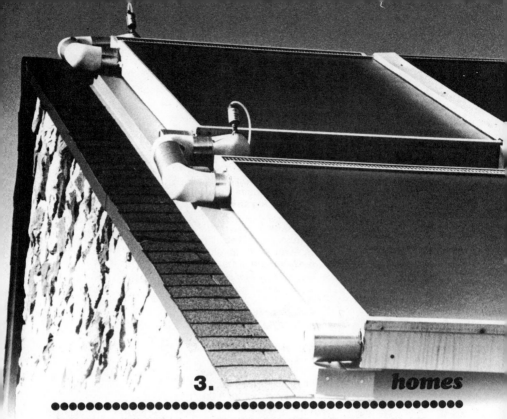

"Most People Don't Want What Architects Want," says
Toronto sociologist William Michelson.[1] His title caught my
eye because, although we've never built a house, I sometimes
feel that new ones I've entered wouldn't suit my needs.

Take kitchens, for example. Whoever invented the modern
corridor kitchen in which you stand to do all your work must
never have had a tired back or varicose veins. An old-fashioned
kitchen table in the middle of things, where you pull up a chair
or stool for time-consuming jobs, is still high on my list of
indispensable kitchen equipment.

But surprisingly, by the time I finished Michelson's piece the
experts were again my friends. He says architects and urban
designers would like to be done with suburban sprawl, fuel
waste, and prize farmland snatched for housing developments
and shopping malls. They would house people in planned
communities featuring compact apartments and townhouses
within walking distance of work, stores, and recreational
facilities.

This is where we come to Michelson's title. According to
studies he quotes, living in a condensed community is simply
not what people want. What a great percentage of the
population clearly prefers is single-family houses on large lots
at the periphery of cities and a car in which to drive to work.[2]

North Americans are not alone in this dream. British writer

Barbara Ward, in a book prepared for the 1976 United Nations
Conference on Human Settlements, leaves out the car and
squeezes the houses closer together, but tends to agree:

> The "home of one's own" that people apparently want
> most to buy is the detached, semidetached or terrace house
> [townhouse] with that blessing for all inventive children and
> industrious parents—the backyard where anything from
> dahlias to pet rabbits to amateur carpentry can make up the
> rich content of "puttering about."[3]

Certainly in a book emphasizing nurture, freedom, and
creativity, we had better not oppose flower gardens and pet
rabbits. Or some provision for a private place where one can
say, "This is where I belong." A home with adequate space and
the right to make decisions about it seems a basic need. People
don't want to be stacked somewhere in boxes out of the rain.
They grow especially restless when the boxes are too full and
some outside power is in charge of restacking them.

Thus we affirm the goodness of choosing how and where to
be at home and having space to putter about. But all's not well
with the dream home researchers say most of us want. First,
many can't afford it and never will. Second, along with the
pleasant aspects of suburbia, we find we're stuck with
communities without sidewalks or safe bikeways, car trips to
buy a loaf of bread, lawns that take half a weekend to groom,
utility bills which swallow two paychecks a family, mortgages
that keep us from sharing with the poor. And the energy crisis.

Expectations for the dream house have gone up and up.
Most new homes of the forties and fifties were quite
comfortable. If we compare these with what people expect in a
new house today, it's clear that the dream isn't static.
Duplication of function abounds with living rooms, family, and
recreation rooms; multiple bathrooms; kitchen eating areas,
formal dining rooms, snack kitchens, and decks. People even
want more and more space *around* the house. The Michelson
article says that "in 1920 the average house lot was one tenth
of an acre. Today it is twice that. And the survey shows people
want still larger lots."[4]

It's doubtful that these larger and more lavish homes
improve communication among family members and increase
fellowship within communities. LeRoy Troyer, an Indiana
architect, says, "In today's buildings we move down corridors
and go into cubicles. We don't have to encounter each other.

"Consider children
who don't eat meals together
and don't have to share
bathrooms and bedrooms.

> They miss an opportunity
> to learn
> interdependence
> and conflict resolution."

A Bible teacher who spent two years visiting Mennonite churches and homes reports, "In all that travel, the most exhausting part was communicating with my hosts and hostesses who provided such lavish accommodations. Things were so tense. I believe wealth is the single most important spiritual crisis facing North American Mennonites. But because I was a guest, it was hard to talk about the way they were living."

Remodeling Dreams

The dream itself—the dream for a perfect home—requires remodeling. Where can we begin?

This world is not my home. Here is the starting point. As good as it is to make a house comfortable, Christians freely admit their longing for Home. No inheritance, real-estate settlement, or faultless house plan fully answers the cry for roots. Christians consciously travel toward a better housing development—a home in the city "whose builder and maker is God."

Living by this hope (not just singing it!) means less time, money, and personal pride invested in housing. Expectations go down, contentment goes up. Furthermore, with the assurance that "in my Father's house are many rooms," we can sometimes accept homelessness, as Jesus did. He became one with the refugees, the shack-dwellers, the evicted of the ages.

The experience of transience helps many understand that home has more to do with friends and love than with expansive family rooms. On the other hand, Jesus' work includes securing decent housing for the homeless.

At home with the earth. For too long we've tried adjusting the environment to our living style.

> Heating and cooling
> we call "climate control."
> It's time to think again
> about controlling
> ourselves.

How much our houses alter the environment, however, is a matter of degree. Adapting is never a 100 percent endeavor.

Any shelter shows distrust of nature's sun, wind, rain, cold, and insects. Any structure we erect changes the face of earth. Still, some people react to chilly evenings with a hand on the thermostat, while others add a sweater. Some build or remodel houses according to fashion, as if they were selecting a scarf; others consider the setting—its natural beauty, existing trees, water-flow patterns, and exposure to sun and wind.

With wise utilization, the environment itself offers solutions. In Davis, California, shade trees are city policy:

> The streets of Davis are lined with 12,000 trees, and 700 new ones are planted each year. One tree is required per lot. The city is partial to those large deciduous trees—oaks, hackberries, and ashes—that provide cooling shade in the summer and lose their leaves in the winter.
>
> Summer . . . temperature generally reaches 95 degrees during the daytime and sometimes exceeds 105 degrees. City officials say that neighborhoods that are covered by leafy canopies are 10 degrees cooler than those that have wide, unshaded streets. A neighborhood that is 10 degrees cooler on a hot day, they add, uses 50 percent less electricity for air conditioning.[5]

Adapting to nature is the oldest human art. Today we need a revival of ancient skills, plus the imagination to develop and accept new innovations designed to be gentle with the environment. This book doesn't provide the technical know-how, which is available elsewhere. Rather, entries in this chapter testify that old ideas like wood heating fit nicely into today's houses; that innovations such as solar power, cave and dome housing, and composting toilets really work for ordinary people. Here one neighbor assures others that solar heating is not as expensive as one thinks, that the composting toilet does not stink.

Adapting to nature with housing is related to conserving nonrenewable resources on all fronts. When selecting a house, *where* that house is located has at least as much to do with saving resources as how the house is heated and cooled. An older house near school and work, if tightened with insulation, may save far more than a new energy-efficient dwelling located where every errand calls for a car.

This old house. When you finish this chapter you may feel like selling the house you live in and making a new beginning. But in reality, you know you can't. You don't change houses like you give up plastic wrap or switch to a smaller car. Many of us are at least figuratively locked in!

Few houses do everything they should—save energy, use space compactly and efficiently, face north or south with many windows one way and few the other, have a proper chimney for wood heat, sit on a location near work, schools, services, and meet all the family's needs. Because you don't get all that by snapping fingers, this chapter is more about retrofitting— making existing structures more energy efficient—than about starting over and doing everything exactly right. Besides, making do with middle-aged and older buildings itself saves resources.

Retrofitting is only a new angle on the old virtue: making do. Usually retrofitting means something like adding a solar system or double-paned glass. While blessing those investments, I like to stretch the meaning even further to include all the energy-saving solutions that are possible here and now: more people in a too-big house, more organization in a small one, more insulation, more long underwear, closing off rooms in winter, and adding awnings and planting trees for summer. We need such actions of a thousand varieties today while we work for more thorough answers tomorrow. Retrofitting means trying to live now the way we should, rather than waiting for the big event that will make it easy to do so.

Listen to testimonies from people busy retrofitting first their dreams and then their houses.

Notes

1
William Michelson, "Most People Don't Want What Architects Want," in *Human Needs in Housing,* eds. Karen Nattrass and Bonnie Maas Morrison (Washington, D.C.: University Press of America, 1977), p. 188.
2
Ibid, p. 190.
3
Barbara Ward, *The Home of Man* (New York: W. W. Norton and Co., Inc., 1976), p. 115.
4
Michelson, p. 194.
5
David Talbot, "Conservatopia, U.S.A.," *Mother Jones* (August 1979), p. 41.

●●●●●●●●●●●●●●●●●●●●●●●●●●

P

Actually, It Was a Terrible House ● During Sunday
dinner with friends our hostess asked, "Did you have a nice
house in India?" I hesitated. We were sitting in an L-shaped
living-dining room furnished in coordinating colors. I
wondered how to define "nice." Before I had a chance to reply,
our eight-year-old son enthusiastically responded, "Oh yes, we
had a real nice house in Calcutta."

Actually, it was a terrible house. After living in it for six
months I was ready to write a manual on coping. This would
include suggestions on how to respond to cockroaches, mice,
and rats coming up drains, torn screens and broken
windowpanes, bats flying through the dining room during
mealtime, blown fuses, broken water pumps, air pockets in the
water pipes, electrical fires, crumbling cement walls, power
cuts, and toilet-flushing instructions for guests. What made
Douglas think it was nice?

I began to reminisce about our various homes. Our first
apartment recalled memories of the growing pains of a
marriage relationship. The house on the mission complex gave
us our first taste of living in another culture where we also
became the proud parents of a daughter. Our older house in
Canada challenged us to repair and rebuild. But as a family we
had our finest hours in our house in Calcutta. We played games
or read. We talked, listened, learned, and sang. We had many
guests. It was also in this house that we sat silent, our minds
churning with whys and hows when we didn't know where to
grab hold of situations that seemed hopeless—but knowing
that answers were expected from us.

In a memo to our successor, I wondered how I could tell
about the frustrating idiosyncrasies of this house without
making them seem a burden. I knew that only the experience of
living in the house could do that but I wished for an
imagination that could make it some kind of sacred ceremony.

Yes, Douglas, we did have a nice house in Calcutta. In fact,
it was a fantastic house. It was our home!
—**Herta Janzen**
  London, Ont.

L

Church in the Whole House ● Fifteen years after first
arriving in Japan we moved to the city of Oita to begin a new
church ministry. Finding nothing suitable to rent, we chose to
have a Japanese home built for us. It is simple and practical.

Straw floors and sliding paper doors for walls are both ideal.
For Sunday worship services and special meetings our
bedroom becomes the extension for the meeting room which
can easily seat forty on the floor. We usually sit on cushions. A
sofa would hinder the flexibility of our living space. We can
easily move our two light easy chairs out of the way for large

gatherings. Peter preaches sitting on his legs. After a while it becomes uncomfortable and even painful. But he would never give up the relaxed atmosphere of our floor life.

We decided our new home had no room for beds. At first Peter put away the bedding from the floor into the closet each morning. As the children grew bigger they learned to do it themselves, leaving their small upstairs rooms empty for play. Jesus' words, "Take up thy bed and walk," took on new meaning for us. Because we have so little furniture, our bedroom can be the family room as well as an extra classroom and Sunday school room.

Our kitchen and dining room are compact but can seat twelve. We always enjoy having guests. Japanese people smile when they come into our home for the first time and see the soft straw floors that are so much a part of their life. They all agree that feelings relax while sitting on the floor.

—*Mary Derksen*
Oita, Japan

●●●●●●●●●●●●●●●●●●●●●●●●●●

One-Celled Living:

Pennsylvania Farm ● Living on the farm in a trailer for some years made me realize how much less I really need. A few car-trunkloads soon filled the cupboards and closets, so we stored the rest.

We did without rugs because we brought in too much dirt. I just used the broom and mop a lot and saved electricity. Since we lacked space we put away the television set. We had no room for knickknacks either. Still, we enjoyed a family dinner with twenty people, though it was a tight squeeze. In the summer our space expanded rapidly as the whole yard became our living room.

We kept things in different places than usual. With only a few drawers for clothing, I folded work clothes and put them in the bottom of the closet. We closely examined the necessity of extra clothes. I put things like sewing projects and some toys into strong bags and hung them in the closets on hangers. For storing mittens, scarves, and stockings I used shoe bags on hangers.

I noticed that people automatically saw us as living a simple lifestyle. Doing with less made me think of the one-celled amoeba. This animal's vital functions all take place in one cell—food intake, digestion, elimination, and reproduction. Our living room reminded me of that. People walked in and said, "My, what a big trailer!" What they didn't think of was that this room was most of it.

—*Karin Hackman*
Hatfield, Pa.

l.

Navajo Reservation • We've lived in Chaco, New Mexico, for two years helping in church growth and development. Our one-room home is situated on Navajo land far from a paved highway and even farther from a town. We have no utilities. Our light comes from the sun, lanterns, or candles. In cold weather we heat and cook with a wood-and-coal-burning stove. In warm weather we use a campstove or outdoor fireplace. Our refrigerator is an ice chest supplemented by our cold windowsills in wintertime. We haul and chop our wood and get our coal from a local strip mine.

Even though we spend lots of time and energy on the basics of living, there's something relaxing about our life here in the quiet, wide-open spaces. We enjoy the fresh air and the big, beautiful sky. Everyone helps with the work and no one's in a hurry. With less leisure time, we also have fewer distractions. We usually get up and go to sleep by the sun. Our eating habits are simple; leftovers must be used soon. With little time to make desserts, we eat fruit.

I don't want to glorify the way we live. It does get lonely at times. I believe the Lord is helping us adapt to our situation and to be content.
—*Eunice E. Stoner*
Bloomfield, N.M.

C

Haitian Town • Our life was so simplified while working in Haiti as medical doctors that it's hard to share this experience. Our home had no running water, electricity, plumbing, refrigerator, or stove. Although we don't advocate this as the way everyone should live, we learned some things from our experience.

We discovered that a lantern or two on a table drew the whole family together for reading. We became very much accustomed to being near each other. We noticed when visiting a larger home that our family all congregated in a bedroom.

A small house is much easier to clean, too. We slept well on thin layers of straw and saved floor space by rolling the mats up during the day. Baths and showers were a luxury. We cleaned ourselves with a small amount of water in a wash basin, some soap, and a washcloth. We kept our doors open, unless the wind blew in rain. Since ants, flies, mice, and rats came in and out of our house, their predators—cats, spiders, and lizards—did the same. Flies breed disease but it was interesting to see that they kept certain hours. We ate breakfast before they got up and dinner after they had gone to bed!

Since we're back in the United States, we wonder what a simple lifestyle means in terms of dollars and cents. We called the local welfare department to find out the allotment for a family of five in food and clothing. Then we put ourselves on this budget. It has certainly made us appreciate the difficulty of staying within these allowances and greatly increased our

respect for the welfare recipient! We are forced to eat simply, as
well as to make do with clothing.
—*Ham and Sue Brown*
  Albuquerque, N.M.

●●●●●●●●●●●●●●●●●●●●●●●●●●●

Privacy in Three Rooms ● In central Vietnam families
were large and homes were small. Sometimes as many as ten
people shared one or two small rooms in refugee camps. Beds
were curtained off for privacy. These were shared by father and
sons and by mother and daughters.

When we lived in Vietnam with our two small children, we
rented a house with three small rooms. We used the front room
as our office and living room. The middle room had a curtain
down the center and served as a dining/sewing room, as well as
a bedroom for a young Vietnamese woman living with us. The
third room was also curtained off to make a bedroom for the
four of us, leaving a walking corridor between the other two
rooms and the kitchen—a small shed built onto the side·of the
house.

Our three children are still small enough to enjoy sharing
the same bedroom. When they get a bit older and want more
privacy, curtaining off their beds is an idea that seems practical
in the United States as well.
—*Pat Hostetter Martin*
  Phoenixville, Pa.

Building Versus Renovating ● While in the United States
I went to a retreat where the focus of discussion was on living
responsibly in light of the world's diminishing resources. A
main point of one presentation was that it is unwise to invest
money in an old house to make it more energy efficient,
suggesting that it is better to build a new house with
permanence in mind: built to last a hundred years.

Tearing down an old house and building a new one, or just
building a new one and selling the old one as it is, is incredibly
more expensive in terms of consuming the world's limited
resources. Tens of thousands of structurally sound houses are
torn down each year in favor of shiny new ones. The new ones
use far more nonrenewable and energy-rich materials like steel,
aluminum, glass, concrete, plastic, and land than the old ones
did. The old ones are built mostly of wood so they require more
labor. But both of these are renewable resources. Good
building materials are destroyed every time a house is
demolished. When an old house has been given proper care, it
doesn't need to be destroyed.
—*Lawrence Yoder*
  Pati, Indonesia

●●●●●●●●●●●●●●●●●●●●●●●●●●●●

P

Spread Out and Pull In ● Most families who can afford to do so arrange housing adequate for their optimum needs. This means that many buy or build a larger home five years before older children leave home because during this time they seem to need more space.

When our four children were small we bought a two-story house with the second floor converted into a separate apartment. We lived on the first floor and rented out the apartment. Later, when we had several teenage children, we were tempted to incorporate the second-floor apartment into our living space.

After looking at all the factors carefully, we decided as a family to upgrade the basement instead. Our temporary family need was met without enlarging the house to the point where space would be excessive later. At the same time we retained the apartment which is occupied by the only neighbors we can choose and by people who invariably become our best friends while giving us a welcome source of income.

If upgrading a basement is not an option, why not consider co-opting the garage for the duration of greatest need? Cars are given far too high a priority in the North American value system. People could use the bedrooms they occupy!
—*Gladys and Edgar Stoesz*
Akron, Pa.

P

One of the smartest things we've ever done (and we were too dumb to know it at the time) was to buy a large two-story frame house with an upstairs apartment. It is within walking distance of all our needs so we don't have to be dependent on an extra car.

Rent from the apartment pays the mortgage and taxes. Some improvements and part of the utilities are tax-deductible. Our lives have been enriched by our tenants and we don't need to worry about leaving the house unattended during vacations.

By the time the children are teenagers and need more space we'll have paid for the house. Then we can install a stairway and use the second floor ourselves. As our parents grow older, we know we would have room to include them in our family, and the children would have the advantage of living with a different generation. Our house can become smaller again and rental income will make retirement more secure.
—*Carolyn Urich*
Bluffton, Ohio

●●●●●●●●●●●●●●●●●●●●●●●●●●●●

Homebuilding:

Choices ● We tried to build a house with low maintenance   ℮
features: a metal roof—no shingles to replace; rough-sawn
siding treated with a wood preservative—no painting; wide
porches—shade from the hot summer sun instead of air
conditioning; plenty of windows to the south—passive solar
heat in the wintertime; and wood floors treated with
polyurethane—no wall-to-wall carpets.
—*Norma Fairfield*
  Singers Glen, Va.

Goals ● Before building our home in the Sierras, we   ℮
outlined our goals. We wanted a God-centered, humble home
where we would feel united and friends could feel comfortable,
a home which was energy-efficient, ecologically sound, and an
extension of the outdoors. We wanted to use as many recycled
materials as possible. Here's how we met these goals.

A lumber company near us was selling the buildings in an
old logging camp. We bought "The Company Store" and
dismantled it for the lumber. The boards are nearly all sound
and the nail holes and crowbar marks add character to the
wood, reminding us also of the trees we saved by reusing them.
We were even able to reuse some of the wiring, plumbing,
cabinets, and cement footings. We purchased windows, sinks,
rugs, and furnishings at rummage sales.

The house is small with few rooms. Most of the area is open.
Two bedrooms serve as quiet retreats for reading and sleeping.
Our beds are pads on the floor that we can roll up out of the
way. We move space-consuming activities to a large
multipurpose room which can also accommodate overnight
visitors in sleeping bags. For the comfort of guests, we have
two bathrooms—one with a shower and tub, the other very
small with only a toilet and washbasin.

Many south-facing windows and a greenhouse which acts as
a solar heater take advantage of the sun's energy. We pipe hot
water through a concrete slab floor to hold the heat. A rock
wall near the stove adds additional thermal inertia.

In summertime we let the sun heat water in tanks at the base
of the greenhouse. A cupola with windows that open for
ventilation acts as a passive air conditioner in the same way as
cupolas on domed buildings in Persia: heat rises, to be carried
out of the cupola by crosswinds.
—*Larry and Ginny Hunt*
  Camp Connell, Calif.

Geodesic Dome Living

● We have chosen to build and live in a geodesic dome. It's located on a regular city street, at 11366 Bird Road, Richmond, British Columbia, V6X 1N9, Canada. Why have we made this choice?

—A dome is warm. Our home costs about 40 percent less to heat and cool because it has 30 percent less surface area exposed to the outside and a unique circulation of air on the inside.

—A dome is strong. It is built of triangles which are twice as strong per pound of material used as the usual rectangles. It is excellent for withstanding high winds, snow, or earthquakes.

—A spherical shape is the cheapest way to enclose space. The triangles can be mass produced and novice workers can put them together. Roofing and dry-walling, however, are more difficult or expensive. Some do-it-yourself builders save 25 percent or more on building expenses.

—We feel a dome is beautiful. It blends more naturally with the shape of the earth and the raindrops around us. Since there is no siding to paint, it takes less maintenance to keep it beautiful.

Our dome is giving freshness and warmth to our family's living experiences. Hard lines converging into tight corners are gone while a continuum of space and light takes their place. The upward sweep of the cathedral ceiling and the new options for decorating new shapes are giving joy to creative spirits.

—Palmer and Ardys Becker
Richmond, B.C.

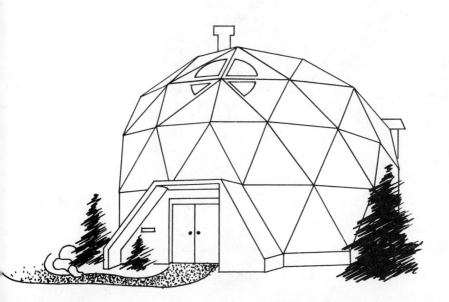

Twentieth-Century Cave ● Many suggested methods of
lowering energy costs sound feasible to the novice. But actually
putting ideas into action sometimes proves that theories are
different from the real thing. Some are just not practical, while
others should have been discovered long ago. Our cave house
which we started in June 1977 seems to be of the latter type.
Building it was quite a venture in faith.

The house is basically octagon in shape with a rectangular
garage. It covers 140 square meters (1,500 square feet) with an
additional 60 square meters (624 square feet) in the garage.

Construction began by bulldozing away the side of a hill.
Next we built the concrete structure. All of the 20-centimeter
(8-inch) thick exterior walls were poured as a slab on the
ground and then set into place with a large crane. The 25-
centimeter (10-inch) thick roof was then poured in its
permanent position and supported by substantial shoring.
Except for the south side, the entire structure was covered with
earth. The weight of the roof and its reinforcing steel
approaches 127 metric tons (140 U.S. tons). Total construction
costs were very similar to that of a conventional home, perhaps
slightly higher.

Even though we followed blueprints prepared by an
architect, the task was not easy nor without problems. We had
difficulty obtaining a building permit and meeting certain local
building codes. Weak lifting cables caused additional problems.

This type of home certainly is not meant for everyone but for
us it seemed to be wise stewardship.

It has no exterior maintenance and no drafts on the floor. It
is virtually fireproof and stormproof. Without exception,
visitors exclaim that it isn't the dark, damp, cold dwelling they
had expected. Instead they find it's light and dry and
comfortably warm even though heated only with a fireplace.
Public interest in the project has been exceptionally high for
these reasons and for the fact that the earth itself helps keep
the home warm. Three meters (10 feet) below the surface, the
earth in our area remains at a fairly constant temperature, near
13C (55–56F). Even in our coldest weather which was −25C
(−12F), our indoor temperature stayed near 7C (45F) without
any heat. In the summer months the same conditions help to
cool it.
—*Gordon Kauffman*
  Middlebury, Ind.

Duplex Living ● Another family needed housing at the
same time as we did. Having several things in common—
limited resources, concerns about lifestyle, fairly good
construction skills, and similar backgrounds including overseas
service—we decided to build a duplex together. We
accomplished this through a contract with a builder who

allowed us to provide the labor for specific jobs, saving us several thousand dollars.

Immediate construction savings also resulted from building a common roof and mutual inner fireproof and soundproof wall. This wall provides ongoing maintenance and heating savings since each unit has one less outside exposure.

Because of our interests in sharing certain facilities, we have both outside and inside entrances into our basements and a door which allows us to move between units without going outside. We walled off a corner of our basement where we pooled our tools. The shared freezer is in our neighbor's basement.

Outside we share a lawnmower and picnic table and do some gardening together. It's great to have someone around for the job that takes an extra hand.

We haven't attempted to move into a communal or spiritual support arrangement. Although we have less noise than in many apartment arrangements in which we've lived, we lose a bit of privacy. Overall, we feel duplex living merits serious consideration.
—*Lowell Detweiler*
  Akron, Pa.

●●●●●●●●●●●●●●●●●●●●●●●●●●●

This Is the House for Us

When we quit farming in 1972, we thought we would build a new home. Providentially, however, we were able to buy a reasonably priced house at public auction. Moving from a five-bedroom farmhouse to a two-bedroom bungalow meant getting rid of extras. We sold, gave to our children, and donated to charity. We find our small house very roomy!
—*Edna Mast*
  Cochranville, Pa.

Our small house was becoming crowded with three young children. We thought about moving and decided that we'd like to live next door to a family from our church. When a suitable house became available, we consulted with a carpenter brother-in-law concerning the structure. A realtor checked the price. The counsel and prayers of our pastor and fellow church members were invaluable in helping us make the decision to purchase.
—*Erv and Ruth Kauffman*
  Portland, Ore.

When my wife and I moved to Hillsboro we found rental housing was not easily available and in the long run, quite expensive. We decided to buy an old house and paid $7,000 for

one that was built in 1919. With some hired labor, the help of friends, and our own efforts, we invested another $4,000 in it. By redoing the kitchen and the bathroom, papering the downstairs and nailing out the upstairs with plywood, we have a clean, warm, comfortable home at a fraction of the cost of most houses.
—*Bill Wiebe*
  Hillsboro, Kan.

●●●●●●●●●●●●●●●●●●●●●●●●●●●

Tightening Up

The house we bought five years ago was wastefully designed. A product of the energy-spending fifties, it was an invitation to a lifestyle we did not want. There is still much to do on it, but here is what has helped so far.

To the 6.5-centimeter (2½-inch) fiberglass batts in the attic, we added 25 centimeters (10 inches) of cellulose fiber insulation. The company had never installed so thick an amount and we paid plenty for it. But we had the satisfaction of saving some trees because the stuff is made from recycled newspapers and our heating bill went down by about 38 percent. The investment should pay for itself in three years. When will Wall Street do as well?

We would not consider having the waste of central air conditioning but now get perhaps half the comfort of it as a free side effect of the winter insulation. One day we returned from a trip in 32C (90F) weather. Inside, with doors and windows closed, it was 21C (70F).

The house has an unheated, glass-walled dining room next to a large screened-in porch with a plastic roof. At winter meals we froze. So I built wooden frames to fit between the posts of the porch, like storm windows, and stapled 4-mil plastic on both sides. Nails held the "storm windows" in place. The porch became, in effect, a solar heater which on sunny days was usually 20 degrees warmer than outside. I'm sure that plastic stapled to the bottoms of the porch rafters, forming a dead air space, would raise the temperature further. I use the porch as a greenhouse now to start the tomatoes for our garden and open up the door to the house when the temperature gets above the 20C (68F) thermostat setting. Nothing like free heat!
—*Ron Conrad*
  Thornhill, Ont.

Old houses *can* be made energy-efficient. After we insulated our 100-year-old farmhouse and added storm windows, we found we could shut off the furnace and heat our entire house comfortably with just one wood-burning stove. Getting an efficient, airtight stove makes a big difference.
—*Judy White*
  Ashland, Ohio

●●●●●●●●●●●●●●●●●●●●●●●●●●●

Solar Retrofits

ℓ I have been in energy conservation as a business for the past
five years, first in retail insulation and now in its manufacture.

With fuel shortages and rising costs, I feel solar heating has
definite economic advantages. It is an inexhaustible source of
energy and is nonpolluting. We decided to install solar
collectors on our own home.

The type of system we put in is called a daytime assist with a
water coil for heating domestic hot water. This is a hot-air
system, so one avoids problems with water pumps, freezing,
corrosion, and leaks.

We used manufactured collectors which are relatively simple
to install. The cost on a system like ours is in the range of
$2,500. However, a tax credit of approximately 55 percent (20
percent Federal, 35 percent Kansas) greatly reduces the initial
cost outlay. We expect the system to save approximately 45
percent on our heating bills.

Because on our house the peak of the roof runs north and
south, we altered our front porch roof to create a southern
exposure for the collectors.
—*James A. Blough*
   Hesston, Kan.

ℓ In our community, New Creation Fellowship, we had the
construction skills and physics training among us to
experiment with solar heating on a major house addition.

In place of the south wall and roof we installed homemade
solar panels that cover about 88 square meters (950 square
feet). On the roof we put double-glazed panels of salvaged glass
underneath with clear fiberglass above. The wall, where the air
temperature is lower, is only covered with fiberglass. The air is
blown through the panels from a duct in the basement up the
wall and roof to the sheetrocked attic which acts as a duct.
Along with a rock storage room and a computerized solar air
mover costing $1,800, the investment was about $4,000 for
materials plus our own labor.

Among other things, we learned a lot about the construction
of airtight walls and roofs (using cartons of silicone sealant),
ducts built with a foil-backed sheetrock, and gaps left for the
glass to expand to temperatures above 94C (200F).

Our experiment was worthwhile for education and gas
conservation. Our gas bill was about half what it would have
been this past winter.

I do not see it as a move toward simple living per se, nor is it
yet a money saver, though that day may soon come.
—*David Janzen*
   Newton, Kan.

In February 1979 Sunflower Energy Works of Goessel, Kansas, installed six of their solar air-heating panels to the roof of our 116 square meter (1250 square foot) house. A duct enters the house from the attic, goes down through the back corner of a closet, and is connected into the regular furnace ducts. A small blower moves the heated air through these ducts and throughout the house. The air then returns through a cold-air duct to the solar panels, completing the cycle. The addition of this solar assist required few changes to our house.

We found that the panels became hot enough to turn on the system by about 10:00 A.M. and warm the house up to the solar thermostat setting of 26C (78F) by afternoon. We allow it to reach this level so that we can maintain a comfortable temperature as long as possible into the night. The house itself acts as storage for the heat. After the system shuts off around 5:00 P.M., the temperature in the house declines slowly, but usually remains in the 20s C (70s F) throughout the evening. Our forced-air gas furnace starts only when the house temperature drops to the regular thermostat setting or on days when there is no sun.

The total cost for our system was about $2,500 for the panels and installation. Federal and state tax credits will return about $1,275 of this cost to us. In comparing the fuel usage with similar months in the past, we estimate a saving of 35–40 percent. We feel that our $1,225 investment was well spent, not just in terms of future savings, but for its clean-operating, nonpolluting, energy-saving, maintenance-free, and comfort-producing qualities.
—*Ron and Carolyn Brunk*
  Hesston, Kan.

●●●●●●●●●●●●●●●●●●●●●●●●●●●●
Heating with Wood

We built an all electric home in 1974. In 1976 we added a wood stove in the basement and a fan above the fireplace. Our savings in electricity look something like this:

1975 we used 38,112 kilowatt hours
1976—31,580
1977—31,092
1978—29,573

I figure that we will have saved approximately $500 this year on our electric bill.
—Delbert Seitz
Harrisonburg, Va.

Our old frame house was heated by an oil furnace. We decided to install a high-efficiency wood stove to lower our heating costs and make use of a renewable fuel. Trees are plentiful in Pennsylvania. We purchased a chain saw jointly with another family.

We placed the stove in the northwest corner of the living room. Laying the flagstone base and installing it were exciting experiences of doing our own work. High up on a nearby wall we made an opening into the next room and installed a 20-centimeter (8-inch) fan. This helps circulate warm air through the downstairs. An alternate method is to use the circulator fan of our central heating system. The cold air intake is in the same room as the stove. The stove reduced our fuel oil consumption about 70 percent the first winter.

We found the stove provides an ongoing family work enterprise, a useful thing in town where there are no cows to milk. Summer and fall Saturdays spent cutting firewood are memorable, as are cold winter evening wood-splitting sessions, illuminated by the streetlight. Wood is truly a great fuel. It warms you twice—once when you cut it and again when you burn it!

The stove provides a center for the family in a way that radiators or air vents never can do. We gather around the open fire in the evening reading stories. That feature alone is worth the original investment. Children and parents can have many warm, healing thoughts while watching an open fire in the security of their own home. As an investment in mental health, it's a lot cheaper than professional counseling. It brings you closer to nature than does watching TV.
—John Stoner
Akron, Pa.

●●●●●●●●●●●●●●●●●●●●●●●●●●●●

Controlling the Temperature

"It doesn't pay to turn down the thermostat at night because the furnace has to run so long in the morning that you use up the fuel you saved." Is this true? Discover the answer for yourself.

Compare the heat in the house to water in a bucket with a hole in the bottom. The more water in the bucket (the higher the temperature in the house), the faster it will run out. As the water gets down to the bottom (the temperature in the house gets nearer to that outside), it runs out more slowly. Similarly, lowering the temperature inside the house makes less heat escape to the outside.

Conduct an experiment with your furnace. Hook up an electric clock parallel with the burner so that the clock runs only when the burner runs. Then note the total time the burner runs overnight at different settings of the thermostat when conditions like temperature and wind are about the same.
—*Willard Unruh*
  Butwal, Nepal

We have our thermostat set at 18C (65F) all winter and wear   ℭ
enough clothes to be warm.

When I use the clothes dryer in wintertime, I set it to vent into the house through a series of filters. This way we keep the heat and the moisture indoors. I keep laundry, dish, and shower water in plugged sinks until it is cold to add heat and humidity. *(Caution: A gas dryer should not be vented indoors because of the possibility of gas fumes escaping.)*
—*Carol Unruh*
  Waterloo, Ont.

During most of the year lovely cross-ventilation from open   ℭ
windows gives me the benefit of night and early morning cool breezes which freshen my entire apartment. This is impossible in most air-conditioned modern structures. In cold weather my room heater provides remarkable economy as opposed to a furnace controlled by a thermostat.
—*Erna J. Fast*
  Hutchinson, Kan.

●●●●●●●●●●●●●●●●●●●●●●●●●●●●

Back to the Fifties in Energy Use ● Residential energy use in Kansas went up about 40 percent from 1950 to 1970.* More than half the increase results from air conditioning— from nil in 1950 to the third largest use in 1970—and the use of various appliances. Space heating changed little and has continued to use the most energy during this period. Water heating is in second place and along with lighting has increased significantly. Energy use for refrigeration has more than doubled.

We use natural gas for space heating, water heating, and cooking. We use only window and room fans for cooling.

Here are changes we made in 1976 to save energy:

1. Turned off lights not being used.
2. Set our thermostat at 20C (68F) the winter of 1976–77 and at 18C (65F) in 1977–78.
3. Replaced a .6 cubic meter (20 cubic foot) frostless side-by-side refrigerator-freezer with a .4 cubic meter (15 cubic foot) automatic defrost refrigerator-freezer.
4. Replaced an old jet water pump with a more energy efficient submersible pump.
5. Turned off the pilot light on the kitchen stove and used matches to light the burners.
6. Filled the outside walls of the house with blown cellulose insulation.
7. Increased the insulation in the attic to a 15-centimeter (6-inch) layer of fiberglass.
8. Insulated some window frames with styrofoam and fiberglass.

One fourth of energy use in the United States is directly under the control of families in their homes. Our experience shows that residential energy use in Kansas could probably be reduced by at least 30 percent within a year or two. If this would be accomplished nationwide, almost 7 percent of our national energy budget would be saved.

—*Dwight Platt*
Newton, Kan.

---

* W. R. Martindale and M. S. Greywall, "Growth of Residential Energy Consumption in Kansas, 1950–1970," *Transactions of the Kansas Academy of Science* (1979), pp. 15–42.

●●●●●●●●●●●●●●●●●●●●●●●●●●●●

℃   **Waterless Composting Toilet**

Living in New Mexico with its semiarid climate makes the precarious status of water more apparent. Estimates say 40 percent of the water used in the average household is flushed down the toilet. To avoid this we installed a waterless composting toilet in our new home. At the same time we provided ourselves with a source of usable compost and avoided putting sewage in a leach field where it contaminates the ground around it.

Waterless composting toilets are available in two basic models. The one we use is a large composting bin, about 1 meter wide, 2 meters long, and 2 meters high (4 feet by 7 feet by 7 feet). This is placed in the basement or under the house to

collect waste from the toilet and kitchen garbage. Both are
essential to the composting process. Once the wastes are in the
bin, the process is similar to a compost pile in the backyard.
Air circulates through the bin by natural convection allowing
the composting process to take place. Approximately 98
percent of the waste products go up the vent pipe in the form of
water vapor. The rest eventually becomes compost which can
be removed and is perfectly safe for use on flower beds or
vegetable gardens.

A second type of composting toilet is a self-contained unit, a
little bigger than 1 cubic meter (a 4-foot cube) which can be
placed in an existing bathroom. It demands a small amount of
electrical energy to speed up the composting process because
the bin is small.

The first question everyone asks us about our unit is, "Does
it stink?" After having used it for almost a year, we've
confirmed that the design virtually eliminates any odor from
the toilet unit. On those rare occasions when natural
convection currents don't eliminate a faint odor, the unit has
an auxiliary fan which can be activated to insure that odors go
up the vent and not into the bathroom. In fact, guests who
have stayed at our house indicate that our bathroom has less
odor problems than those using the conventional system.
—*Mel Goering*
  Sante Fe, N.M.

●●●●●●●●●●●●●●●●●●●●●●●●●●●●

*In our business, which is
recycling newspaper
into insulation, we get
cores from newsprint.
We cut these into 50-
centimeter (20-inch)
lengths and use them for
fuel for our heating
stove and our neighbors'
fireplaces.*
—*Mary Hochstedler*
  Kokomo, Ind.

*We have two
thermostats, one set at a
lower temperature for
night and during working
hours away from home.
A timer automatically
makes the change from
the lower to the higher
setting at designated
times.*
—*Floyd Zehr*
  New Wilmington, Del.

For $75 I had the body of a school bus moved to my farm. After removing most of the seats, I installed shelves along the sides and center. The space has proven suitable as a library for my books and magazines.
—Wilmer M. Landis
  Harrisonburg, Va.

The setting sun is reflected from the windows of the almshouse as brightly as from the rich man's house. The snow melts before its door as early in the spring.
—Thoreau

. . . If a man offered for love
  all the wealth of his house
    it would be utterly scorned.
—Song of Solomon 8:7

Paul's Law: The more elegant the kitchen, the less cooking goes on in it.
—Paul Longacre
  Akron, Pa.

To relieve her baby's heat irritation, I often saw an African mother pour cool water over the baby's head with her cupped hands. The child gasped and sputtered but was soon content and asleep wrapped in a towel. Where water was scarce, cooling the head and the back of the neck were effective.
—Sara Regier
  North Newton, Kan.

During the hot season in India we learned to keep cool in bed by dampening a sheet and covering ourselves from head to foot, or even rolling up in it like a cocoon. On our cotton webbing cots, which allowed air to circulate beneath us, we were soon comfortable on the hottest afternoon or muggiest night.
—LaVonne Platt
  Newton, Kan.

Koreans heat the anpang—combination sitting and master bedroom—while cooking. Flues run from the sunken kitchen in the stone work under the floors and smoke rises from a chimney on the opposite side of the house. In the anpang, the part of the floor nearest the kitchen is the warmest. Generally Koreans sleep with their feet on this part.
—Helen Tieszen
  Seoul, Korea

At bedtime the Japanese turn off their stoves until the next morning. During our ten years in Japan, we gradually learned to appreciate the warmth of several layers of blankets and comforters in a chilly room. Now we continue this practice in our centrally heated American home.
—Sue Richard
  Iowa City, Iowa

Japanese houses are almost always built with sliding door-length windows to the south to add warmth in winter. Using portable kerosene heaters, only one or two rooms are heated at a time.
—Fritz and Ellen Sprunger
  Miyakonojo, Japan

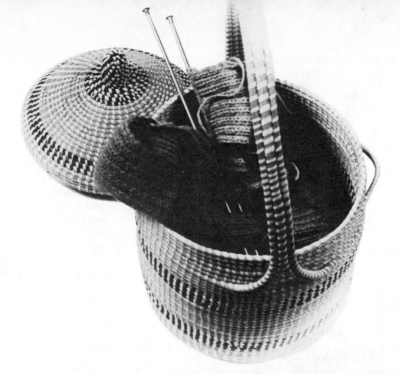

4.   *homekeeping*

●●●

A neighbor who moved from England to our small
Pennsylvania town said this about her adjustment: "The first
few months I went out every day and washed or swept the
front steps. Then one day I looked up and down the street and
realized that nobody else bothered much with what in England
is a real mark of a good housekeeper. So I quit cleaning my
steps! But what is it that one has to do here?"

Every community and culture has its unspoken standards. In
Indonesia you swept the packed earth around your house at
least once, if not twice, a day. Thirty years ago in North
America it was the way you did the washing. Laundry was a
real job—remember bluing, starch, tubs, and wringers? To
accomplish it properly required skill and dedication. If we can
believe the stories, people watched to see who got the sheets
fluttering on the line first on a sunny Monday morning, and
checked if they were white! But modern laundry equipment
and easy-care fabrics changed all that.

Maybe it's just as well we don't check the neighbor's sheets
anymore, for keeping tabs on each other isn't the point. People
should feel free to set their own style of homekeeping. But it
can't hurt for each of us to take a good look at ourselves. In
spite of no-wax linoleum and no-iron shirts, keeping things
livable still eats up a tidy share of our time and energy.
Whoever makes such a sizable personal investment in one

activity must occasionally ask the question, "Is there some *meaning* to this whole business?"

So Who's Independent?
More than that, we can't afford to act too independently in our homekeeping. As long as one house is connected to every other house through power lines, water and sewer pipes, garbage trucks, and the incessant stream of products and services moving in and out, how we keep our homes *is* the affair of everyone. Curiously, the past few decades landed us all in a contradiction. We act as if we're personally independent and can make our own decisions our own way; in reality, most people are entirely dependent on others for food, fuel to cook it, water, heat—in short, anything they really must have.

What then are the guidelines today for doing well the ordinary tasks? Entries to this chapter show people changing their priorities. Old questions warrant new answers.

Is It Clean?
Our grandparents didn't have hot running water and shelves of detergent, or antibiotics to take whenever they caught a germ. No wonder they came up with "cleanliness is next to godliness." Keeping things neat was honest work, deservedly filling much time. It's still important. A grease-splattered stove and grimy bathtub don't mean you're living simply or that you've done something more significant with your time than cleaning. It may even mean that you're sloppy about your environment and other important matters.

But the opposite approach has more potential for disaster. In contrast to our grandparents, most of us now have every chance for reasonably clean homes, clothing, and bodies— without undue effort. We ought to be delighted with this development and know where to stop, contented. Instead, we believe the advertisers that somewhere there is a sanitary land of soaps, sprays, and cleaning machines featuring cleaner than clean, whiter than white, and no smells but nice ones.

If our culture buried
people with their
favorite tools,
some North American
housekeepers
would go to their final rest
with a paper towel
in one hand,

an aerosol disinfectant
in the other,
and a deodorant
laid at the feet.

Is It Pretty?

The word *decorate,* as applied to making a home attractive,
smacks of the same mentality as *entertain* in reference to
serving guests. *Adorn* and *glamorize* are synonyms of *decorate.*
We need to rearrange our thinking before we start moving
furniture and sewing curtains.

Where do you start in deciding how a home should look?
With the Sears advertising pages in a women's magazine? With
what's available in the furniture store? With what's "in" this
year, whether rattan or hanging plants or Oriental rugs or
quilted bedspreads? Should you plop into a living-room chair,
sit chin in hand, and meditate on what will give the place some
zing, or just give up and call a professional decorator? (There's
that word again.)

Should you consciously decide at all how your home should
look? Designer Victor Papanek says our current obsession with
the look-of-things has given us an ugly world that doesn't even
work well! He declares that "in a world brought nearly to its
knees by abject want, a preoccupation with 'making things
pretty' is a crime against humanity."[1]

Lest I dismiss the whole subject and come off a hypocrite, I
confess that arranging objects, colors, and designs in our house
is an aspect of homekeeping I dearly love. It's a great creative
adventure, one that I won't give up without a fuss. An
attractive home buoys my spirits.

Everywhere in the world people arrange for some beauty,
some expression of their ability to invent interesting subjects
for their eyes and fingertips.

The plainest cooking area
behind a hut in Somalia
boasts an intricately
carved
stool or colorful
basket.

Cooks across Asia encourage their charcoal fires with
attractively woven fans. People in Belgium spend 2 percent of
the national income on fresh flowers.[2]

But starting with "What will make this place pretty?" only

puts you at the mercy of the latest magazine spreads. It actually quenches your spirit. You pay the bill and you might stand on a stool to hang drapes, but that's all the look of your house will have to do with who you are and where your values lie.

Instead, ask first, "Who are we?" and "What will we do in this room?" Designers call that *form following function.* The home serves the people in it rather than the way someone else thinks a home should look.

After you figure that one out, other questions follow. Since new materials of practically every kind are scarce and expensive, what do you have now that's useful to the function you have in mind? Is someone else discarding what you can repair and use? If you must appropriate a new material or object, is it designed to last, or is it just a fad? Does it have only one use, or multiple uses?

Will the item eventually become a disposal problem? Few people today carry this question far enough. It's not only a matter of styrofoam cups. A wicker laundry basket can be composted, but not a plastic one. You can refinish a wood floor and scatter cotton and wool area rugs, or you can cover it with nylon shag. The synthetic carpet is a petroleum product. And when it becomes worn and soiled, the earth has no good place for it. But natural fibers make good rugs, paper, or mulch. You can refinish the wood floor again and again.

Finally, demand meaning from anything nonfunctional which you bring into your home. Replace furniture store art with your own child's drawing or your grandfather's portrait. Buy an artist's work, but only if it has meaning for you. This, as much as anything, makes the difference between a home and what is only a decorated living space.

One caution, however. With our society's overemphasis on material things, the battle is usually to unclutter and streamline, not to add more. Home should be a sanctuary from our noisy, overstimulating world. That requires some bare walls and corners, for when treasures are few, they become more valuable. Says Anne Morrow Lindbergh, in *Gift from the Sea:*

It is only framed in space that beauty blooms. Only in space are events and objects and people unique and significant—and therefore beautiful. A tree has significance if one sees it against the empty face of sky. A note in music gains significance from the silences on either side. . . . Even small and casual things take on significance if they are washed in space.[3]

Is It New and Strong?

Every system has its idols. Advertisers know by now which gods the North American householder will obey. One more-with-less principle for homekeeping is to recognize these on sight and refuse to worship.

The first is simply *New*. Flip through a magazine and see how many ads carry that word. For actual new products it works with a degree of honesty. But when ads for old faithfuls try to weave in the newness idea, things get strained.

"Wait till you taste the new raisins," shouts a full-page raisin bran ad. New raisins? A new genetic strain that doesn't wrinkle, maybe? Tell the prune people, they will be interested. But no. Fine print explains that with the year's turning, a fresh crop of raisins is now in, allowing raisin bran headquarters to add "new raisins" to every box. Never mind that cereals have a shelf life of a year or more.

"It's new" framed on the package with sunburst lines means "it's better." But new is a high, a temporary glow that sputters out when edges fray and chip. Newness saturation produces a longing for roots, for the comfort and even the status of old things. Thus little antique shops flourish down the street from giant discount stores. Cooks who feel compelled to line their kitchen counters with new appliances scour flea markets for old graters to hang on the wall, though they no longer know how to dismantle a cabbage without the food processor.

The second idol is *Strong*. "I need something *strong*," wails a coughing drugstore customer. Something to solve my problem quickly, efficiently, once for all, comes the unspoken message. Never mind side effects.

Strong has brother and sister gods. One of them, probably born because things got *too* strong, is *Mild*, as in "now even milder." Sometimes Strong and Mild appear comfortably on the same package. I once bought a hand lotion which boasted "new adult strength" together with "baby fresh mildness." Obviously, advertisers for home products hire smart psychologists, for all this works beautifully, year in and out. Entries to this chapter discuss ways of escape.

Where's the Off-On Switch?

When we planned this book we couldn't assign energy conservation to one section, because it belongs everywhere. Certainly it applies here, and may be the single most important aspect of a new way of keeping the home.

Enough times we've been told to turn off the lights. But even specific good habits don't apply broadly enough. For example, now we're told to buy only energy-efficient appliances. And certain appliances like the crockpot and microwave get billed that way. But what the electric company leaflet doesn't mention is that every new appliance requires energy to manufacture, market, and eventually receive a proper burial. To sort all these angles, we need a conservation ethic which makes us think along many fronts.

Principles gleaned from testimonies on homekeeping include:

1. **Set a reasonable standard for cleanliness** and pare cleaning and beauty products to the basics.
2. **Reduce purchase of all products and materials** involved with homekeeping which are either nonrenewable or not biodegradable. Begin with small disposables like styrofoam tableware and plastic wrap; then include larger items such as plastic containers and furniture, synthetic rugs and fabrics.
3. **Systematically recycle** glass, paper, and aluminum. Compost organic materials from the kitchen and yard. Work for integrating recycling services into community garbage collection and processing.
4. **Save energy supplies** by doing some chores the slow way and by hiring people to help, rather than by buying more machines. Redeem menial tasks by sharing them. Use the time to think, pray, and identify with those who have less. This can be a modern expression of servanthood or foot washing.
5. **Let meaning and function determine** the look of objects, rooms, and yards. Plan around people, their needs and activities.
6. **Arrange your home to bring the people in it into closer fellowship.** Having only one bathroom teaches consideration for others. One warm room draws the family together on winter evenings. Children want to play near the place where their parents work. Highlight enjoying each other, not the things you own.
7. **Don't let lack of space or facility keep you from doing what's important**—inviting guests for meals and lodging, expanding your household, enjoying various kinds of family fun, cooking from scratch. Make do.
8. **Look to other cultures** for ideas on living well and flexibly in a small space.

Notes

1
Victor Papanek, *Design for the Real World* (New York: Bantam Books, 1973), p. 324.
2
Michael Perelman, *Farming for Profit in a Hungry World* (Montclair, N.J.: Allenheld/Osmun, and Co., Inc., 1977), p. 115.
3
Anne Morrow Lindbergh, *Gift from the Sea* (New York: Pantheon, Inc., 1955), pp. 114–115.

●●●●●●●●●●●●●●●●●●●●●●●●●●

The Challenge of Limitations ● While living in the   I.
interior of Brazil we simply had to adapt to new situations.
There were no alternatives. We used the resources we had. This
included little things like beating egg whites with a fork and
learning to sleep in a hammock.

I find it's a challenge to continue this attitude now that we're
back in North America. I mentally put myself in a position of
limited resources and ask myself, "What do I have right now
that can be used in this situation?"

First Timothy 6:7–8 helps me keep things in perspective:
". . . we brought nothing into the world, and we cannot take
anything out of the world; but if we have food and clothing,
with these we shall be content."
—*Anette Eisenbeis*
  Marion, S.D.

Baskets: Function and Beauty ● While living in East   I.
Africa, I saw baskets that combine artistic expression and
practical livelihood.

What could be more beautiful than the women with their
basket displays waiting for customers along the road to the Rift
Valley? What could be more graceful than a delicately
balanced basket atop the head of a brightly clothed Buhaya
woman on her way to market? And what could be more
practical than the basket itself for carrying clothes from the
scrub board to the bushes for drying? I soon adopted the
custom of using baskets as my neighbors did.

Today as baskets grace the various corners in our home, they
link me with memories of our stay in Africa. Each has a story
of its own. One serves as identity for a certain tribal group.
Another recaptures friendship with a neighbor who gave it as a
farewell gift. With still another, I remember the excitement of
bargaining over its worth. My basket collection is a kind of
course in cultural anthropology and African art.

But the baskets also fill many functional roles. The plain
market basket is a clothes hamper, wash basket, or picnic
basket. I fit plants into suitable baskets or turn baskets upside
down for plant stands. Others hold my knitting or crocheting
projects. Then there are the all-purpose tote bag, the handbag,
the wastebaskets, sewing basket, bread basket, magazine
basket, and lunch money basket. My favorite is a plain shallow
one with which I created a wall clock using straw flowers from
Mt. Kilimanjaro for the hour markers.

Perhaps the most valuable aspect of these baskets is that all
were hand-created by using available resources like reeds and
banana fibers. Eventually all can return to the earth with no
disposal problem.
—*Ruth Detweiler*
  Akron, Pa.

l.

Improvising Furniture ● We've learned to enjoy swinging and relaxing in a big braided hammock. I can't say for sure what this does to one's back, but I know it is good for tired legs and varicose veins. We'd rather have a hammock than an expensive couch.
—*Pat Sharp*
  San José, Costa Rica

e

In the fall our Portuguese neighbors in Winnipeg purchased boxes of grapes for wine making. A few days after the grape shipment arrived the alleys were full of discarded wooden crates. We hauled them in by the dozen. After washing them we glued and nailed them together in various ways to make end tables, a telephone stand, a plant stand, a TV case, and a coffee table. The finishing touch was a walnut stain. We were quite proud of our Portuguese Provincial furniture!
—*Joan Gerig*
—*Orlando Redekopp*
  Gaborone, Botswana

f

While attending graduate school, we improvised much of our furniture. Our bed was a foam rubber mattress on a heavy plywood sheet set on a series of cement blocks. Our study desk was also a long sheet of plywood set on cement blocks, each stack of blocks decorated with colorful cotton cloth to protect our shins. An old buffet with its legs cut off and two side doors removed became our record and games cabinet. For ten dollars we bought a three-chair section of wooden seating, cleaned it with soap and water, and rubbed it to a soft glow with scratch remover and furniture oil. This augmented the sofa in the living room without taking much room. All these items were easily acquired and more easily sold and given away on our departure.
—*Paul Longacre*
  Akron, Pa.

●●●●●●●●●●●●●●●●●●●●●●●●●●

How-To:

Frame a Picture ● I often use this frame for large posters and designs. It's simple to construct, requires few materials, and is inexpensive. Hardware stores will cut glass to your dimensions.
● Materials Needed:
  —item to frame ⎫
  —hardboard backing ⎬ exact same size
  —sheet of glass ⎭
  —four strips of wood (scraps)
  —framing clips (available from art supply stores)
  —nails, wire

● Directions:
1. Nail the strips of wood to the back of the hardboard in a square or rectangular shape. This sets the picture off from the wall and prevents warping.
2. Attach wire for hanging the picture to the wood strips.
3. Place the picture between the glass and the backing.
4. Join together with framing clips.

—Alfred Siemens
Vancouver, B.C.

Learn to mat pictures. Instruction books are available at libraries.

Beds ● Most of our beds at New Creation Fellowship are family hand-me-downs or garage-sale specials. But those we built reflect our need to pack as many people as we can into limited bedroom space. One design is a plywood box the size of a single bed foam pad with three drawers cut into the side for storage. Casters on the corners make it mobile.

Another design which our children have loved but will soon outgrow is the "hutch." This is a bunk elevated above a closet rod and desk, as illustrated.

Space can be added to bedrooms where the ceilings are high by building lofts and suspending beds with desk space beneath them.

—David Janzen
Newton, Kan.

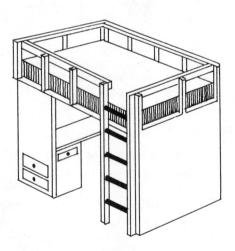

Bedding ● We had three extra woolen comforters which weren't getting much use. I bought three long heavy-duty zippers and sewed them to the comforters to make sleeping bags. They can still be used as extra covers on a bed and after ten years have gone to camp many times.

—Ada Beachy
Goshen, Ind.

We're relearning the joys of flannel sheets and a hot-water bottle now that the nights are cold and there is no heat in the house after the fire goes out.
—*Joan Gerig*
Gaborone, Botswana

When I was expecting our first child I didn't want to spend a lot of money on receiving blankets. I bought one full-size white blanket and cut it up into five small ones. I sewed binding around the edges and added liquid embroidery designs. While saving money I had the satisfaction of creating something special for our baby.
—*Bev Martin*
Stevens, Pa.

Make Pocket Wall Hangings ● With two families in one small house, I have five of these to save drawer and floor space.

Use sturdy cloth of desired length and width. I sometimes contrast the pockets and the backing. The size of the pockets depends on what is to be kept in them.

These can be used as holders for small kitchen utensils, shoes, socks, hankies, scarves, art and craft items, toys, books, and cleaning supplies. Providing pockets for children's clothes and toys expresses love and nurtures orderliness. Pocket hangings may be placed on or behind doors, in closets, in play areas, and in basements—wherever they're useful.
● Materials Needed:
  —sturdy fabric
  —cord or twill tape for loops
● Directions:
  1. Cut the backing to the desired size.
  2. Cut pockets, allowing for two small pleats in each.
  3. Hem the top edge of each pocket.
  4. Sew pockets onto backing, double-stitching for extra strength.
  5. Hem outside edges and add loops at the top for hanging.
—*Alta Erb*
Scottdale, Pa.

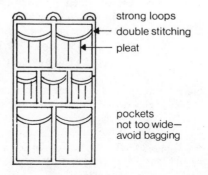

strong loops
double stitching
pleat

pockets
not too wide—
avoid bagging

Cleanliness ● The main function of cleanliness is to
prevent illness. People of all cultures clean themselves in one
way or another. Even animals do it. In our civilization,
however, we make cleanliness into a god.

I use soap only when necessary. Clear water cleans my body
sufficiently since dead skin is sloughed off anyway. Many
people—Eskimos and desert nomads—don't have access to
water for body care for months at a time.

I stopped using facial creams. The beauty effect is caused less
by the cream than by the facial massage. When no soap is used
I seldom need cream because skin moisturizes itself.
—*Ingeborg V. Keutz*
Ingolstadt, Germany

●●●●●●●●●●●●●●●●●●●●●●●●●●●●

Cleaning: Alternative Solutions*

How can you save money, improve home safety, and throw
away fewer plastic bottles, aerosols, and other odd containers?
Don't buy expensively packaged, single-purpose cleaning
products. With a few basic, multiple-use generic items you can
clean just as well and mix your own combinations for specific
jobs. The following directions are summarized from *Super-
Economy Housecleaning,* by Lois Libien and Margaret Strong,
William Morrow and Company, 1976, pages 27–31. Various
entries emphasized the same techniques and confirm that they
work.

Basic Cleaning Supplies
Ammonia cuts through grease and grime and is an excellent
heavy-duty cleaner when diluted with water. But it is a
powerful chemical and reacts with other chemicals to form
poisonous gases. NEVER mix ammonia with chlorine bleach,
commercial oven cleaners, or anything else that is not
specifically recommended. Read the label on the ammonia
container carefully before using.

Use ammonia full strength to "fume" clean the oven. Set a
cupful of undiluted ammonia in the oven overnight. With the
oven door shut, the ammonia will loosen burned-on crust. Next
day pour the cup of ammonia into a bucket of warm water, add
a few tablespoons of washing soda, dip in some newspaper, and
wipe the oven clean using steel wool to rub away any tough
spots.

Baking soda or bicarbonate of soda is a versatile, nontoxic
cleaning product. Use it as a no-scratch powder for scrubbing

---

* The title "Alternative Solutions" also comes from *Super-Economy
Housecleaning,* a delightful book written in the more-with-less spirit.

chrome, porcelain, and all but aluminum cooking utensils. Dilute it in water to clean and deodorize refrigerators, freezers, thermos bottles, and lunch boxes. On a damp cloth, it will even clean silver. If there's a grease fire in your kitchen, sprinkle it liberally with baking soda and it's out!

Chlorine Bleach not only bleaches and disinfects laundry, it also cleans stains from sinks, bathtubs, coffeepots, teapots, and cups. Use it to disinfect chopping blocks, remove soil and mildew from shower curtains and painted surfaces, and to deodorize and disinfect the toilet bowl. Because it is a powerful chemical, NEVER mix chlorine bleach with ammonia, toilet bowl cleaners, or oven cleaners. Read the label on the bottle before using.

Vinegar (distilled, white) used alone or in combination with ammonia or washing soda cleans soap scum off bathroom tiles. Use it in dishwater to make glassware gleam. A cup of vinegar in an open container will rid a room of stale odors in less than an hour.

Washing Soda, also known as sodium carbonate or sal soda, acts as a water softener and cleaner. Use it to scrub burned food from pots and pans other than aluminum ware and to keep drains and traps clean without corroding.

Liquid Dishwashing Detergent does more than clean dishes. Use it to remove stains from rugs, upholstery, and from washable and nonwashable clothing, as well as for handwashing delicate fabrics.

How to Mix Your Own Homemade Cleaners

As with commercial products, these solutions should be stored in carefully labeled, well-closed containers and kept safely out of reach of children.

—**Multipurpose Cleaner**
Mix ½ cup ammonia and ⅓ cup of washing soda in 4 liters (1 gallon) of water. Use the whole batch on floors or other large surface.

—**Cleaner for Walls and Painted Surfaces**
Mix 1 cup ammonia, ½ cup vinegar, and ¼ cup baking soda with 4 liters (1 gallon) of warm water.

—**Window Cleaner**
Put 3 tablespoons ammonia and 1 tablespoon vinegar into a cup and add water to fill. Use in a spray bottle. If you wish, add a few drops of blue food coloring to approximate the commercial product.

—**Once-a-Year Wood Polish**
Mix 1 cup each of turpentine, vinegar, and boiled linseed oil.

—**Brass, Copper, and Pewter Cleaner**
Mix ¼ cup of salt with enough vinegar to dissolve it. Add flour to make a fairly dry paste.

—Low-Abrasion Scouring Powder
Mix 9 parts of fine-grade whiting (available in hardware
stores) with 1 part detergent powder.

—Upholstery and Rug Shampoo Foam
Add ¼ cup liquid dishwashing detergent to 1 cup warm
water in a large bowl. Beat to a dry, sudsy foam. Use
immediately.

●●●●●●●●●●●●●●●●●●●●●●●●●●●

Laundry

We switched from our automatic washer and dryer to a
wringer washer, laundry tubs, and clothesline. I do six loads of
wash once a week in an hour and a half with one washer full of
hot water. I rinse in cold water.
—Norma Fairfield
   Singers Glen, Va.

I have been using a sud-saver with our automatic washer ever
since it was purchased fifteen years ago. This is a great saving
in water and soap.
—Winifred Wall
   Carlock, Ill.

After seeing how Europeans air their sheets, only washing
them once every few months, we decided we could do much
less laundry by adjusting sheet-washing to the weather. Even
in Nigeria with its constant 90 percent humidity and high
temperatures, we put the top sheet to the bottom for a second
week of use before washing.
—Stan and Delores Friesen
   Accra, Ghana

Clothes Drying

In Hong Kong none of my Chinese friends had clothes dryers.
I learned to do as they did. To conserve space we clipped socks
and washcloths to the lower edge of other things. We hung
shirts, blouses, and dresses on hangers before putting them on
the line. I became efficient at stringing underwear on a bamboo
pole.
    Now that I'm back in the States, I still do the same. If it's
not a good drying day, I simply postpone the job.
Remembering others who work much harder to do their
laundry has become my regular prayer reminder for them. I
can't help noticing how people spend money for labor-saving
devices, then more money for exercisers. This is hard to explain
to Asian friends.
—Margaret Metzler
   Kokomo, Ind.

C We began using drying racks to reduce trips to the laundromat while living in student housing. We found that our apartment was more comfortable in winter because of the added humidity.
—*Ann Naylor*
Arendtsville, Pa.

I use the dryer only for the clothes that would otherwise need to be ironed, sometimes for only a few minutes to fluff them.
—*Winifred Wall*
Carlock, Ill.

●●●●●●●●●●●●●●●●●●●●●●●●●●

Water Conservation

When I was in Belgium, I discovered that the people conserve water by bathing only once or twice a week and taking sponge baths in between.
—*Barry Rands*
Los Angeles, Calif.

L An Austrian friend taught me an economical way to shower. Positioning himself under the shower head, he turns on the water just long enough to wet his entire body. With the water off, he applies soap and thoroughly scrubs himself. Then back he goes under the shower using only enough water to rinse off the soap. His total water consumption time is about one minute. Following his example, I now use one tenth of the water I previously thought was necessary for showering.
—*Archie A. Harms*
Ancaster, Ont.

We place one or two big buckets under the shower and with a small bucket use that water to flush the toilet. This saves several thousand liters a year, and is only a small trouble.
—*C. B. Spee*
Etten-leur, Netherlands

C Because of our limited water supply on our farm, it seemed natural to send our bath water out to the lawn instead of down the septic tank. Now that we live in town we've installed a bypass to carry water outside rather than to the sewer. A shut-off in the bypass prevents freezing in winter and a fine wire mesh at the end of the hose keeps bugs from entering in summer. As Grandma Strausz always said, roses love used soap water!
—*James Klassen*
Newton, Kan.

I keep a jug at the sink into which I run water until it's hot instead of letting it go down the drain. I use it later to wash vegetables or water houseplants.
—*Mary Brubaker*
  Harrisonburg, Va.
—*Laura Wolfgang*
  Bally, Pa.

I immersed a plastic container full of sand at one end of the toilet tank bowl. This saves 4 liters (about one gallon) of water with each flush.
—*Edward L. Kauffman*
  Phoenix, Ariz.

A typical American family of four uses 100 gallons of water per day for flushing the toilet.
—*College of Home Economics*
  Knoxville, Tenn. 1977

We use water from a dehumidifier as distilled water in irons and batteries and to water houseplants.
—*Abe Dyck*
  Akron, Pa.

●●●●●●●●●●●●●●●●●●●●●●●●●●●

Water Heating

We keep our water heater temperature at 50C (120F). This provides our family of four with plenty of hot water and eliminates the danger of accidental scalding. When we did this in conjunction with greatly reducing the use of our clothes dryer, our monthly electric bill dropped by one fourth.
—*Reg Toews*
  Akron, Pa.

When my family left for three weeks' vacation without me, I turned our gas-fueled water heater off except for the pilot light. This kept the water warm enough for summertime showering. I heated water on the stove for dishwashing every other day. With the money saved we'll all go on vacation next year when we'll turn off even the pilot light!
—*Donald Reist*
  Scottdale, Pa.

We heat our water with a solar collector on the roof of a greenhouse we built on the south side of the house. By locating our hot water tank on the second floor, higher than the collector, we take advantage of the fact that hot water rises. This eliminates the need for a pump.
—*Judy White*
  Ashland, Ohio

Make a habit of washing your hands with cold water from the
COLD faucet. When we turn on the HOT faucet we usually
don't wait for the warm water to come. All we do is add cold
water to the water heater, wasting more energy.
—*Erma Wenger*
  Musoma, Tanzania

●●●●●●●●●●●●●●●●●●●●●●●●●

Cordless Crockpots

During our stay at the Thokoza Conference Center in
Mbabane, I saw demonstrated what I'm calling an African
crockpot. This is a fairly deep, simple grass basket stuffed full
of crumpled newspaper. You make an impression at the top to
hold the pot. In the morning, boil soaked dry beans for fifteen
minutes. Then nestle the pot down in the newspaper inside the
basket. Put a heavy blanket or pillow on top to keep in the
heat. At suppertime the beans are soft, hot, and ready to eat.
—*Darlene Keller*
  Mbabane, Swaziland

On a return trip to Canada after three years in Asia, I stopped
to visit an aunt in Germany. It was a beautiful December
morning. Snow started falling softly. I suggested we go for a
walk but realized immediately this probably was impossible
since my aunt had just begun cooking a pot of rice and milk.
  "Oh, that's no problem," she said. "We'll just put it to bed."
And she did. She put a thick layer of newspaper on her
mattress, next the pot with boiling rice and milk, and another
layer of paper. Then she tucked it all snugly under the feather
tick and we were off. We walked and talked for over an hour.
When we came home our meal was ready.
  Now I frequently cook rice this way although not in the bed.
I bring it to boil in a heavy pot, turn the heat off, and cover the
pot with a thick towel. I can go to church or out to the garden,
or just stay home and still conserve energy.
—*Anne Warkentin Dyck*
  Swift Current, Sask.

●●●●●●●●●●●●●●●●●●●●●●●●●

Less Cooking, Less Waste

In the course of a conversation with a Chinese Indonesian
friend, she asked me how much bottled gas my household used.
When I replied that a thirteen-kilogram (thirty-pound) tank
usually lasted from ten days to two weeks, she was
flabbergasted.
  "How is that possible?" she asked.
  I replied that bottled gas was our only source of cooking

fuel, that we used it for boiling our water and for cooking three times a day.

"*Three* times a day!" she exclaimed.

"Yes, of course," I answered, "breakfast, lunch, and dinner."

Now it was my turn to be surprised. My friend told me she cooked once a day, heating only what was necessary for subsequent meals. I discovered that most Indonesians do it this way. Another friend of mine cooks double on Saturdays so she does not need to fuss with cooking on Sundays when she could be visiting with friends who drop in.

Because it is cheaper I began to use a kerosene burner for cooking rice and boiling water for drinking or doing dishes. I now use the gas stove only for occasional baking or cooking and have reduced consumption to one tank in three months! Often I cook only at noon. In the evenings I heat what is left from lunch and add a fresh salad or other variation.
—*Shirlee K. Yoder*
Pati, Indonesia

I like knowing that even in small ways I can reduce energy consumption and experience greater well-being.

My hot breakfast usually included an egg, toast, and coffee, all of which required electrical equipment for preparation. When I gave up the egg and toast in favor of homemade granola with milk I soon realized that I was not only feeling better but the satiety value of the new menu was greater. It was exciting to discover that my calorie intake had decreased while proteins were increased, especially when my body weight tended to stabilize. I began using a percolator to make my coffee when I discovered that the drip-method needed twice as much electricity as the percolator method.
—*Catherine R. Mumaw*
Goshen, Ind.

●●●●●●●●●●●●●●●●●●●●●●●●●●●

Thermos for Hot and Cold

It seems we had to come to Southeast Asia to discover the thermos bottle as an energy-saving tool. All our Filipino friends here use thermos bottles to save on expensive gas or wood used for heating tea or coffee water. We were pleased to discover how much less frequently we had to use the stove by following their example.
—*Gene Stoltzfus*
Davao, Philippines

After an early summer picnic, our disorganization was evident—the eight-liter (two-gallon) thermos didn't get back to

the basement. Then we made a marvelous discovery! By filling
it with ice and water every morning we had instant cold drinks
available all day. I'm convinced that our refrigerator was
opened about 6,000 fewer times during the three hot months!
—Muriel Thiessen Stackley
Newton, Kan.

●●●●●●●●●●●●●●●●●●●●●●●●●●

Living Without Wasting:

What Shall We Do with These Plates? ● On their way to
the Mennonite World Conference in Wichita a group of eight
Kenyan musicians spent several hours at the Mennonite
Central Committee offices in Akron, Pennsylvania. They were
invited to join the MCC staff in a chicken barbecue on the
lawn.

Having been first through the serving line, the Kenyan
visitors were also first to be finished. When they came to the
hostess asking where to put their dishes and trash, she
indicated two large plastic buckets—one for flatware, the other
for garbage. They scraped the chicken bones and watermelon
rinds into one bucket and put the flatware into the other, but
kept the paper plates and cups.

After walking around for another few minutes with these in
their hands, wondering where to place them, they finally
approached the hostess again.

"But what shall we do with these plates?" they asked her.

"Oh, you can put those in with the rest of the trash," she
responded, pointing to the bucket.

Still somewhat baffled, they did as they had been directed.
As they backed away one explained to the others, "In this
country they use plates only once and then throw them away."
—Jon Jantzen
Albuquerque, N.M.

Extra Work or the Easy Way? ● After seven years
overseas, we were startled to see many things discarded which
we wished we could transport to East Africa. For example,
styrofoam hamburger containers would have made lovely
storage trays for any number of small items at Rosslyn
Academy! After two years of living in the States, I still keep
plastic and paper bags. I cannot throw away a glass jar or a
metal can with a plastic lid.

Not finding places actively involved in recycling has been
discouraging. One paper recycling firm I contacted was being
forced out of business because of fire regulations. A clinic I
called was unable to accept small jars and bottles because of
government regulations. How our East African clinic rejoiced
to receive anything like pill bottles and mustard jars!

With our heritage of frugality and thrift, we Mennonites should be pioneers in reprocessing. It's extra work to collect or store items for recycling and much easier to throw things away but are we looking for the easy way?
—*Jo Sensenig*
  New Holland, Pa.

●●●●●●●●●●●●●●●●●●●●●●●●●●●

Living Without Wasting:

Paper Products

When I was eight years old Mother finally consented to let me   **P**
use the sewing machine. She cut up old white shirt tails in hanky-size pieces which I hemmed. Our supply of hankies lasted for years. How much less waste than the modern paper tissue way of life!
—*Martha K. Kauffman*
  Atglen, Pa.

I use handkerchiefs instead of tissues. This isn't so hard to do when tissues aren't available or one box costs over a dollar.
—*Selma Unruh*
  Butwal, Nepal

I've learned to save all table napkins from airplanes, restaurants, or homes. I use them as handkerchiefs or toilet tissue.
—*Tillie Hunsberger*
  Port-au-Prince, Haiti

I resurrected napkin holders for our family. The napkins had been idle in my linen drawer too long. They can be used more than once before laundering.
—*Amanda Toews*
  Scio, Ore.

Napkins and hankies can be pressed under a few heavy books.
—*Erma Wenger*
  Musoma, Tanzania

I don't let advertisers con me into buying those soft, strong   ℬ
absorbent whatevers. We use old towels, tea towels, tablecloths, sheets, and underwear for cleaning, dusting, and mopping-up operations. We tuck clean, folded rags into picnic baskets for clean-up jobs. A cloth or two in the car is handy for cleaning the windshield or wiping the dipstick, as well as for bandages or wiping sticky fingers while traveling.
—*Vivian Lautermilch*
  Calgary, Alta.

In Ghana I learned to save wax paper from cereal boxes. I
continue to do this and never need to buy it in rolls.
—*Margaret Ingold*
Goshen, Ind.

I use brown paper bags as cooling racks for cookies and other
baked goods and to drain fried foods.
—*Jo Sensenig*
New Holland, Pa.

When I go shopping I take my own paper bag in spite of raised
eyebrows. This often causes people to question me and is an
opportunity for me to say something about saving trees and
avoiding pollution.
—*Sylvia Horst*
New York, N.Y.
—*Rebecca Yoder*
Goshen, Ind.

Thrift shops need assorted sizes of bags, particularly flat ones,
in which to put merchandise.
—*Gladys Stoesz*
Akron, Pa.

While camping in Europe and buying food for lunches at the
local stores we learned that you pay the equivalent of thirty
cents for each grocery bag the store supplies. That explained
why everyone came to the store equipped with a large market
basket. If we did this in North America, think of the trees we
would save!
—*Margaret Metzler*
Kokomo, Ind.

We never bought paper supplies at home. My mother kept a
stack of newspapers cut in half-sheet sizes in a convenient
place. One can be generous with them and use them for sifting
dry ingredients, peeling and cutting vegetables and fruits, and
as cooling racks for bread and cookies. They can be easily
discarded with the mess.
—*Sara Regier*
North Newton, Kan.

I use newspapers to insulate cold or hot food when storing or
transporting, to wrap sweet potatoes individually for winter
storage, and to absorb fat or grease from pans or dishes before
washing them. In wet weather I place several layers inside the
entrance to our house. They make a good mat for wet or dirty
boots.
—*Christine Burkholder*
Singers Glen, Va.

Washing windows with newspapers is just as easy as using

paper towels. I find it quite satisfactory. Just crumple two
sheets of newspapers, dampening one for washing and using
the other for drying and shining.
—*Betty Miller*
  Berlin, Ohio

Our church youth group has a monthly paper drive to earn   ℮
money for special projects and activities. Newspapers are in
great demand for making shredded fire-resistant insulation
material for buildings.
    Some collection centers accept other types of paper—
magazines, catalogs, junk mail, food cartons, carboard boxes—
depending on the use to be made of the recycled product.
—*Rosemary Moyer*
  North Newton, Kan.

Mulching with newspapers and grass clippings enables me to   ℮
enjoy gardening. I always hated to hoe the garden and pull
weeds in the heat of the summer. Now I need to do practically
none of this.
    Either when I plant the garden or just after plants appear, I
put five layers of newspaper between the rows and also between
such plants as tomatoes and cabbage. I space rows so the
newspapers will easily fit, covering the edges with dirt to hold
the paper in place until I can cover them with grass clippings.
As plants get large, I place grass clippings right against them.
    Because the grass and paper hold moisture, plants grow
better. The few weeds which appear are easily pulled out. By
the end of the summer the paper deteriorates and with the
grass adds humus to the soil.
    One word of caution—you may need to spread a bit of lime
on the garden during the winter since the grass clippings tend
to add acidity to the soil. Some experts suggest avoiding the use
of colored newspaper pages for mulch.
—*Paul Leatherman*
  Akron, Pa.

●●●●●●●●●●●●●●●●●●●●●●●●●●
Nondegradable Products

What's wrong with using aluminum drink cans, trays, and foil?   ℮
    —For one thing, the process wastes millions of tons of
precious raw material *that can never be replaced*. But more
importantly, aluminum is a material that breaks down very
slowly. For nearly a thousand years we will have to live with
the beer cans thrown in the garbage today, or tossed casually
out of an automobile last night. . . .
    Aluminum foils, while thinner, are every bit as resistant to
rust, corrosion, and biological breakdown as cans. Used

aluminum foil clutters up our dumps and acts as an effective shield against "breathing" by the top layer of the soil. This in turn directly affects rain absorption as well as the course of subterranean streams and natural water reservoirs. . . . As well as creating minor climatic changes within small ecological systems, this also creates a tendency for garbage-shielded dumps to retain vital minerals, and prevent their absorption by the adjacent useful farmland.*

We use foil sparingly, washing it for reuse as long as it remains intact. We put old clean foil into a box with other aluminum for recycling. Some companies buy used aluminum by weight. Foil pans are convenient when taking pies to friends, for carry-in meals, or at relief sales. It's tempting to discard them but they can be used repeatedly if washed.
—Rosemary Moyer
North Newton, Kan.

Oven-heat dinner rolls in a brown paper bag sprinkled with water instead of wrapping them in foil. Turn off the oven when the bag is dry, or resprinkle. A covered roaster or casserole dish will also do the job.
—Author's Entry

Instead of foil or plastic wrap to cover food for storage, use
—a jar with a lid
—a covered dish
—a recycled plastic bag
—a plate to cover the dish
—Author's Entry

Why habitually buy products in plastic containers? I'm glad we can get our milk from a farmer and so reuse the containers rather than accumulate more each week. I also buy margarine in paper containers.
—Janet Stoner
Akron, Pa.

I seldom throw away a plastic bag. I wash them with my dishes, rinse well, and hang to dry over a rack my children made out of tinker toys.
—LaVonne Platt
Newton, Kan.

We keep our use of styrofoam, aluminum, and plastic at a minimum, even on outings. The few extra minutes needed to wash the dishes is well worth the effort, for in so doing we're expressing our respect for the environment.
—Mary Alice Troyer
Austin, Tex.

---

* Papanek, *Design for the Real World*, pp. 251–52.

Styrofoam trays used by supermarkets for packaging fruit,   ℮
vegetables, and meat are handy for refilling with an assortment
of fruits, breads, or cookies to give as gifts to shut-ins or
friends.

These trays may also be recycled as picnic plates, but if
possible, buy meat and fresh produce at places where it's not
packaged in this way.
—Ruth Umble
Corning, N.Y.
—Gladys Stoesz
Akron, Pa.

We return all egg cartons to the farmer from whom we buy
eggs or take them to a thrift shop where farmers can buy them
for reuse.
—Jo Sensenig
New Holland, Pa.

I use disposable diapers only for traveling.   ℮

My reasons for not using them are:
—They are expensive—twelve for $1.79.
—They create pollution. Not everything in the diapers
  decomposes so they clutter up landfills all over the country.
—They can cause diaper rash because air cannot circulate
  through plastic and paper fibers as it can through cloth.
  When my child had disposables on for a week at a time he
  had more diaper rash than with cloth diapers. Disposables
  are supposed to be more absorbent, so babies are often left
  with wet paper against their skin for a long time.
—I like washing and folding nice soft diapers for my child.
—I believe cloth diapers are more comfortable and less
  confining.
—Bev Martin
Stevens, Pa.

Tin Cans

A scrap metal dealer in one of our neighboring cities accepts   ℮
clean, flattened cans for recylcing. He doesn't pay us for them,
but we're satisfied to know they are being used again. Cans are
easily flattened by cutting out both ends, inserting the ends into
the can, and flattening the can with your foot.
—Rosemary Moyer
North Newton, Kan.

Glass

Glass-recycling centers accept nearly any kind of clean, whole,
or broken glass. This is reprocessed into new glass products;
sometimes it is crushed and used in road surfacing or building
materials.

Our local thrift shop accepts assorted glass containers.
—*Rosemary Moyer*
North Newton, Kan.

Gallon jars may often be obtained for the asking from
restaurants or dining halls. These make attractive canisters.
—*Janet Stoner*
Akron, Pa.

●●●●●●●●●●●●●●●●●●●●●●●●●●

Priorities

P We want our home to accommodate guests easily. For this
reason we shopped until we found a secondhand table with
eight boards. It has a good varnish finish that doesn't need a
tablecloth. In the basement we have several single bed foam
rubber mats covered with fitted sheets. When not used as beds
they're stacked to provide a place to sit.
—*Sara Regier*
North Newton, Kan.

I'm spending a few weeks of study and solitude at the Overseas
Missionary Study Center, Ventnor, New Jersey. Because the
apartment here is furnished with no frills or duplicates,
housecleaning is easy. When I return to Kansas in several
months, I want to unclutter.

Today I wrote these instructions for myself.

"Get rid of all duplicates. Sell or give away everything we
don't need. Be involved only in that which is truly of merit and
brings peace, fulfillment, or benefit to someone. Examine every
purchase, every block of time spent, every square foot of your
house, every effort including cooking and cleaning habits.
Rework to trim, eliminate, or change in order to focus on
tranquility, peace, and service."
—*Marie Wiens*
Hillsboro, Kan.

●●●●●●●●●●●●●●●●●●●●●●●●●●

*Housekeeping: With
Alternative Solutions*

*After the dishes are
done I add about half a
cup of ammonia to my
dishwater to soak the
drip bowls from my
stove's cooking units. In
a few minutes I can wash
them with little scouring.
—Sara Regier
 North Newton, Kan.*

*I make scratchless
scrubbers for washing
sinks, pots, and pans
using the plastic mesh
bags in which some
fresh produce is sold.
—Mildred Steiner
 Goshen, Ind.*

*Copper-bottomed pans
or brass items clean
almost instantly when
you use a few teaspoons
of vinegar and then*

sprinkle with salt. Children love to watch the magic!
—Grace Whitehead
  Kokomo, Ind.

For several years I've used witch hazel as an after-shave lotion. It has a soothing effect, does not have an offensive odor, and costs about one tenth of the price of after-shave lotion.
—Edward L. Kauffman
  Phoenix, Ariz.

Petroleum jelly is an economical product. I keep a little jar of it in my purse to use for chapped lips or dry noses. It is also good for diaper rash.
—Erma Wenger
  Musoma, Tanzania

Many dollars are wasted on bathroom deodorants. The flame from one or two matches will eliminate odors. This is better than adding other foreign gases to the air. Of course, special safety precautions must be taken where children are involved.
—Mary Kathryn Yoder
  Garden City, Mo.

●●●●●●●●●●●●
With Less Cooking

Before leaving for Sunday morning worship, I sometimes set a package of frozen dinner rolls on a sunny windowsill. They are nicely warmed for our noon meal.
—Kathy Hostetler
  Akron, Pa.

I make iced tea with solar heat. Put two teabags or two teaspoons of tea leaves in a large (about eight cup) glass jar of tepid water. Allow to stand seven to eight hours in full sun. Store in the refrigerator.
—Hilda Newcomer
  Seville, Ohio

A friend of mine cooks rice in the bottom of a double boiler while heating the meat sauce in the top.
—Linda Goering
  Gaborone, Botswana

I prepare many meals using only one burner. I simply slide one pan to the side while I heat a vegetable. The first dish remains hot enough.
—Judy Schrag
  Newton, Kan.

For years now I have been batch baking to save energy. I schedule this for one afternoon each week. The last item is a casserole for our family dinner.
—Ursula Harms
  Ancaster, Ont.

●●●●●●●●●●●●
With Beauty Plus Thrift

In Japan fresh flowers are a sign of welcome to the guest. I embarked on a flower-arranging course and discovered that a single rose is as much admired as a large bouquet. Simplicity lends elegance!
—Mary Derksen
  Oita, Japan

Instead of making our living room curtains of the expensive fabric which matched our wallpaper, I bought just one yard of it for curtain tiebacks and quilted throw pillows.
—Becky Horst
  Lederach, Pa.

●●●●●●●●●●●●
With Beds

We sleep on woven mats without mattresses or beds. This isn't nearly as spartan as it sounds. A pillow adds a great deal to the comfort. The first week we woke frequently and felt a little stiff but now we sleep as soundly as on the finest bed.
—Dorothy Beidler
  Kalimantan, Indonesia

●●●●●●●●●●●
**With Living Without
Wasting**

*I'm known as the
ultimate scotch mother.
My reputation was fixed
one year at Halloween
when I removed all the
toilet paper from the
trees before a rain so
that we could use it in
our bathroom.*
*—Areta G. Lehman
　Goshen, Ind.*

*Free wallpaper sample
books are a must at our
house. Some of the ways
we use them are for
shelf paper, drawer
liners, children's art
projects, wrapping
paper, flowerpot covers,
place mats, table covers,
greeting cards, posters,
and book covers.*
*—Verla Fae Haas
　Bluesky, Alberta*

*We share a subscription
to the daily paper with
our neighbors.*
*—John and Helene Janzen
　Elbing, Kan.*

*I paint unfinished pine
yard fencing with used
motor oil. The idea came
from a Swedish neighbor
who said that many 500-
and 600-year-old houses
in Sweden are treated
only with used motor oil.
In about a day or two the
oil soaks in and dries
giving the wood a very
nice light color. No sign
of the engine dirt is
evident. When I changed
the oil in our car, my
eight-year-old daughter
did most of the painting.*
*—James L. Eigsti
　Ann Arbor, Mich.*

*I need disposable bags
for my sweeper but I
empty and reuse them
until they tear. It's a
dusty job which I always
do before a shampoo
and bath. A package of
bags lasts indefinitely.*
*—Edna Mast
　Cochranville, Pa.*

*When faced with minor
household repairs I
check in the public
library for do-it-yourself
home-repair books. They
explain each step
carefully in everyday
language, and are
usually well supplied
with diagrams.*
*—Jeremy Wilkins
　Vancouver, B.C.*
*—Floyd Zehr
　New Wilmington, Pa.*

*An appliance repairman
told me to put petroleum
jelly on the gasket of the
refrigerator and freezer
doors. This serves a dual
purpose: it prevents the
gasket from getting
brittle and it creates a
better door seal.*
*—Joyce Rosenberger
　Quakertown, Pa.*

*One strategically located
light left on to illuminate
one room brings us
together and saves
electricity. Our dining
table has ample room for
the four of us to work
and relax on long winter
evenings.*
*—Vera Kauffman
　Buckhannon, W.Va.*

*By the time we could
afford a garbage
disposal, our priorities
had changed. We began
to ask: Why spend
money on another
appliance requiring
electricity and water?
Why add to the city's
waste-disposal system?
Why buy commercial
fertilizer for our garden
while sending potential
compost down the
drain?*
*—Rosemary Moyer
　North Newton, Kan.*

*In winter when our
vegetable supply is
decreasing and the
temperature is below
freezing outdoors, I put
pans of water out to
make ice. By storing it in
the freezer for later
summer food
processing, I save the
electrical energy needed
for ice making.*
*—Mabel Eshleman
　Lancaster, Pa.*

*A push lawnmower is
great! It always starts, is
quiet enough to use
early in the morning
without waking
neighbors, and
efficiently combines
exercise with a
necessary chore.*
*—Richard Harris
　Manhattan, Kan.*

a ● Energy Consumption
● Per Capita
● in Twenty Most Populous
● Countries, 1974

Country	Kilograms of Coal Equivalent[1]
United States	11,485
Federal Republic of Germany	5,689
United Kingdom	5,464
USSR	5,252
France	4,330
Japan	3,839
Italy	3,227
Spain	2,063
Mexico	1,269
Brazil	646
People's Republic of China	632
Turkey	628
Egypt	322
Philippines	309
Thailand	300
India	201
Pakistan	188
Indonesia	158
Nigeria	94
Bangladesh	31

[1] Excludes firewood and dung.
Source: United Nations

b

**Energy Efficiency—
Passenger Travel**

Inter-City Passenger Transport
Fuel Efficiencies
by Vehicle Type

Vehicle Type	Average Seating	Fuel Economy: Average Miles Per Gallon	Average Fuel Efficiencies: Seat-Miles Per Gallon	Passenger-Miles Per Gallon
Automobile:				
Luxury, 4000 lb.	6	14	84	42
Standard, 2500–4000 lb.	5	18	90	45
Compact 2500 lb.	4	26	104	52
Bus, Highway Diesel	50	7	350	158
Rail, Diesel/ Electric	100	2.5	250	100
Airplane				
Short-Range	130	.43	56	28
Medium-Range	260	.27	70	35
Long-Range	164	.17	28	14
Jumbo-Jet	435	.14	59	30

The average passenger-miles per gallon have
been computed using load factors encountered
under typical urban operating conditions:
automobile, 50 percent; bus, 45 percent; railroad,
40 percent; and airplane 50 percent.

From *Energy Prospects to 1985,* Volume II,
Organization for Economic Cooperation and
Development, Paris, 1974.

C Relative Cost of Operating
Household Appliances

Appliance	Average Wattage	Estimated Use Per Day	Annual KWH Consumed	Average Monthly Cost*
Water Heater (Standard)	2,474	4.7 hr.	4,244	$17.68
Refrigerator-Freezer (Frostless-14 cu.ft.)	615	8.2 hr.	1,841	7.67
Refrigerator-Freezer (14 cu.ft.)	326	9.6 hr.	1,142	4.76
Food Freezer (Frostless-15 cu.ft.)	440	11.0 hr.	1,767	7.36
Food Freezer (15 cu.ft.)	341	9.6 hr.	1,195	4.98
Air conditioner	1,566	2.4 hr.	1,372	5.72
Range	12,207	16.0 min.	1,188	4.95
Clothes Dryer	4,856	34.0 min.	1,004	4.18
Television (color)	332	4.1 hr.	497	2.07
Dishwasher	1,201	50.0 min.	365	1.52
House Fan (medium)	370	2.2 hr.	297	1.24
Frying Pan	1,196	26.0 min.	189	.79
Electric Blanket	177	2.3 hr.	149	.62
Washing Machine	512	33.0 min.	103	.43
Radio	71	3.3 hr.	86	.36
Vacuum Cleaner	630	10.8 min.	41	.17
Toaster	1,146	5.6 min.	39	.16
Clock	2	24.0 hr.	18	.07
Food Blender	386	6.0 min.	14	.06

Adapted from *In Celebration of Small Things* by Sharon Cadwallader, published by Houghton Mifflin Co. Copyright © 1974 by Sharon Cadwallader. Reprinted by permission.

* Calculated at $.05 per kilowatt hour. This was a typical charge for residential use in eastern Pennsylvania in February 1980.

d

Spending with Different Levels of Income

Summary of annual budgets
for a four-person family
at three levels of living,
urban United States,
autumn, 1978.

	Lower Budget	Intermediate Budget	Higher Budget
Total	$11,546	$18,622	$27,420
Food	3,574	4,609	5,806
Housing	2,233	4,182	6,345
Transportation	856	1,572	2,043
Clothing	847	1,209	1,768
Personal Care	301	403	570
Medical Care	1,065	1,070	1,116
Miscellaneous	515	956	1,578
Social Security & Disability	719	1,073	1,091
Other Items	502	810	1,365
Personal Income Taxes	935	2,738	5,739

Note: Because of rounding, sums of individual items may not equal totals.

From United States Department of Labor, Bureau of Labor Statistics, April 29, 1979

**End Uses of Energy,
United States, 1968**

	%	Totals
Refrigeration	1.	
Water Heating	1.	
Feedstocks	1.6	
Air Conditioning	2.	
Space Heating	7.	
All Other	1.6	14.4% Commercial
Air Conditioning	1.	
Refrigeration	1.	
Cooking	1.	
Water Heating	3.	
Space Heating	11.	
All Other	2.2	
		19.2% Residential
Railroads	1.	
Airplanes	2.	
Trucks	5.	
Automobiles	13.	
All other	4.2	
		25.2% Transportation
Stone, Glass, Clay, etc	2.	
Paper, etc.	2.	
Food, etc.	2.	
Petroleum Refining, etc.	5.	
Chemical and Allied Products	8.	
Primary Metals	9.	
All Other	13.2	
		41.2% Industrial

100

From *Exploring Energy Choices,* Energy
Policy Project of The Ford Foundation,
Washington, D.C., 1974.

On the power of small things:
When spiderwebs unite,
they can tie up a lion.
—Ethiopian proverb

There is no cure that does not cost.
—Kenyan proverb

About half the time
when people ask me
what's the reason for
simple living,
I say,
"It's more fun."
—John Alexander
*   Philadelphia, Pa.*

5. transportation and travel

●●●

Americans traveled twice as much in 1977 as they did the decade before, according to a July 2, 1979, *U.S. News and World Report* article, "A Nation on the Go." Eighty-two percent of inter-city travel alone was by automobile. This mushrooming use suggests that the family car must be a prime focus of concern for responsible living. Focusing on cars in North America is probably not too difficult. It comes naturally.

In my high school sophomore class one person received considerably more popularity than his academic or athletic prowess seemed to merit. He owned a car. His parents were more affluent and certainly more liberal with their funds than most parents in the 1950s. We referred to him as the fellow with the "four-wheeled personality."

With the proliferation of cars in high school parking lots today, "four-wheeled personalities" get little status. Or do they? A quick glance at automobile advertisements reveals that such personality extension is still with us. One ad features a 1980 Chrysler Cordoba with a business executive saying, "I like what they're doing to my car." The big print above a Chrysler LeBaron reads, "A new measure of prestige."

North Americans and cars are synonymous to many visitors from overseas. Elizabeth Huettmann, a Mennonite Central Committee Exchange Visitor, wrote about her first impressions in the United States. "When we left Kennedy Airport we saw the big cars. Then I knew I was in America." Elizabeth and her colleagues in the 1978–79 program were invited to submit ideas for this book. Of the fourteen responses, ten mentioned cars as an area of extravagance.

Katie Funk Wiebe, writer from Hillsboro, Kansas, says, "Americans prefer to keep in touch with their cars rather than their friends. Some have owned more cars than they have had friends.

> "They can list
> with faithful accuracy
> each model they acquired
> through the years,
> how much they paid
> for each one,
> its main faults,
> and why they traded it in—
> but they couldn't list
> as many close friends.

"Americans grow up with several cars at a time and give them names as if they were family pets. They jump in and out of them daily. They curse them, praise them, polish them and repair them, and sacrifice to make payments and keep them running. They aren't ready to do the same for friends."

Of all the automobiles in the world, 45 percent are in North America. The United States has one for every two persons.[1] Transportation eats up 25.2 percent of total commercial energy in the United States. More than half of this is used in automobiles.[2] Viewing our cars judiciously and using them temperately will contribute to responsible living.

Following are four principles to help us:

1. **Drive less.** Walk, bicycle, start a carpool, use public transportation, and combine trips. Pare down the family fleet from three to two cars, two to one, or one to none, if possible.

2. **Drive smaller, more fuel-efficient cars.** Europe and Japan show us that we do not need the 300-cubic-inch engines that consume our limited fuel supply when 100-cubic-inch engines will do. If your driving is minimal, however, buying an older, less fuel-efficient car may be a good choice. Recycling older cars can save energy which would be needed to manufacture new cars.

3. **Drive tenderly.** Insurance company executives report that most accidents are preventable. Safe driving is directly

related to achieving greater fuel economy. Lower speeds, slower starts, and gradual acceleration translate into significant fuel savings.

Fuel economy is decreased 8.1 percent by driving 80 kilometers (50 miles) per hour, rather than 65 kilometers (40 miles) per hour. It decreases an additional 11.3 percent at speeds of 100 kilometers (60 miles) and another 17.3 percent at 115 kilometers (70 miles) per hour.[3]

4. **Maintain your automobile properly.** Regular tune-ups, adequate tire pressure, and systematic oil changes and lubrication add miles per gallon.

Tender driving and proper maintenance will not only stretch the kilometers on a liter of fuel but will extend the life of a car. That, too, is energy and resources saved—yours and the earth's.

The U.S. News and World Report article mentioned earlier states that much of our travel—37 percent—involves visiting friends and relatives. For a book that places high value on nurturing people and strengthening each other, this is good news. Other pleasure trips rank second, comprising 26 percent. These precede business trips and other reasons for traveling.

The entries in this chapter speak to more than just judicious car use. They discuss the second-highest category—pleasure trips—and suggest that the following principles should influence our vacation travels.

1. **Travel with design.** Pleasure trips should build personal relationships and bring renewal. "Getting away from it all" is fine, but unhealthy if it's the only purpose for traveling.

2. **Fewer trips—better planning.** The one well-planned trip a year or a lifetime is better than many quick, frequent trips. Fewer excursions allow more time for savoring the pleasures and absorbing the experiences. One cannot visit all the picturesque or interesting places in the world. Paring down the possible is not deprivation—it's often getting more with less.

3. **Balance the well-planned with the spontaneous.** The "Let's climb that ridge" or "Stop at that craft shop" needs to be balanced with "Tomorrow we will be in Jasper" or "Flight LH413 leaves Frankfurt at 13:20 for London." Too rigid a schedule can leave nerves tattered. Too many uncertainties can cause a run on the aspirin bottle.

4. **Explore local sights.** Picturesque places need not be four provinces or states away to qualify. Several years ago our neighbors told us of their exciting two-week vacation visiting historical and natural spots in their own county. No motels were required. They never drove further than forty-five miles from home.

5. **Gather few but lasting mementos.** Well-selected souvenirs help one relive and enjoy a trip. Picture-taking helps one

recall pleasant travel memories, but a persistent need for the
perfect shot may force you to miss the enjoyment and
splendor of the actual experience. A missionary friend
dubbed the camera "the white man's burden" after seeing
wave after wave of tourists descend on Hong Kong.

6. **Think who benefits.** Living responsibly calls us to consider
who gets our vacation dollars. Small inns, shops, and
market stalls need the money more than big hotels or
restaurant chains. Where we go, what we plan to learn, and
how we spend money can nurture people, do justice, and
show that we cherish the earth.

This chapter's entries share how people are getting more
with less in their transportation and travel. Energy is being
saved with smaller cars and shorter and better planned
vacation trips. Still, the best energy saver may be staying at
home.

Time with yourself,
with your family,
and with your God
may prove to be
the ultimate saving.

Notes

1
Lester Brown, Christopher Flavin, and Colin
Norman, *The Future of the Automobile in an Oil-
Short World,* Worldwatch Paper 32 (Washington,
D.C.: Worldwatch Institute, September 1979), p.
10.

2
Robert L. Loftness, *Energy Handbook* (New
York: Van Nostrand Reinhold Co., 1978), p. 158.

3
Ibid., p. 417.

●●●●●●●●●●●●●●●●●●●●●●●●●●●

Buying a Car

Secondhand ● Buying used cars saves on taxes, insurance, and initial cost. Also, most of the lemons show their nature after the first 16,000 kilometers (10,000 miles)!

Before buying we check Frequency-of-Repair records in *Consumer Reports* to warn us away from certain years and models. We test-drive and inspect the car in daylight, pay our mechanic to check it out before we buy, and deal with a reputable dealer. We also try to contact the former owner.
—Connie Buller
Blair, Neb.

New ● We recently bought a new car. To get one without air conditioning, power steering, extra cylinders, and fancy interiors or exteriors, we needed to wait from six to eight weeks after ordering. Since we've never had these, we knew we'd never miss them if we didn't learn to depend on them.
—Martha Zimmerly
Orrville, Ohio

Bigger Barns on Wheels ● Many North Americans concerned about the energy pinch will sell their gas hogs and buy new, more economical cars. By selling an old car we're probably hastening its way to the junkyard. Once there, great amounts of energy will be needed to recycle the iron and steel. None of the plastics, glass, rubber, or cloth will be reused. Instead they will poison the environment when they're burned. By buying a new car, we cause great amounts of energy and nonrenewable resources to be expended—just so we can get an extra mile or so to the gallon. It would be better to reduce gas consumption by driving less.

Trading in a good car for a new one is nothing but a modern version of tearing down barns to build bigger ones. The guilt for irresponsible consumption is added to greed.
—Lawrence Yoder
Pati, Indonesia

●●●●●●●●●●●●●●●●●●●●●●●●●●

Sharing Cars

When I came to Hesston College to teach, I moved into an apartment together with a friend. We decided to share my car, thus lowering our transportation expenses for gasoline and maintenance.

Two years later when the car was in need of major repairs, Shirley bought a car. We traded mine in on it and I lent her some money, interest-free. Again we shared maintenance and gasoline expenses.

Learning to work together and compromise enriched our
relationship. We cut out unnecessary trips, since the car wasn't
always accessible. We spent time going to and from places
discussing our spiritual, emotional, physical, and social
growth. Working on many of these areas jointly was exciting.
—*Korrene Thiessen*
Manhattan, Kan.

P Members of our church group live near each other for support
and enrichment. Some of us have quite old undependable cars,
a few have nearly new compact cars, and several have none.
We often share vehicles. The problem, of course, is how to
determine their availability and share maintenance costs
equally.

We encourage use of public transportation whenever
possible. We keep mileage records to reimburse each other
according to a predetermined rate. When possible, carloads go
places together and share in running errands. We seriously
discuss whether or not to buy cars when the concern arises.
—*Weldon and Marg Nisly*
Philadelphia, Pa.

●●●●●●●●●●●●●●●●●●●●●●●●●●

Till Death Us Do Part

C By our wedding anniversary in 1978, our 1970 model car had
traveled about 176,000 kilometers (110,000 miles). We've
about reached the conclusion that we'll drive it till it dies, and
in the meantime enjoy the advantages of owning an older car.
1. No car payments.
2. No collision insurance.
3. Lack of worry about scratches or dents. Fortunately, we
   haven't had any major scrapes.
4. A continual reminder that one's car should not be a symbol
   of one's security or self-esteem.
—*Dale and Harriet Bicksler*
Harrisburg, Pa.

●●●●●●●●●●●●●●●●●●●●●●●●●●

You Don't Have a CAR?

It's surprising how shocked, and sometimes offended, people
are when they learn that we have chosen to live without a car.

For the past several years our work has freed us from the
necessity of a car while also making it financially impossible to
own one.

Our legs get us where we need to go, either on foot or on a
bike. In times of emergency we rent a car from family or

friends. Using public transportation isn't as handy as jumping
into a car and going, but it makes us evaluate the necessity of
the trip.

We don't say that no one should own a car, but we do say
fewer people need cars. It seems that there could be sharing in
this area, both of ownership and use. Maybe someday we'll
own a car with another family, if the situation warrants it.
—Millie and Dave Holderread
Corvallis, Ore.

In September 1978 a terrific jolt from a high-speed pickup
caused my car to sail through the air, landing roof-side down in
the center lane of a busy five-lane highway. Miraculously, I
crawled out of the shattered rear window with only minor
injuries.

In the weeks that followed I made a list of the pros and cons
of buying another car. On the positive side were convenience,
usefulness, and independence.

But in the end the cons won. Here's the list that affected the
decision-making:
—A car pollutes, a bicycle doesn't.
—A car is expensive. I'm trying to live simply so that I can
share more.
—A car is bothersome to my nontechnical mind.
—Owning a car is extravagant since I have access to other
vehicles.
—A car is unjustifiable in the face of poverty.
—Interdependence through sharing rides and expenses with
others brings joy.
—Walking and bicycling give me time for meditation and
physical fitness.
—My home is located near stores, work, and schools.
—Hedy Sawadsky
Elkhart, Ind.

●●●●●●●●●●●●●●●●●●●●●●●●●●●●

Use a Bicycle

American families seem to expect mom to chauffeur her
children everywhere—to music lessons, scout meetings, church
or school activities, shopping, newspaper routes, or friends'
homes.

Being a parent of six children and living in the country, I
wasn't willing to become a taxi service. We gave our children
bicycles as soon as they could handle them, around four or five
years old. When they were capable of riding on main roads we
went with them on short excursions. Under our supervision
they began to watch for stop signs and cars. By seven or eight
years of age they could be trusted to go short distances on their

own. After our eight-day bicycle trip this summer, four miles to music lessons seem easy. Our older children strap their violins to their backs but we haven't solved the problem of an eight-year-old taking off with a cello!

My husband has always watched the condition of the children's bicycles, but has seldom repaired them. He teaches and helps them to keep their bicycles oiled and safe. That way, when they are left to their own resources, they are capable of handling the situation.
—*Kathy Histand*
Sellersville, Pa.

The first thing I noticed when I arrived in Vietnam was that people really knew how to use bicycles. The streets of Saigon were crowded with them carrying whole families, literally four or five people. While Americans only ride a bicycle, Vietnamese also walked with it, using it as a wheelbarrow. They carried tables, chairs, bricks, wooden planks, bamboo, dozens of chickens or ducks, or even several pigs tucked into baskets.

I now live in New York and use a bicycle every day. I commute to work and save at least half an hour and one dollar daily. With a sturdy carrier for the back, I use it to take the wash to the laundry, pick up boxes at the post office, and carry friends. I keep a strap cut from an inner tube on the carrier to secure boxes. In order to use my bicycle as a wheelbarrow, my left hand brake is the rear brake. I can push heavy loads with my right hand on the seat or boxes while using my left hand to steer and brake.

A well-built bicycle is a work of art. It is one of the most efficient machines ever designed. It uses only human energy and is even more ecological than mass transit. It uses few resources in production or maintenance and doesn't pollute. It's quiet enough to let you think. In a congested city, bicycles actually save time over cars. A well-functioning one pays for itself in several months.
—*Doug Hostetter*
New York, N.Y.

Genuine Horsepower • While living in Detroit, Michigan, we saw how pollution contributes to human suffering through diseases like cancer and emphysema.

A factory three blocks from our home produced padded dashboards for safer automobiles. Each year this factory paid a fine to continue polluting the air. Three of our neighbors died of emphysema during our two years there. All three were men in their forties. Only one smoked. These people couldn't afford to own cars or live in a better part of town. They were forced to stay in an unsafe environment, making safety devices for those who could afford them.

Our response to this experience after leaving Detroit was to
sell our car. We walked and used bicycles but traveled mainly
by horse and buggy. Many times we stayed home. Our pace of
life slowed.

A trip to town was a once-a-week event with an hour visiting
and sightseeing on the way and another coming home. Because
we weren't paying for a car, insurance, license, fuel, and
upkeep, we realized how much of our income had been used
for transportation in the past.

Now that we're again involved in our wider church
conference work, we've bought a car to use for long trips. We
know a horse and buggy cannot be practical for everyone, but
we still find it very enjoyable.
—*David and Annie Donaldson*
  Hythe, Alta.

●●●●●●●●●●●●●●●●●●●●●●●●●●

Instead of a Second Car

Both my husband and I have jobs that demand transportation
throughout the day, not just to and from work. To save energy
and money we purchased a moped as a second vehicle. It drives
about 240 kilometers (150 miles) to one Imperial gallon of
gasoline (1.2 U.S. gallons). Usually we have free parking space
downtown, since a moped may be parked in bicycle racks. We
also benefit from fresh air on our trips.

Most of the summer the car is in the driveway. In the winter
the moped is there. During the time we can't use the moped we
schedule the use of the car more carefully and use public
transportation.

We sometimes hear interesting comments about the preacher
and his wife helmeted for travel! Several colleagues at my place
of work are considering purchasing mopeds for the same
reasons we did.
—*Anna Mary Brubacher*
  Kitchener, Ont.

I had been adding about 64,000 kilometers (40,000 miles) on
the family car each year, most of it commuting to work. When
I changed jobs and we moved to another community during
the 1973–74 energy crisis, we decided to buy a house close
enough to work so that I could walk. We had to wait over a
year for a suitable one.

The benefits are well worth the wait. While saving money
and fuel, I get exercise walking to work. I can eat lunch at
home with my family. I don't tie up the car during the week so
my wife has access to it, saving us the extra expense and waste
of a second car.
—*Richard A. Kauffman*
  Scottdale, Pa.

●●●●●●●●●●●●●●●●●●●●●●●●●●●

C **Prevent versus Repent** ● Every person who drives ought
to take a maintenance course to become aware of the basics of
car care. It is the nature of mechanical equipment that it rarely
fails without advance warning. By the same token, it does not
heal itself. Costly repairs can often be avoided by taking care of
small items, even as little as tightening a bolt.

Every driver can do the following simple things to drive
more economically:

1. Check gasoline mileage and take corrective action when it
   drops. Points, spark plugs, and timing affect amount of
   gasoline used.
2. Change oil and filter and do other lubrication on time. You
   can save a tidy sum by doing the job yourself. One
   indication of oil condition is its appearance on the dipstick.
   Another is clicking valve lifters, a tapping sound that
   sometimes disappears after the engine is warm. Heavy or
   prolonged knocking will ruin an engine in a short time.
3. Check tires at least monthly. Keeping them properly
   inflated will extend tire life and reduce gasoline
   consumption. Rapid or uneven wear on front tires will
   require front-end alignment.
4. Avoid cold starts. The life of the engine is directly related to
   the number of cold starts it makes. A very high-heat
   thermostat is a must if you make short trips in winter. Not
   turning on the heater and defroster immediately also helps
   the engine warm up faster. Avoid pumping the accelerator
   and *never* race your engine.
5. Check out new noises and erratic operation. Unusual
   behavior could be a sign of coming trouble which can be
   prevented by prompt action.
6. Learn to work with your repairman by describing the car's
   problem clearly and accurately. Don't switch mechanics
   until you've given yours a fair chance to satisfy you.

—Willard Unruh
Butwal, Nepal
—Dave Kelly
Glendale, R.I.

L **Traveling Light** ● I experienced my first lesson in traveling
light in Vietnam during the 1968 Tet Offensive when I lost
everything I had. At first I reacted a bit by buying a bunch of
stuff. Later I began to realize that I didn't need all those things.

When I began working and traveling in India, I got tired of
checking luggage in and out. Now I just grab my briefcase. In
it (and it strains the hinges a little bit) can go three changes of
clothes, the papers I need, and, because I'm an avid reader,
books. I usually carry a little clock (since I don't use a
wristwatch), a towel, a shaver, toothpaste, and a toothbrush. I
don't carry any high-powered shaving cream. The soap that I

have, I use. Sometimes I carry a wee bottle of deodorant and
sometimes I don't. That's it. Five minutes before I'm ready to
go, I throw things into my briefcase and I'm off. I usually wear
a trench coat and maybe a long-sleeved shirt in case it gets
cooler.

I think it is important to keep clean and neat looking. I've
discovered, however, that if you're tied up in the security of
things, that's all people see. If you're working with ideas, then
people see the person.
—*Paul Kennel*
 Calcutta, India

●●●●●●●●●●●●●●●●●●●●●●●●●●●●

The Stewardship of Travel: I ● Our family enjoys   **P**
traveling and values it highly. Sometimes we plan for trips
several years ahead of time. We study *National Geographics,*
maps, and brochures to locate places that interest us most.

In making our travel schedule we mark off the time it will
take to get to our destination and back. Then we fill in the rest
of the spaces on our calendar with the sights we want to see,
leaving a sensible amount of driving time in between. If our
travels include Sundays, we choose a place of worship—maybe
a historic church or an outdoor worship service.

Roadside lunches have become our trademark. While saving
time and money and determining our own menu, we get to pick
the decor of our dining area. It's not hard to beat the plastic
plants, fake brick, and styrofoam beams of the fast food places.

We avoid big-name motels, choosing instead to stay in
guesthouses, small country inns, and private homes. In many
states and provinces retired couples and widows rent rooms to
travelers. We watch for small signs in the yard and always
carry sleeping bags with us so more of us can share a room.

Along the way we collect picture postcards in a scrapbook
together with our tickets to museums, clippings from the
brochures, and our own photos. Later we'll relive the trip
many times over!
—*Jan Gleysteen*
 Scottdale, Pa.

The Stewardship of Travel: II ● Especially in a first
experience abroad, a group tour led by a qualified leader may
be worth considering. A well-conducted tour gives a basic
introduction to countries without the traveler having to know
the languages. It is considerably less expensive than an
individual tour.

While I recommend an organized tour, I caution vacationers
to be aware of several facts.

Find out exactly what you are getting. A brochure sent to a
friend describing an eight-day trip to Switzerland for only

$888, New York and back, featured glamorous full-colored pictures of Alpine peaks (always under blue skies!), spectacular mountain railways, gorgeous dinners served in romantic settings, and steamships gliding through emerald lakes. The folder mentioned places which could be seen in Switzerland and neighboring Austria. Nowhere in the folder did one read that these *would* be seen. In the final analysis the tour only promised airfare to and from Zurich, six nights and breakfasts at a decent hotel, and a single excursion in downtown Zurich. It was the most overpriced plane ticket on the market!

Find out who the tour leader is and his/her qualifications. Guided tours and escorted tours are not the same. A guide, a leader, or a director is someone who is knowledgable and experienced. An escort merely gets X number of people together and doesn't pretend to know anything about the countries visited. Being able to present a good Bible study does not qualify a minister to lead a tour to Israel. A good tour director has lived or studied in the areas to be visited, speaks the languages, is recognized in his/her field, can handle emergencies, relates well to people, and understands group process.

Beware of "celebrity tours." Recently a nationally known radio speaker led a cruise to the Pacific billed as a Christian tour. Twenty busloads of people were turned over to local guides to visit the standard tourist spots while the "celeb" limited his input to several inspirational talks in an auditorium.
—*Jan Gleysteen*
  Scottdale, Pa.

Tourists, Be Aware! ● Everyone in the world travels on a more-with-less plan except North Americans. We're the only ones who spend our life's savings to go on that one fantastic trip abroad without getting the most for our money.

While in Venice last spring, I came upon a group of bewildered tourists clutching their travel bags and staring at St. Mark's Basilica. Although we became friends quite easily—we found we were all from the Vancouver area—it was impossible to convince them to venture anywhere without their guide. They had been told to wait for his return in an hour and a half and were afraid to leave that exact pillar even to walk through a nearby market or to go fifty steps to a museum. They had just come through Germany, driving a whole day without ever setting foot in the country. All were German-speaking Mennonites!

I never take a guided tour. Rather, I study budget books, especially those written by retired people who've traveled economically. I ask friends and acquaintances about their trips. I don't book all transportation from an agent at home because sometimes I've saved by buying passage abroad. Although it isn't restful, traveling by train at night saves on hotel bills. I always buy insurance through the International Association of Medical Assistance to Travelers (IAMAT), which claims English-speaking doctors and moderate rates. I keep my luggage to a minimum and carry nothing of great value.

I've learned to expect and rather look forward to the differences in people and customs I'm bound to encounter when traveling. Some things always surprise me and some are unpleasant. I deliberately choose low-priced hotel accommodations; all I want is a place to sleep and refresh myself. I don't waste money at places that cater to North American appetites. I usually begin by buying fresh produce and cheese at a market. Often I eat in my room. Finding the authentic dish of any region requires several days of observing, exploring, and inquiring.
—*Tom Graff*
Vancouver, B.C.

Mennonite-Your-Way ● We will never forget the summer of 1975 when our family of five, including two under two years of age, headed for a Mennonite Church Conference in Illinois. The drag of the miles, the tensions in relationships, and the almost prohibitive food and lodging bills forced us to search for a better way.

An idea was born! With an eye toward good stewardship and a heart toward fellowship, we wondered whether there might be a network of people across Canada and the United States who would open their homes (driveways, beds, yards, etc.) to host travelers. Such a hospitality listing could be compiled into a directory and made available to travelers. We spread the word and in about two months a listing of 1,700 host units was gathered from more than forty states and seven provinces.

In June 1976 the *Mennonite-Your-Way Directory* was published. The title came naturally from an already common denominational idiom for lodging with friends. We made the directory available for anyone to use. About fifty host families listed are not Mennonites. A few suggestions standardize expectations of both the traveler and host.

We published a second edition of *Mennonite-Your-Way Directory* in 1979. In addition to host locations in the United States and Canada, a few international hosts are added. Copies of the current *Mennonite-Your-Way Directory* are available for sale. Other groups could organize such a network. For more information write: Leon and Nancy Stauffer, Box 1525, Salunga, Pa. 17538.
—*Leon and Nancy Stauffer*
Salunga, Pa.

ℳ **A Trip We Didn't Take** • While living in Botswana we've found it tempting to use our vacation time to travel to the Cape of Good Hope and other fascinating sites in South Africa. But through our contact with refugees from South Africa we were reminded that those relaxing vacations are provided for us by the hard work of black people in that country: people who receive low wages, whose separation from their families is enforced by law, who are not allowed to own homes, and cannot even eat in the same restaurants we do.

As a result we choose not to vacation there but take opportunities to discover how to identify with them. We can't take a holiday from our convictions.
—Orlando Redekopp
Gaborone, Botswana

●●●●●●●●●●●●●●●●●●●●●●●●●●●●
When We Go Camping . . .

℮ We try to leave everything home but the bare essentials. Instead of taking a lantern, we schedule our activities from sunup to sundown. We have one-pot dinners or simple meals which require no cooking. Two pots and a cup and a spoon for each person are all the utensils we need. Large cans make excellent camping pots. We buy dried foods in grocery stores. These are more economical than freeze-dried foods found in camping-supply stores. They are just as lightweight and are packed in boxes or bags which we can burn rather than in foil which has to be carried out. We prefer a fire for cooking but use a camp stove where this isn't possible.

Our shelter is a sheet of tarpaulin. It keeps off the rain and lets in the feelings. We don't have special clothes for camping. Sturdy, comfortable shoes, rugged dirt-colored clothing, and extra warm apparel is all we need.
—Larry and Ginny Hunt
Camp Connell, Calif.

℮ Nearly every summer my husband and I have an inexpensive and restful week camping in a national or state park. We've used the same tent for twenty-five years. Our other equipment includes sleeping bags, a two-burner gas cooker, a kerosene lantern, a flashlight, a small folding table, and two folding chairs.

Our tent fits into an old suitcase. An old broom with a shortened handle, a piece of plastic laid on the ground under the tent area, and an old rug in the doorway keep the floor dry and clean. The trunk of our car becomes a handy pantry.

During the daytime we read, hike, and watch wildlife. In the evenings we play games, visit with our neighbors, or sit around

the campfire. Park Service provides free hikes, guided ranger
tours, talks, wildlife movies, and church services.

One Sunday just prior to the benediction, a deer stalked out
of the forest to within several feet of the minister, looked
around curiously, lifted her head as if in gratitude, and nibbled
leaves from a tree overhead. We had a sudden sensation of
being in the Garden of Eden.
—*Evelyn Fisher*
  Akron, Pa.

●●●●●●●●●●●

With Cars

*In 1915, my wife's
grandparents wanted to
buy a new automobile.
They decided to forego
this purchase, however,
because there were
many fellow Christians in
their church who could
not afford a similar
"necessity."*
—*Mel Boehr*
  Blair, Neb.

*The higher cost of
transportation may help
us realize we don't need
to bring in the celebrity
to whip up enthusiasm in
the congregation. God
has supplied each
church with all parts of
the body of Christ. We
don't need to go looking
for a leg or an ear or a
mouth in another body.*
—*Katie Funk Wiebe
  Hillsboro, Kan.*

*A friend of ours has a
heated garage and
allows others to use it to
do maintenance work on
their cars. He is skilled at
car repairs and
frequently puts in half a
Saturday teaching a
novice.*
—*Ruth Guengerich
  Ann Arbor, Mich.*

We function without a second car. We use bicycles, taxi, public transportation, and the word "no" to simplify our transportation needs.
—Mary Sue Rosenberger
  Louisville, Ohio

When we attended high school in a town four miles from our farm, we rode with members of several other neighbor families. None of us ever drove in separate family cars. The resulting friendship ties were strong and good.
—Bertha Fast Harder
  Elkhart, Ind.

I put an old six-cylinder engine in our VW van. The transplant cost less to purchase and put in than the estimate to repair the old engine. VW owners may be interested in a book by John Muir, How to Keep Your VW Alive. A Manual of Step By Step Procedures for the Compleat Idiot. It works!
—Harold Kraybill
  Lancaster, Pa.

Indonesians are able to make old American cars last twenty or twenty-five years. New American cars are not marketed in Indonesia because they are too big.
—Lawrence Yoder
  Pati, Indonesia

When we have to travel long distances we do it in our 1971 compact car. We take along a small ice chest, an electric hot-water pot, and supplies for simple breakfasts in our motel room. We stop at supermarkets for lunches and buy a wholesome meal for supper.
—James and
  Norma Fairfield
  Singers Glen, Va.

While visiting in India several years ago, I noticed that one large New Delhi congregation met each Sunday morning as a body, but divided into five or six groups for the evening service to save travel expenses. They kept costs down but fellowship strong.
—Katie Funk Wiebe
  Hillsboro, Kan.

●●●●●●●●●●●●

With Cycling

Although we live in a hilly area we do just fine with two-speed bicycles. If the hills are too steep we just walk for awhile and enjoy the change of pace.
—Norma Fairfield
  Singers Glen, Va.

Riding my bicycle I am free and open. I see what is happening around me and talk to other cyclists. I don't threaten others because it is a person-sized machine.
—Doug Hostetter
  New York, N.Y.

Neighborhoods are more beautiful on a bicycle than from cars.
—Grace S. Bergey
  Hatfield, Pa.

●●●●●●●●●●●●

With Vacation Travel

After staying in a private home during a church conference, a Kansas couple offered to pay for the hospitality. When their hosts refused they mutually agreed that a contribution to a famine relief project would be an excellent way to resolve the problem. They sent Mennonite Central Committee one hundred dollars.
—WMSC Voice
  August 1978

On a vacation trip we consider it a waste of money to drive right past places of scenic and historic interest just for the purpose of reaching a particular destination.
—Mary Emma
  Showalter Eby
  Harrisonburg, Va.

We go on weekend camping trips close to home which are possible more frequently than the thousand-milers and are more ecologically sound, more restful, and more fun.
—Lois Franz Bartel
  LaJunta, Colo.

We own a pop-up camper with a neighbor family to reduce costs.
—Vera Schmucker
  Goshen, Ind.

6.   *celebrations*

●●

Writers' conference speakers tell you there is no subject on
which you cannot write something significant. I disagree.

When products or services having to do with weddings,
Christmas, or Easter must be advertised, people *do* find
themselves writing on subjects about which there is absolutely
nothing sensible to say. And write they must, or lose their jobs!
This dynamic produces literature that either makes you laugh
or cry.

Take the "Spring Bridal Supplement," which yearly comes
stuffed into our small-town newspaper. It's a collection of ads
mixed with banalities in news article style and is all about how
to get married and dazzle your friends at the same time. The
day it comes no one needs the funnies.

First a photographer promotes "new posing and lighting
techniques" and says, "We do more double and triple
exposures than ever." Next is a wedding cake with blinking
electric lights and a real water fountain which, miraculously,
will not squirt onto either the icing or the bridal gown. A
fashion column, wary of being caught a few days behind the
trends, plays it safe with "couples this spring will middle-aisle
it in traditional updated styling."

Some years the whole business fills me with pity for brides.
Ads cajole them to buy everything from Super Shooter Food
Guns for cake decorating to special alarm clocks for the

wedding morning. Brides have it hard. But this year I wept for the grooms.

Kindergarten boys would fold under the put-downs. "Brides, please don't trust anyone else with your groom!" says a men's store. An ad for tuxedo rental begins smoothly, "He's in the wedding, too, looking handsome," and ends, "in finely tailored formal-wear you think was cut just for him." A list of "The Bride's Obligations," given similar importance to the Ten Commandments, ends with "get wedding present for the groom." And the groom thought that ballpoint pen she gave him was her own idea, born of true love!

These creative writers carefully handle the subject of the groom's feet. Perhaps this is a reaction against a few overly casual pasture weddings of recent years in which he went barefoot. And *that* was in reaction to stiff shiny shoes which pinched his toes. Last-minute tips for the groom remind him to "line up clean underwear and appropriate socks beforehand, check to see all zippers are performing as they should, and, if using rented shoes, make sure one is for the left foot and the other for the right." Like an airplane pilot poised for flight, he checks all systems: up-down on the zipper, left-right on the shoes . . .

Since life is short, we may as well laugh. And then determine that our celebrations will indeed center on praising God, not mammon. By God's grace we can make both holy and merry the unique events which mark our years.

The testimonies in this chapter best speak for themselves. Here is a summary of some important principles:

1. **Celebrate the meaning of life** at births, birthdays, marriages, deaths, various anniversaries, and special times. Living more with less does not mean abolishing commemorations and festivals.
2. **Celebrations are more than entertainment.** They should nurture people and strengthen faith. Activities which joyfully accomplish that are appropriate.
3. As much as possible, **separate celebrations from commercial interests.** Sometimes paid services are useful, but their availability must not dictate how we celebrate.
4. **Money may be well spent on celebrating.** But in our day overspending is the greatest temptation. Look for moderation and simplicity.
5. **Even at celebrative times, cherish nature by saving energy and by avoiding products that litter and pollute.**
6. **Gifts given during celebrations serve the receiver's genuine needs or reflect the giver's desire to show love, or both.** In the case of simply wanting to show love, a gift of time, personal expression, or other innovation may accomplish the purpose best.

7. Weddings do not belong only to the bride (it's your day!) or birthdays to the child (you can have anything you want at your party) or funerals to the one who died (but that's what father would have wanted). Celebrations belong also to families and churches and communities. Therefore, **considering the feelings and involvement of many is important.**

8. **Celebrations are not only for today.** They become our history. For once-in-a-lifetime events, like weddings and funerals, handle tradition sensitively. Make room for new ideas, but carefully weed out what is cheap and frivolous. Rented shoes or bare feet may embarrass you when you look back in twenty years.

The Alternative Organization has an excellent resource available entitled *Alternative Celebrations Catalogue* as well as other materials on voluntary simplicity. Order from: 4274 Oaklawn Dr., Jackson, Miss. 39206.

●●●●●●●●●●●●●●●●●●●●●●●●●●

Marriage:

The Wedding

We wanted our wedding to convey the biblical idea of celebration. We knew a prepackaged ceremony would not reflect our values. We didn't want a bride-centered pageant following guidelines set by Amy Vanderbilt or *Bride's Magazine.* Our search for alternatives gave us joy and satisfaction.

1. We designed our own invitation. Printers found this inconvenient; presses are set for gold-embossed lettering, not brown ink writing.

2. We avoided formal attire because of the wealth and status it communicates, choosing instead cotton made special with hand embroidery. Now our clothes are acceptable for other occasions.

3. We excluded the services of a professional photographer since, to us, this reflected a Hollywood mentality of self-importance. We didn't want the informality and fun spoiled by a hired camera. Several friends captured the celebration on film for us.

4. Rather than flawless arrangements from a florist, our bouquets came from neighbors' gardens, grainfields, and ditches. These reflected the thistles as well as the wheat and daisies in our relationship.

5. In lieu of fancy packages, we asked for gifts of participation—singing, praying, counseling, joy—or a monetary contribution to Mennonite Central Committee.

This freed us from the dilemma of owning three toasters or a deluxe electric can opener!

6. Our wedding feast broadened the traditional idea of temperance. To include wise use of food, we served whole-grain rolls with soy spreads and alfalfa sprouts.

7. Since silverware seemed already to impose a dishwashing burden, we decided to use paper plates and cups. We intentionally left out nondegradable dishes.

We don't recommend this sort of wedding celebration to anyone not committed to the work involved. Even simple weddings get complicated. Choosing from already existing lists in a bridal shop is less hassle. But we feel that comparing our wedding to a traditional one is like comparing home cooking to a TV dinner. The satisfaction of the process and outcome speaks for itself.

—*Dale and Jane Yoder-Short*
Lafayette, Ind.

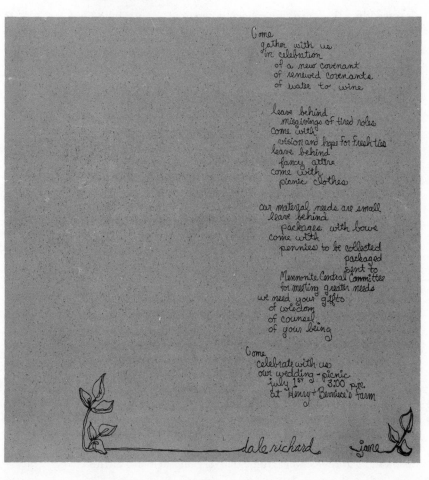

Come
gather with us
in celebration
of a new covenant
of renewed covenants
of water to wine

leave behind
misgivings of tired roles
come with
vision and hope for fresh ties
leave behind
fancy attire
come with
picnic clothes

our material needs are small
leave behind
packages with bows
come with
pennies to be collected
packaged
sent to
Mennonite Central Committee
for meeting greater needs
we need your gifts
of wisdom
of counsel
of your being

Come
celebrate with us
our wedding - picnic
July 1st 3:00 p.m.
at Henry + Berniece's Farm

dale richard   jane

For our marriage celebration we invited our families and
friends to a church camp midway between our homes—
Winnipeg, Manitoba, and Wayland, Iowa. For two days we
learned to know one another through activities such as
swimming, washing dishes, and worshiping together. We
shared our backgrounds as both families brought traditionally
favorite foods.

Instead of hiring caterers we cooked the simple meals
ourselves. A sister's gift was organizing the guests into working
crews. With the campground beauty there was no need for
florists' bouquets, new gowns, or rented tuxedos. The camp
rent, our largest bill, supported a church-sponsored project.
—*Joan Gerig*
—*Orlando Redekopp*
   Gaborone, Botswana

The Rings

Our wedding rings are symbolic and personal. People who like
them at first sight still like them when they learn their history.
Creating them was an occasion!

While visiting Peter's family we enlisted brother William to
straighten with pliers the chosen raw material—paper clips. I
held the clip strands as Peter and William braided; two bronze-
colored clips to represent our lives and one silver clip to
represent the kingdom woven throughout to qualify the
relationship. A friend loaned us his soldering gun to close the
metal braid.

Our family agreed the results were well worth the wearing!
The rings are sturdy and don't discolor our fingers. We do
anticipate possible breakdowns. This reminds us that marriage
cannot be taken for granted but requires care and sometimes
repair. The strands have all turned silver—a parable of the all-
pervasive and mysterious growth of the kingdom.
—*Mary Sprunger-Froese*
   Saskatoon, Sask.

●●●●●●●●●●●●●●●●●●●●●●●●●●

Birth—A Celebration ● As a nurse-midwife I meet many
childbearing families who want to participate in decisions
surrounding birth. Some wish to have family members present.
All want to give birth in a peaceful, happy, and loving
environment. They especially want the opportunity of holding
the new baby right after birth.

The midwifery center in Reading gives women this choice.
When a pregnant woman first visits the center, she is
thoroughly examined, at least once by a doctor. Normal or
low-risk patients may elect to have their babies at home, in the
hospital, or at the center. Home delivery and delivery at the

center, where a mother may go home several hours after the birth, are less expensive than a routine hospital delivery.

When we plan to deliver a client's baby at home, we visit that home at least once before the delivery to acquaint ourselves with the physical layout. We try to develop a special relationship with each patient and her family. We respect the couple's rights to know all the medical facts.

Birth is truly a celebration! The joyful get-acquainted period when parents are so involved with their baby that they are oblivious of everything else confirms this. I thank God for allowing me to help make this possible.
—*Esther Mack*
  Reading, Pa.

Birth Announcement for the World's Children ● When our child was born we wrote a letter to friends, instead of using more typical birth announcements. We gave details of Ryan's birth but also focused on our dreams for the kind of world in which he and all other children will live. One paragraph said:

> In this time of great joy and concern we are all challenged by the vision of a "new earth" of peace, plenty, and justice spoken of in Isaiah 65. In this world there will be no weeping, no calling for help. Babies will no longer die in infancy and all people will live out their life-span. People will build houses and get to live in them—they will not be used by someone else. Wolves and lambs will eat together; lions will eat straw as cattle do.

We concluded by suggesting that those who wanted to share our joy and concern write their government urging changed national priorities, or send a gift in Ryan's name to a church agency to further peace and development work around the world.
—*Duane and Ramona Smith Moore*
  North Manchester, Ind.

●●●●●●●●●●●●●●●●●●●●●●●●●●●

Death:

Mourning with Those Who Mourn ● Silence settled on the street as the late afternoon sun sent down its last rays. Shops closed and people left for home. Suddenly the stillness was broken by a wailing that gripped my heart and stopped my breath. I ran to the veranda overlooking the street. A woman, stripped to the waist, with ashes falling from her disheveled hair, stumbled down the street. Other women were supporting her but her anguish seemed too deep to share. As they moved toward the river, the wailing increased.

I remembered then that yesterday a teenage boy had

drowned in that river. The men were still searching for his
body. This was his mother.

Another missionary to whom I related this experience said,
"Isn't it wonderful that we Christians have a hope and don't
need to let ourselves go like that?" Later, I learned that this
African mother *was* a Christian and that at the church funeral
she had been calm and almost serene. Today she was
expressing her grief in her own way.

How do Christians mourn? Are we immune to the pain of
death? Do we deny our deeper emotions too carefully? In
Africa death is a fact and treated as such. There is no hiding
behind soft music and heavily perfumed flowers.

We were studying and adjusting to a new culture while
waiting for our first baby to be born. Unexpectedly, he arrived
six weeks prematurely and was gone as quickly as he came.
While I was alone in the hospital room trying to come to grips
with what had happened, a middle-aged African woman came
softly into the room. As she began cleaning she turned to me
and said a few words in a language I didn't understand. I
shrugged my shoulders to indicate that I didn't know what she
was saying. She reverted to sign language and now I knew she
was asking about my baby. How was I to tell her that he had
died? I tried, then just shook my head. Overcome with grief, I
burst into tears. Her eyes told me that she understood. She was
a complete stranger and yet she began to weep with me. As she
went about her work she mourned softly. Her caring comforted
me. I learned something that day about mourning with those
who mourn.

—Elfrieda Schroeder
   Kinshasa, Zaire

Vietnam Lessons About Death ● In Vietnam people
seem to be at home with death. Losing a loved one is a sad
occasion, but the event isn't mystified by an unfamiliar,
professional undertaker. The body stays at home, is washed
and clothed by relatives, placed in a simple wood coffin, and,
on an auspicious day, carried to the graveyard and lowered
into a hand-dug grave. One custom I especially noticed was
that family members dropped handfuls of dirt into the grave.

When my father died several years ago, our small son, Minh,
was most uncomfortable with the sight of Grandpop's casket.
He didn't want to go into the funeral home and clung to his
mother and me at the graveside. After most of our friends had
left, we stood around the grave. One after another, sons,
daughters, and grandchildren each dropped a handful of dirt
into the grave. It was the turning point for Minh.

Participating in the event freed him of his apprehension. He
began to speak freely about how we buried Grandpop. He liked
to return to the graveside occasionally with flowers.

Children are able to contemplate death. When we find a
dead bird or animal near our home, the children carry it out to
the pine trees where we dig a little hole, lay the animal into the
soil, and cover it. Then, following Vietnamese custom, we plant
several sticks of smoldering incense by the new grave.

Commemorating death dates is another custom in Vietnam.
Getting together on the first anniversary of Pop's death was a
special occasion for each member of my family, including our
mother. We met at the farm where we grew up, shared a meal,
had fun, and reminisced. We came away feeling good about our
roots.
—*Earl Martin*
Phoenixville, Pa.

Coffin: Money or Meaning ● When my father died of a
heart attack, the whole family was present. We had a time of
singing, praying, and crying in his hospital room after his spirit
had gone.

Father lived a simple life in which he carried out his beliefs.
He often expressed a desire to be buried with no attempts to
cover the reality of death. The thought of making a coffin for
him was not foreign to any of us.

The first funeral director we contacted said he could not
accommodate us if we did not purchase a casket from him. The
second undertaker, who had experienced customs of Amish
and conservative Mennonites, was willing to comply. In the
days that followed, he consulted with us several times before
carrying out details that he normally assumed as his
responsibility. We deeply appreciated his cooperation and his
advice on construction of the coffin.

In planning the box, as we called it, we drew a design that
was strong, simple, and beautiful. We selected pine wood—a
favorite of father's and easy to use. My brother and I have
woodworking experience. Friends were willing to help. About
twenty-five people, including children, helped sand, saw, or
turn screws. Mother and my three sisters made the pillow and
lining from bed sheets. We had time to stop and reflect, eat a
hamburger provided by friends, discuss events of the past day,
and shed tears.

In keeping with father's wishes and our own thinking, the
coffin was not placed at the front of the church during the
service. We concentrated on the message being shared,
realizing father was in glory. At the cemetery we didn't use
artificial grass or a casket-lowering device. Six pallbearers, all
fellow pastors of "Brother Roy," lowered the coffin.

In retrospect, building the box was a difficult but beautiful
experience. Even though work involved was perhaps greater
than if we had bought a coffin, we were rewarded by feeling the
caring of friends. Working together brought joy, releasing

tensions and memories for years to come. The actual cost, which we felt was the most minor consideration, was about one fourth that of the least expensive commercial wood coffin.

This record is meant to encourage others to consider breaking some practices of the past. We're often made to feel that the best can only be bought, that no expense should be spared for a loved one. Money rather than meaning seems to be the code by which we live. That needs to be changed. Our children are watching.
—*R. Wesley Newswanger*
Strasburg, Pa.

●●●●●●●●●●●●●●●●●●●●●●●●●●●●

Birthdays

One mother told me that she doesn't let her children have birthday parties. This is her way of avoiding an overabundance of gifts.

When our children have birthdays, our gift to them is the party and the cake. We organize special games and fun like baking cookies or stringing popcorn necklaces to take home. Sometimes we ask guests to bring gifts they themselves have made. A favorite one year was a fuzzy-wuzzy caterpillar in a jar!

Rather than a material gift, an invitation for a mystery trip fascinates our children. Unknown to them until they get there, the destination may be a park, zoo, or swimming pool.

Once our eight-year-old daughter came home from a party absolutely thrilled. The birthday child's mother had sewn cloth dolls before the celebration. At the party the children stuffed them and dressed them up with an assortment of remnants, lace, and other odds and ends. They took them home along with happy memories.
—*Margot Fieguth*
Mississauga, Ont.

To celebrate our preteen children's birthdays we sometimes invite one friend plus her family for a special dinner.

For Cara's birthday one year we turned our dining room into an Italian restaurant with checkered tablecloth, drippy candles, fresh fruit bowl, and soft music. We made a posterboard restaurant sign for the porch and matching menus which listed all sorts of Italian specialties. Daughter Marta, dressed as a waitress, informed the diners that we were temporarily out of everything on the menu except spaghetti, garlic bread, salad, and cheesecake. On the back of the menu was a quiz about Italy with information taken from the encyclopedia. We gave funny prizes for the lowest and highest scores.

The next year we turned the family room into a Bedouin tent. We pushed all the furniture into an adjoining room. For a tent atmosphere I made big string loops on the corners of plaid blankets and hung them at various angles from high bookshelves and plant hooks on the ceiling. We set several cement blocks on the floor in the middle and laid an old door on top for a low table. Candlelight and all the sofa pillows in the house improved the atmosphere. We took off our shoes, sat on the floor, and ate Arab pocket bread with lettuce, tomatoes, grated cheese, and bean filling. After the meal we stayed around the low table to play games.

For both parties, our children quickly caught the spirit and did much of the work involved. We decorated with what we had. Neither party cost us a cent beyond the food we served. The mix of ages meant I had fun myself and didn't have a houseful of young ones to supervise alone.
—*Author's Entry*

●●●●●●●●●●●●●●●●●●●●●●●●●●●
Christmas

A Navajo Celebration ● After prayer meeting on Christmas Eve a Navajo woman motioned me aside. Because I was geared to giving rather than receiving I was surprised when she invited me to spend Christmas Day at her mother's home. This turned out to be one of the most meaningful Christmases I've ever spent anywhere.

Sitting on the dirt floor we ate a dinner of mutton stew, Navajo fried bread, raw hot green peppers, and coffee. A gunny sack served as a tablecloth. There weren't enough bowls and spoons to go around but no one seemed to mind waiting until another had eaten and the bowl was washed. Leftover food and the gunny sack were put away carefully at the end of the meal.

By then I felt deeply the care and love this family shared together. They had so little material wealth and when they included me in their gift-giving I was overwhelmed. Each one treasured a sack treat including an orange, peanuts, and hard candy. Before the guests left, the grandmother asked me to read aloud the Christmas story.

My Christmas Day in the hogan is a beautiful memory. The warmth of friendship and the presence of Christ's love gave a new meaning to the lowly birth of Christ.
—*Edith Mae Merkey*
Bloomfield, N.M.

Commemorating God's Gift ● This year during vacation our extended family—parents, three married couples, and one single brother—discussed how we could make Christmas a time of sharing the good news of Jesus with all the world. We finally decided not to exchange Christmas presents within the family. We plan to replace gift-giving in three ways.

First, each family unit will make a contribution to a joint fund. This money will be given to projects and agencies working on world hunger and peace concerns. Second, we will share one Christmas project that will minister to poor or lonely people in our home community. Inviting elderly people to share a meal or giving a program at one of the institutions near us are possibilities. Third, we plan to have a special family worship service in which we will dedicate the offering of money that would have gone toward personal gifts. At this time we'll have what we call a gifting of each other when we recognize the gifts of love, labor, emotional support, spiritual insights, and vision each person gives to the family.
—*Ramona Smith Moore*
North Manchester, Ind.

Halloween • "Don't beg for things," we tell our children, but one night a year we disguise them and send them out to collect as much loot as possible. Halloweening was forbidden or discouraged when we were children, but no alternatives were given. Our own children felt left out when their friends at school described treats they'd collected the night before. In our search for a more suitable celebration, we tried and enjoyed several alternatives.

One year we planned an evening of games with each adult in the household responsible for an activity in a different room. We let the children bob for apples, follow his/her own string maze to find a prize at the end, eat a doughnut dangling from a string, and compete in a ball-rolling game.

Another Halloween we planned a special candlelit dinner for the five children. We all dressed in our finest. Then each adult waited on one child. After the meal, the adults hid somewhere in the house. Upon finding one of us, the children received a piece of candy each—a rare treat.

One afternoon close to October 31, we rang doorbells and offered homemade bread to senior citizens living near us. When trick-or-treaters came to our house we invited them inside for their homemade treat. We admired their costumes and watched them unmask so we could identify them. This helped our smallest ones to be less fearful of the spooks and goblins.
—*Herb and Sarah Myers*
Rheems, Pa.
—*Ken and Libby Nissley*
Mt. Joy, Pa.

World Holidays • Identifying with people from cultures that waste fewer resources than we do is one way of helping maintain a firm commitment to living more with less.

Celebrating holidays of other cultures helps establish that

sense of identity. Having lived in India, our family still celebrates Indian festivals. With the help of the UNICEF calendar and other publications, we've also enjoyed celebrating with people from countries we've never visited.

What fun it was one morning in the middle of December to awaken to the music of a Swedish folk song and be treated to a Santa Lucia breakfast by our daughter! She discovered that in Sweden December 13 is the day when the eldest daughter serves a special breakfast to her family, wearing atop her head a wreath of greenery surrounding tall candles. She had been up secretly since 2:00 A.M. to make "Cat's Eyes"—the currant yeast buns described on the calendar.
—*LaVonne Platt*
 Newton, Kan.

Nine O'Clock Dessert ● At our house we have tea and dessert around nine o'clock instead of right after dinner. This gives all of us in our shared household another time to be together and minimizes the need for fancy foods at dinner.

We celebrate birthdays, anniversaries, and special events, such as Tom receiving Canadian citizenship, at our nine o'clock gathering. One evening we were led into a darkened room, a friend played a trumpet fanfare, and suddenly room lights revealed Gathie's new paintings. After viewing, discussing, and applauding her work, we had cake and tea. A marvelous event!
—*Elizabeth Klassen*
—*Alfred Siemens*
 Vancouver, B.C.

Tea Will Be Ready in Three Minutes ● While living in Indonesia I was often invited to sit down and drink a glass of *strop* (cold, sweet fruit drink) or a cup of Javanese coffee before delivering my brief message or conducting a business transaction. Because of poor or nonexistent telephone service, personal visits were frequent; because of the socializing ritual, they consumed much more time than in North America. This greatly reduced the number of errands I could accomplish in a day but enhanced communication and socialization. The slower pace and liquid refreshment also made the heat and humidity bearable.

Since returning to the United States we've tried to institute more tea-drinking opportunities with friends who drop by our house. We buy tea inexpensively in bulk rather than in tea bags. A fine tea strainer provides a clear drink for guests, although I don't mind plenty of fodder in mine. With an assortment of herb teas next to the teapot, we're usually able to make good on our invitation: "Sit down—tea will be ready in three minutes."
—*Paul Longacre*
 Akron, Pa.

An Answer to Buying Parties ● Each year I get
invitations to buying parties—Tupperware, Stanley,
Dutchmaid, or Sarah Coventry. Although I enjoy the fun of
being with friends, I'm bothered by the whole idea behind the
parties. They encourage me to buy things I don't need and to
schedule a party so my hostess and I can win lovely gifts. If I
agree, the overbuying continues.

I designed a different kind of party to replace the buying
kind. In October I invited friends for a craft party. We made
small Christmas tree ornaments which were then given to a
thrift shop in our area. I supplied the materials and light
refreshments.

The fellowship of this evening easily equaled a buying party.
Guests had the satisfaction of learning to make something and
of helping a worthy cause. The thrift shop manager was
delighted to have seasonal handmade items to sell. And I was
able to play hostess with a clear conscience.
—*Susan Hurst*
New Holland, Pa.

●●●●●●●●●●●●●●●●●●●●●●●●●●●●

Eating and Drinking

A Soft Approach to Alcohol ● Darlene and I have
evolved a style of abstinence from alcohol which we find
comfortable and satisfying.

Both of us grew up in solidly rural Mennonite communities
in Oklahoma and Saskatchewan. Drinking was generally
frowned upon. Of course, there were always those who opened
a bottle of wine at festive occasions like weddings and pig-
slaughterings! Moderation and abstinence were practiced side
by side. It was not until later that an emphasis on
fundamentalism labeled anyone who drank unchristian.

We've now lived in the city for twenty-five years.
Occasionally we attend parties at the university where I work.
When offered a drink we ask for "something soft." We've never
been embarrassed at these events. There are always some who
do not drink because they don't like the taste, or for religious
reasons, or because they are with Alcoholics Anonymous. The
act of drinking together as a symbol of friendship is more
important than what one drinks.

Our intensive Canada-wide research of Mennonite drinking
patterns shows that about one-third drink. Regretfully, this
trend appears to be on the rise in urban centers. Abstinence is a
simple way of doing more with less. It isn't a sacrifice. It is
another way of cutting out something we do not need.
—*Leo Driedger*
Winnipeg, Man.

A Vegetarian Diet ● I've been a vegetarian for twenty-five

years. Actually, I am a lacto-ovo-vegetarian: I do eat milk, cheese, and eggs. My wife, Elfrieda, is a tremendous cook, as good a reason for my health as my vegetarianism.

Sometimes our dinner guests wonder whether they are eating veal or beef or another kind of meat. It's always interesting to see their faces and hear the comments when they discover that the casserole is basically soybeans with no meat at all. Of course I can't resist the temptation to say that it contains as much protein as meat, and that if more of us would abstain from beef there would be more food available for the hungry people of the world.

What I have in mind is the unfavorable conversion rate of vegetable protein to animal protein in the case of cattle fed in feedlots—about six to one. Poultry is a better converter at the rate of three to one and the catfish is the absolute ultimate in efficiency with a ratio of one to one. Saying this, I can be sure of a lively discussion or even an argument. Some of the responses are predictable.

Do I wear leather or plastic shoes? What about taking the life that is dormant in the egg? I know that game. The intent is to neutralize or weaken the force of an argument by pointing out its inconsistencies. So I answer, with tongue in cheek, that my shoes are leather but the cow died a natural death and I eat only unfertilized eggs.

Elfrieda keeps accurate record of our food costs and has documentary evidence that we've saved thousands of dollars over the years. We've eaten well but in thirty-four years of marriage we've never bought a roast of beef.

What about inconvenience? For me there is none. But I've been a nuisance to many a good homemaker. After having caused additional trouble and some anxiety when visiting in homes, I gave it another thought. I didn't want to be too rigid and inflexible. So for a brief period I reverted to a carnivorous diet. Now, my rule when visiting in private homes is to eat what is set before me. At home and in restaurants I maintain a vegetarian diet.

Elfrieda isn't committed to the vegetarian principle and occasionally will prepare a separate dish for herself. It may be a bit more work but has never been an occasion for tension. We've never argued over either diet but thank the good Lord for both.

The deeper motivation for being a vegetarian has to do with my world view and philosophy of life, my concept of creation and redemption. It has to do with reverence for life—all life. In a sense it is simply an extension of the pacifist or nonresistent principle.
—Peter J. Dyck
Akron, Pa.

Gift Giving

●●●●●●●●●●●●●●●●●●●●●●●●●●●●●

When our children were young, Truman was a student pastor. **P**
I never thought it made sense to use his limited income to buy
his birthday gift. Then I read about Jackie Kennedy
memorizing poetry with her children as a gift to John. It made
me realize that the wealthy also need to look for meaningful
giving that cannot be bought with money.

Our daughter Kathy was learning to play the piano. She
chose to memorize "Bridge over Troubled Waters" for her
dad's birthday. She practiced long and hard to perfect it. It was
a favorite gift, and Truman often requested her to play it for
him.
—Betty Brunk
  Akron, Pa.

At one end of our garden is a small tree nursery. I buy large **C**
nursery pots in bulk from a local supplier, and each spring go
about the property digging up shade tree seedlings that come
up voluntarily. Some years I visit the woods to dig out
overcrowded little sugar maples and ironwoods. I put each in a
container, or if too small, in a row in the garden.

I water the trees once a week unless it rains, and in winter
heap earth up around the pots for protection. When a tree is
about a meter (three feet) tall, we give it to a visitor or take it as
a gift to someone. I still can't believe how people fall for trees!
Almost nobody who has room for one can resist. When people
return the container, I use it again.
—Ron Conrad
  Thornhill, Ont.

My mom called one day to find out what our five-year-old
wanted for his birthday. "Gee, Grandma, I dunno," he
puzzled. "I have everything I need in my backpack!"
—Ruth Martin
  Ephrata, Pa.

I wanted to give a Mother's Day gift that would last **P**
throughout the year and remind Mom of our friendship while I
was away. I made a calendar with personal notations for each
day including the special events in Mom's life. Among them
were:

"Today is your anniversary—have a candlelight supper."
"The swimming pool opens tomorrow—do ten sit-ups."
"Remember Matthew 11:25–30."
"Do a favor for a stranger today."
Mom often says how much the calendar meant to her. She

checked it often and even though the year is over, she still
hasn't thrown it away.
—Bobbie Hamman
Athens, Ohio

One family we know gave a gift of coupons for several evenings
of free babysitting to a couple with young children.
—Carolyn Yoder
Pittsburgh, Pa.

●●●●●●●●●●●●●●●●●●●●●●●●●●

Gift Wrapping

It's become a tradition to see how many Christmases I can
create an attractive package using the same piece of gift wrap. I
make bows from discarded strips of wrapping paper cut with
pinking shears.
—Corlene Schulz
Burr Oak, Mich.

I use brown paper bags for wrapping gifts for my twenty-one
grandchildren. I decorate them with construction paper
cutouts also using these as name tags.
—Mary Brubaker
Hesston, Kan.

Our children enjoy making their own wrapping paper by
coloring, painting, or pasting pictures on plain newsprint or
other scrap paper. We use scraps of cloth, felt, or yarn to make
a bow. Real or artificial flowers, fall leaves, or evergreen
branches sometimes decorate our gifts. We make tags from old
greetings cards.
—Mary Jane Hoober
Hesston, Kan.

Newspaper can make a distinctive package. For a baby gift, I
circle the baby's birth announcement in the newspaper with a
red felt-tip pen and use that page as gift wrap, making sure the
announcement is in a strategic position on the package.
    I use the same idea with an engagement announcement to
wrap a wedding gift, the sports page for a sports enthusiast,
and a comic page for a child's gift.
—Erma Wenger
Musoma, Tanzania

To make a bow, I cut newspaper strips, then pull the strips
between my finger and an open pair of scissors to curl them. I
fasten several together with tape or a staple.
—Sandy Lord
Tehachapi, Calif.

Greeting Cards

I used to spend hours looking for just the right card for a
particular occasion until I realized this was a trite attempt at
building a relationship with someone. Now, during daily
devotions, I note verses that would be appropriate for various
times—a birthday, a death, or an encouragement. Then I use
these to compose my own greeting cards on plain stationery.
—*Sara Regier*
  North Newton, Kan.

I have fun decorating greeting cards using pressed flowers,
weeds, or leaves, cutouts from magazines and seed catalogs,
and used greeting cards. The base can be anything—maybe the
cardboard that comes with some clothing. I often use a felt pen
to trim a torn edge. I keep a file folder of collected items for
this purpose.
—*Hedy Sawadsky*
  Elkhart, Ind.

I started creating birthday cards when I lived where none were
available. I like to use checked fabric and, with contrasting
embroidery thread, cross-stitch an initial of the friend's name. I
paste this to the front of the card and write a message inside.
My trademark—"No Jo Cards"—appears on the back.
—*Norma Johnson*
  Akron, Pa.

More from Your Cards

Only good greeting cards deserve to be recycled. I choose those
that honor Christ, celebrate the season, or speak of friendship.
I may use them as postcards, notepaper, or bookmarks.
Sometimes they become parts of mobiles or collages.
—*Elizabeth Showalter*
  Harrisonburg, Va.

When I'm performing with my Autoharp or singing and
holding a microphone, a small card with typed words is
preferable to sheet music. I use the clean half of used greeting
cards for this. In the nervous moments of waiting in a church
or auditorium, I look at the picture with my small penciled
reminder of the sender's name. It gives me a special feeling of
warmth at a time when it is much needed.
—*Connie Isaac*
  Fresno, Calif.

●●●●●●●●●●●●●●●●●●●●●●●●●●

Letters Are for People

P I like to write letters. First of all, there are the milestones in life: birthdays and weddings, an ordination or a promotion, the death of a dear friend or a nephew's graduation. I get involved in these moments, even though not always on time.

There are other reasons to write: a promising young man decides to go to seminary to prepare himself for the ministry, a friend offers her talents to serve for three years in a needy country far away, or an older couple has left the community to retire in another state. When traveling I like to send picture postcards to older people, shut-ins, and children.

But what about those business letters? Here I also like to think of the recipient as a person. If a pastor had an outstanding sermon published recently I'll comment on that before answering his questions. Much as I regret it, sometimes I must communicate with a mass-produced letter. I try to write such letters in a warm, personal style as if I were writing to each person in particular. When these letters are ready to mail, I often add a few words of personal greeting.

Undoubtedly personalized correspondence contributes to sales and good public relations. But for me the real motivation is that I believe in the church as the family of God. In such a church the Christian should show concern, care, and love to humanize the world and to counteract the fearful impersonality of that stuff marked "Occupant."
—*Jan Gleysteen*
   Scottdale, Pa.

The most interesting stationery I've received is from a friend who fashions his own. Often letters from John are typed on plain white paper with a little photo or cutout pasted in one corner. Once his letter had the word *censored* rubber-stamped on it several times. You can imagine how carefully we read that one! Another time we received a large, fancy candy bar wrapper in the mail with our address on it. We opened up the wrapper to discover a mouth-watering letter from John.

I've taken to brush-stroking red Chinese characters for Pat's and my name in the corner of a sheet of plain inexpensive typing paper. I like to think it makes quite elegant stationery at half a cent a page!

And then there's Art. Every letter we've received from him over the past years has been sent in a recycled envelope. He just scribbles out the address on the one side, writes our address on the back, pastes it shut, and sends it on its way. The letter is written on the back of junk mail or, more often, on the back of some printout announcing a disarmament rally or community action program.
—*Earl Martin*
   Phoenixville, Pa.

Envelopes:

Recycle Them

I save envelopes which haven't been sealed. I paste a colored patch over the name and sometimes decorate it with cutouts from other used colored envelopes.
—Corlene Schulz
  Burr Oak, Mich.

I use church bulletins or wallpaper samples to make envelopes. As a result I haven't had to buy any in four years and have discovered artistic talent in myself which I never knew was there.
—Susan Shenk
  Lititz, Pa.

Eliminate Them

When using a large page for a note or letter, a simple folding can eliminate the envelope altogether. It can hold an enclosure or second page of a letter.
- Materials Needed:
  —a sheet of paper about 22 x 30cm (8½" x 11")
- Directions:

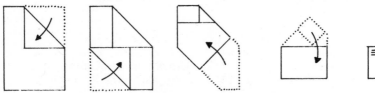

1. Fold down the upper right corner to within 4cm (1½") of the left edge. (Fig. 1)
2. Fold up the lower left corner to fit the lower edge of the first fold. (Fig. 2)
3. Fold the lower point up so its edge is even with the upper edge. (Fig. 3)
4. Bring the upper point down so that the crease is horizontal to the lower edge. (Fig. 4)
5. Turn the final point over the edge and secure with a postage stamp. (Fig. 5)
6. Address as usual. (Fig. 6)

—Hedy Sawadsky
  Elkhart, Ind.

●●●●●●●●●●●●●●●●●●●●●●●●●●●

Many old people suffer
from the ugliness of their
environment. Much
healing could be offered
to older people by
helping them to make
their home and room a
little more beautiful. With
real plants which grow
and die as they do and
ask for care and
attention as they do,
their lives might be less
lonely. Real flowers
about which and to
which we can speak can
have more healing
power than well-chosen
words about the
meaning of life and
death.
—From Clowning in Rome
   by Henri Nouwen

We all enjoyed having
international students or
families in our home
over the Christmas
holidays. While we
shared our home and
family we also learned
more about Somalia,
Nigeria, and Japan,
which previously were
just spots on the globe.
Sometimes our guests
prepared a typical meal
from their country—a
special treat.
—Ken and Libby Nissley
   Mt. Joy, Pa.
—Herb and Sarah Myers
   Rheems, Pa.

We were away on
vacation for a week
during the time that
friends were hosting
wedding guests. We
offered our house to use
as a motel. Siblings and
relatives who hadn't
been together for
several years
appreciated deeply the
quiet of a home setting
for this occasion.
—Mary Smucker
   Goshen, Ind.

For our daughter's birthday we hid coupons at the end of ribbons that wound around furniture. These were for a kitten to be selected at the Humane Society, for yogurt from the store (a treat, since we usually have only plain, homemade yogurt), and for a trip to a skating rink.
—Judy White
    Ashland, Ohio

The Longacre family and our family wanted to share an evening meal with a third family visiting from Canada. The weather was too cold for a picnic and our houses were inadequate for adult conversation plus a play area for ten lively children.
    We checked the church schedule and found the evening open. We took food and games and enjoyed plenty of elbow space in two fellowship rooms. At the end of the evening we were careful to tidy up and turn off lights.
—Margaret Brubacher
    Akron, Pa.

Each Christmas our children receive something we've made for them. A castle playhouse made from a huge carton and a dragon playhouse made of papier-mâché over chicken wire lasted for over a year before they finally self-destructed—much more play value than from toys we've bought.
—Judy White
    Ashland, Ohio

I've attended many professionally catered wedding receptions but none held a candle to the beauty and simplicity created by our friends for our daughter's backyard wedding. Love and care were the important ingredients.
—Loretta M. Leatherman
    Akron, Pa.

7. *recreation*

●●

A funny thing happened this morning on the way to writing
this chapter about fun. I left home at 7:45 A.M. and walked five
blocks to the office with my brain already busily sorting ideas
on recreation. On arrival I used my right hand to set my
brown-bag lunch behind the desk as usual. Only then did I
notice that my left hand held our fifth-grade daughter's Snoopy
lunch pail. I had been oblivious to it bumping against my side
for half a mile.

Fifteen minutes later Snoopy was back at the elementary
school. I lost a bit of time, but took the whole thing as a last-
minute reminder, before beginning to write, that ordinary days
are peppered with crazy surprises and relaxing grins.

If we turn down speed and noise enough to notice, life is
ready with free thrills and gifts of beauty. Yesterday on a walk
through one of Akron's wooded areas I stumbled upon a large
natural garden of lavender and white phlox—right after I
complained to someone that I had seen all the spring wild
flowers in our area and was tired of hiking there.

And a week earlier on another walk a teenager and I came
upon an aeronautics show. Just as we passed a grove of maple
trees, those windy gusts which precede a rainstorm hit. Within
moments the air spun with thousands of two-inch
helicopters—winged maple seeds whirligigging around us in
nature's wild tree-planting frenzy. Choosing favorites and

shouting through the wind, we watched some of them sail
above the houses for blocks.

Smiling Spirits

More-with-less standards for living never imply that we
should stop the fun.

Certainly these are grave days. Still, more with less does not
mean a somber lifestyle which preaches only responsibility and
condemns beauty, excitement, and humor. It doesn't even
mean rejecting the new. Although I shudder every time
another advertisement shrills forth, "It's new!" in another way,
newness is what we need. For it is in the very hope of a new
kingdom, brought about by the eternal recreative Spirit of
God, that we may dare to laugh every day.

> Recreation
> is the saving chuckle
> of the soul.
> It happens
> when we see a new thing,
> or discover
> a new way of seeing.

It is making a new thing and being remade, hearing a new
sound and singing it. Nothing could be more in keeping with
the nature of God.

In the Apostle John's vision of the order to come (Revelation
21), newness is a strong theme. At last God finds a dwelling
place with us. The older order passes away. Then the one who
sits on the throne cries, "Behold! I am making all things new!"
That's at the end of the Bible, not the beginning. The God who
made heaven and earth, who created us and is redeeming us, is
not finished yet! Creation and re-creation never stop.

Leisure Without Rest

The process of re-creation requires leisure and rest. People in
the Western world have leisure. We do not need to slave every
minute in order to eat. But only a few appear to have rest.
Cheap energy supplies in the past decade allowed running to
and fro at speeds and with a frequency never before possible.
Profit-making work began to swallow Sundays and holidays.
No wonder everyone has been getting so tired.

Obviously much of this fatigue takes place in the name of
making more money, even though the pantry's already
stocked. After all, by burning a little more gas and working one

more evening a week, it *is* possible to chase down one more account, open another store, or farm another field. But it may not be possible to love a spouse, children, and the friendless poor at the same time.

Others wear themselves out proving they are indeed worthwhile people. Get those new drapes up and the spring cleaning finished before Aunt Matilda arrives. Publish three articles a year or perish professionally. Fertilize the lawn, support every bake sale. Keep that schedule untangled and keep those children on the run—soccer practice, violin lessons, art class, library day.

Then one can write a Christmas letter that tops them all: "Jeffrey goes out for sports, took the lead in the class play, went backpacking, is first-chair trombone, and never dawdles a moment. We insist that he be precocious and have as much fun as everyone else is having. Frankly, you are lucky to know his parents as old college friends."

You know as well as I that many letters barely veil that message. I wait for the one that reads, "We were pleased to get Lisa toilet-trained the day before kindergarten opened" or "Matt is doing better in school. This year he went down second in the spelling bee."

A third way to justify exhausting yourself is to say "you're busy saving souls, for the night is coming" or "It's the Lord's work." This excuse is the one for which children and spouses are supposed to have no answer. But Jesus himself sometimes deliberately avoided crowds who waited for him to speak. He proposed a downright nasty end for those who offend children and made it clear that little ones had a right to his time (Mark 10). He retreated to hills and private rooms to pray. His center was as much the garden as the throng.

Holy Leisure

Forced by the energy shortage, the best recreation may still turn out to be staying home and fine-tuning our senses. Not being able to go away so often won't spoil our lives, for happiness is seldom a place. Thoreau said, "I wish ever to live as to derive my satisfactions and inspirations from the commonest events, everyday phenomena, so that what my senses hourly perceive—my daily walk, the conversation of my neighbors—may inspire me."[1]

In a more modern piece, Richard J. Foster writes:

The church Fathers often spoke of *Otium Sanctum:* "holy leisure." It refers to a sense of balance in the life, an ability to be at peace through the activities of the day, an ability to rest and take time to enjoy beauty, an ability to pace ourselves. With our tendency to define people in terms of what they produce, we would do well to cultivate "holy leisure."

And if we expect to succeed in the contemplative arts, we must pursue "holy leisure" with a determination that is ruthless to our datebooks.[2]

This isn't suggesting that we cut out all travel, meetings on important issues, vacation, or trips to visit relatives. It does suggest living by rhythms and priorities. Claim the freedom to say "no" both to good causes and to frantic, counterproductive efforts to have fun.

Happily, persons who choose to conserve energy supplies, save money, and nurture their spirits and relationships normally don't have problems finding recreation. Rarely in a discussion on simple living have I heard the question, "But what can we do for fun?" The more critical danger is that those who allow themselves everything they want become unable to enjoy it. Less with more flies home to roost.

Testimonies on recreation offer these principles:

1. **Beware of living in a way which allows no free time.** Do not feel guilty for taking regular periods to muse, meditate, be silent, and unoccupied. You'll do more praying.

2. **Blur the distinction between work and recreation.** Invent ways to make dull work enjoyable. Redeem menial tasks by working together and by sharing them across lines of age, sex, race, and profession. Leisure activities might teach a skill, improve your home, augment your food supply, or serve others' needs. Rhythm and change are more important than whether you "work" or "have fun."

3. **Choose activities carefully.** For any form of recreation, ask a positive question: "Does this strengthen my own spirit and my relationships with others?" and a negative one: "Is it expensive in terms of money, energy supplies, or the natural environment?" Since so many activities are available which answer yes to the first and no to the second, don't accept many trade-offs. Investigate free possibilities close to home. When choosing toys select fewer, longer-lasting items which encourage cooperation and creativity. Prefer simple baby dolls or stuffed animals to Barbie dolls, balls and blocks to war games. Look for toys made of wood or cotton rather than plastic, for mechanical rather than battery-powered ones. Help children learn to play imaginatively with household odds and ends. Find ways to involve children playfully in adult work.

4. **Live *now* the way you honestly would like to live.** "We'll take more time together when we've made enough to retire or when I get off all these church boards" can trail into "But then he had that heart attack." "I'll spend evenings with the children after these night classes are over" might end "But the children aren't home evenings anymore."

5. **Use some recreation time for physical exercise.** Exercise is great preventive medicine and a more-with-less remedy for depression and overweight.
6. **A frequent desire to "get away from it all" signals other needs.** Look for the real problem. Make home a place in which you and your family enjoy staying.

Notes

1

Thoreau, *Thoreau on Man and Nature,* p. 14.

2

Richard J. Foster, *Celebration of Discipline* (New York: Harper and Row, 1978), pp. 20–21.

●●●●●●●●●●●●●●●●●●●●●●●●●●●●

More with Less

Our family of seven enjoys active recreation and could run up   **P**
quite a bill for entertainment. Since lots of interesting activities
cost very little, we substitute these for more expensive sports:
—hiking instead of car rides
—bicycling instead of riding horseback
—playing croquet instead of miniature golf
—using canoes or rowboats instead of motorboats
—sledding instead of skiing or snowmobiling
—ice skating on the pond in season instead of indoors
—roller skating on the sidewalk instead of at a rink
—reading good books aloud to one another instead of going to
   the movies
—camping instead of using motels
   Our low-cost recreation program continues in other ways.
We enjoy a supervised trampoline which is available two days
a week all summer in our town. We made some of our
recreational equipment such as a knock hockey board,
chinning bar, rabbit cages, and bow and arrow. We encourage
group games in the backyard like "Kick the Can" and "Run,
Sheep, Run."
   Although we pay for recreation by buying some sports
equipment and do go out bowling or miniature golfing
occasionally, we avoid getting regularly involved in sports
which take a new wad of money for each game played.
—Janet Stoner
   Akron, Pa.

While on a Goshen College student program in Haiti, I saw   **L**
many cheap and delightful toys in use. Because most Haitians
struggle to exist, I was impressed by their joy of living reflected
in toys and games.
   The most common toy consisted of a ring and a stick.
Children ran up and down a street pushing and rolling the ring
along, the challenge being to keep it upright. The ring might be
an old bike tire while the push tool could be a sturdy, curled
leaf.
   People of all ages played ball. Rags packed together, either
tied or sewn, formed one kind of ball. These weren't always
spherical nor consistently firm, and sometimes had a rock in
the middle for weight and momentum. Sometimes they kicked
a soft, small ball and kept it in the air for long periods of time.
All sides of the feet, and all positions of the leg were used for
kicking and keeping the ball in the air.
   In addition to marbles, they used pebbles, cashews, or bottle
caps. They drew a hopscotch design in the dirt with fingers or a

stick, made jump ropes from leaves twisted into a cord, and used a long blade of grass for a whistle.
—*Susan Kenagy*
  Goshen, Ind.

●●●●●●●●●●●●●●●●●●●●●●●●●

Enjoying Nature

Walking ● Three pairs of grimy hands offered Mom limp bouquets of desert wild flowers. It was the end of a Saturday afternoon walk through the sagebrush for my brother and sister and me.

Beginning in childhood I learned the simple but exquisite pleasure of taking walks. I recall many adult hands that took mine as we set off gladly for a walk.

During adolescence and through my college years, life was often a whirl of activities which excluded taking walks. Zairean friends finally brought back to me the full pleasure of *la promenade*. In a setting with no external entertainment possibilities we set off over the hill to pick mangoes, into the valley to look for a monkey, or just down the road singing!

Walking costs nothing, yet it exercises the body and relieves daily pressures. It gives me a chance to observe God's world and time to converse with friends. Today when someone says, "Let's go for a walk," I respond with pleasure.
—*Nancy Heisey*
  Lancaster, Pa.

Cross-City Skiing ● For the past six years Betty and I have enjoyed cross-country skiing. We love the stillness of the woods and are always impressed by the beauty of life when it is approached without extra contrivances.

Last winter we were blessed with an abundance of snow here in New York City. This made it ideal for skiing up the sidewalk to Central Park, spending an evening there, and skiing back. Old railroad right-of-ways are excellent for skiing, too.

Since it's such an inexpensive form of recreation, we've met many families and elderly people out cross-country skiing. Asking directions and sharing food and ski wax is always a way of meeting and learning to know people. It surely beats standing in noisy crowded ticket lines going up and down the same hill all day.
—*Jim King*
  New York, N.Y.

Picnics Early and Late ● Picnics can be fun anytime and with almost any kind of food. We enjoy picnics often by making do with what we have. We keep a basket ready to go with a tablecloth, a few dishes, and an old blanket. We don't look for a picnic table or bother with chairs except for older people.

Sometimes we have a breakfast picnic at sunrise. We take the black skillet, some unpeeled potatoes, margarine, and eggs. Everyone helps gather brush to keep the fire going. We slice the potatoes as thinly as possible and start the frying, a delightful aroma rising in the early morning air. When the potatoes are tender, we add eggs. We listen for the birds and try to identify them while the food cooks.

A picnic at dusk can be equally enjoyable when birds gather for nesting time. We stay out until the stars shine in full brilliance. Lying flat on our backs we identify the constellations.

—*Marie M. Moyer*
  Telford, Pa.

Stargazing ● We find stargazing a challenging and enjoyable family activity. As a child I tried to learn constellations from a book alone, but quickly became discouraged and overwhelmed.

An important rule is to start simply and take small steps. All you need to begin is a guidebook to the stars—a star map is even better—a flashlight, and a place to go beyond the reach of streetlights. It takes ten minutes for eyes to readjust to night darkness, so we dim the flashlight with a cloth and rubber band.

Even small children can find the Milky Way and the Big and Little Dippers. Next we find the North Star and the star within the Big Dipper that is actually a double star. Native Americans used this as a test of good vision.

In winter we find majestic Orion surrounded by the Pleiades, Taurus the bull, and Leo the lion. In summer, Cassiopeia and Cygnus the swan are the easiest large constellations to find.

Any almanac shows the phases of the moon and when various planets are visible. After a while you might even tackle some of the brighter stars such as Vega, Sirius, and Arcturus.

We find that the more we learn about the sky, the greater grows our wonder at God's creation. Watching stars stretches our thoughts. We imagine what star-travel and other worlds might be like, and we put our earth and its troubles in perspective.

—*Becky Horst*
  Lederach, Pa.

Zoo Membership ● With a tax-deductible contribution of twenty-five dollars I became a member for one year of the New York Zoological Society, providing free admission to the New York Aquarium on Coney Island and to the Bronx Zoo. This includes a limited number of tickets for special exhibits, rides, and free parking.

Since I live beside the zoo, I find this a terrific place to bring friends and relatives. It's educational and interesting, and provides outdoor exercise. Nonmembers may choose a free admission day—Tuesday, Wednesday, and Thursday—to avoid weekend crowds.
—*Mildred Miller*
Bronx, N.Y.

●●●●●●●●●●●●●●●●●●●●●●●●●●

For the Fun of It

P

Sixty years ago we didn't have many store-bought toys in our family. Our mother, however, was good at improvising.

Seating us around the oilcloth-covered table, she inspired our imaginations with a pile of popped corn. We soon found cats, dogs, chickens, giraffes, elephants, and bearded faces. We made fences from the duds and traded with each other, all the while eating to our hearts' content.

A wooden apple box became a bobsled when Mother put a short board across it for a seat. Father's big work shoes were excellent horses and the shoelaces became reins. We had a small whip made from string tied to a stick. After dressing our dolls warmly we filled our drawstring purses with necessary shopping items, tucked ourselves in snugly with a lap robe, and rode to an imaginary town.
—*Amanda Toews*
Scio, Ore.

Our children's favorite toy here is the Sears Catalog. They love to see how many things on each page are unnecessary, ridiculous, or useless. They quickly sense the difference between their handmade Raggedy Ann dolls and the factory version, or the futility of a bubble gum machine.

Maybe adults could also satisfy their thirst for consumer goods by browsing through a catalog rather than the nearest mall. How about looking for things you don't need and don't want? It's more fun to choose the one dress on each page you really can't stand than it is to eye one on every page that you wish you had.
—*Delores Friesen*
Accra, Ghana

P

I've seen grown men on the floor racing spool tractors to the delight of themselves and their children.

To make them, insert a rubber band through the hole of a spool and secure it at one end with half a matchstick. Thumbtack this end so that the matchstick cannot go around. At the other end, put a longer matchstick that extends over the edges of the spool. Wind up the rubber band by turning the long

matchstick until it is tight. The tractor travels on the floor as
the band unwinds.
—*Martha Zimmerly*
  Orrville, Ohio

In Morocco we often passed shop after shop in which used tires   ℮
were being made into buckets and jugs of all shapes and sizes.
   After seeing a twelve-sided rubber tire shape at an outdoor
art exhibit in Virginia, my husband was inspired to create one
like it to serve as a climbing toy. The twelve tires bolted
together can be pulled or pushed onto any of its sides. Our
children crawl through it, climb over it, rock it, use it as a cave,
or pretend it's a deep well.
   Another type of jungle gym we've seen has tires bolted
together and attached to a metal frame which is securely
fastened to the ground.
   Other tire toy possibilities are a crawl-through S-shaped
snake, a rubber tire man, a tire swing, or even a small
playhouse.
—*Barbara J. Miller*
  Harrisonburg, Va.

As I approached my seventies, a desire to begin doing Fraktur
grew upon me so I took advantage of an evening course offered
at our high school. Here I acquired the rudiments of
calligraphic lettering. Since then, when I want to do something
different, I sit down and produce what I call a piece of art.
   I make Fraktur pieces for anniversaries, birthdays, and fund-
raising events. I haven't sold any, and don't intend to make it a
commercial venture. I do it for fun!
   It is a good way to cleanse my mind from the cares of this
life.
—*John E. Lapp*
  Souderton, Pa.

●●●●●●●●●●●●●●●●●●●●●●●●●●●

At Home:

Home Movies ● We enjoy viewing films which we rent
together with a group of friends. We choose from a wide range
of subjects including nature, exploration, science, and religion.
Embassies are willing to lend films depicting their countries.
This is a good way to expose our children to the world in a
selective way.
—*Katie Myers*
  Dacca, Bangladesh

Family Reading ● As far back as I can remember, Mom   P
and Dad took time to read with me. I grew up loving to read—
the classics, fairy tales, novels, history, and especially poetry.

Some of my happiest recollections are of family evenings when the three of us shared a special silence, each engrossed in a book. I remember winter hours spent in a warm kitchen, eating popcorn and listening to Mom reading aloud. Joy in reading— a treasured gift from my parents—has become a part of my being.
—*Jenny Coward*
Akron, Pa.

Making Music • We invite other families to our house one evening a month for a potluck. After supper we make music together. Particular skills and talents determine the kind of music we choose.

Music making is not just for professionals. Even young children sense the pleasure and value of music by actively participating.
—*Shirley S. King*
Newton, Kan.

●●●●●●●●●●●●●●●●●●●●●●●●●

Television

Generally we limit ourselves to an hour of TV watching a day. The children's viewing is confined to educational programming, unless a parent is watching with them.

We try to use the content of the program or commercial as a springboard to introduce our own values to the children. For instance, our comment after a dog food commercial might be: "It seems strange that dog food can sound so important when many people in the world are hungry."

After a hair-coloring or cosmetic commercial, I've said: "They make it sound as if it's wrong to grow old."
—*Mary Sue Rosenberger*
Louisville, Ohio

We use television as an alternative source of family entertainment. Instead of spending money for movies, we may watch a special program together—a musical, a Christmas drama, or an educational feature.
—*Marlene Kropf*
Portland, Ore.

●●●●●●●●●●●●●●●●●●●●●●●

Old-time Adventure • Because we wanted our children to have these experiences at least once, we made them family experiments:
—Maple-sugaring—we tapped one tree.
—Cider-pressing—we tried it with an antique hand press.

—Apple-butter making—we used a copper kettle and arranged
for a family gathering.
—Bobsledding—we gathered the neighborhood children.
—Washing wool—we did this in the stream and again invited
neighborhood children.
—Making dyes—we used walnut hulls and goldenrod.
—Coloring Easter eggs—we used onion skins.
—Martha Zimmerly
Orrville, Ohio

Playing and Learning • When I taught sewing classes my
three-year-old daughter usually went along. When she wanted
to sew I supplied her with a scrap of cloth and threaded needle,
knotted so as not to come apart. By her fourth birthday she
had embroidered a number of designs in straight stitch on quilt
patches. Sewing on my treadle machine was her next interest.
She made a patchwork cushion by sewing along a marked line
on patches I pinned together. Her attention span was short—
she worked only five or ten minutes at a time—but in a few
months she gained more skills, perseverance, and self-
satisfaction than most educational toys provide.
—Erma Wenger
Musoma, Tanzania

Sabbath Rest • My husband and I spent part of a
sabbatical year in a remote fishing village on a warm island.
While there we planned two ways to carry the calm
atmosphere of that Eden back into our congested lives at home.
Both have helped us immeasurably, but both took herculean
amounts of willpower to initiate.

First we gave away our television set before we could
become readdicted. In the evenings, instead of canned laughter,
we hear crickets. Our son has had no trouble learning to count
without Sesame Street. We read our news and survive quite
happily without televised accounts of Philadelphia's fires and
robberies to feed our anxieties. We spend more time talking,
reading, going outdoors, and inventing recreation than we did
before. We are also forced to face our problems more quickly
since we can't hide our silences behind the TV noise.

Our second method of calming down is a ritual we call our
Sabbath. It is planned for a time when we're all tired and tense.
We prepare ahead of time to keep ourselves from being caught
up in schedules. No one works that day. After turning off our
phone, we sleep in or have a quiet morning and some family
activity in the afternoon—maybe a hike, a picnic, or a movie.
We avoid driving far or spending much money. We
rediscovered local streams and parks we'd ignored for years.
Driving slowly we talk and explore, relaxing to recharge
mental energy. We visit others only by consent of everyone in
the family. Sometime during the day we include devotions. Our

five-year-old son particularly likes to turn out the lights, light a
candle, pop corn, and listen to religious music. This is
amazingly calming, like a campfire.

Our Sabbath does wonders for our entire family. It is a way
of saying we come first to each other and to God, and that
there are times when no one may make demands on us.
—*Mary Lou Cummings*
Quakertown, Pa.

Physical Fitness

Just One Serving ● About a year ago, it became obvious to
me that I should do something about my eating habits. At age
thirty-seven I was somewhat overweight. Then I discovered
that my cholesterol level was high. With a family history of
heart problems, I needed to reduce weight, increase my
exercise, and control my cholesterol intake.

I decided to limit myself to one helping only of the main
meal of each day. To keep from eating excessively, I also
committed myself to avoiding smorgasbords.

I kept my commitment quite well except for Christmas Day,
when I had extra turkey. Several times throughout the year I
attended smorgasbords, after all. While eight dollars is a high
price to pay for one plateful of food, it gave me the opportunity
to speak to those who were going back for third, fourth, and
fifth helpings.

Even though I've lost weight and my cholesterol level is
down, I continue to find desserts more tempting than exercise.

I liked the affirmation of a friend who reminded me of my
decision at a high school dinner when he held up his finger
saying, "Just one helping, Larry, just one!"
—*Larry W. Newswanger*
Lancaster, Pa.

Make Mine Exercise ● I believe commitment to a healthful
diet should be matched by an equally strong habit of consistent
exercise. God gave me my body—a beautiful and complicated
piece of machinery. It's part of my witness to keep it strong,
clean, and fit. Because I work in a sedentary occupation, I
examined the "three square meals a day" rule. I don't need
that much food. By adding calories which my body can't burn
I merely add weight to my frame. I decided to substitute
exercise for eating at least once a day.

Studies show the importance of a balanced breakfast to a
productive day. The evening meal is a time of refreshment with
my family after the work is done. Since lunch often makes me
feel sleepy and sluggish in the afternoon, I decided to take the
noon break without food.

For a time I used my lunch hour to clean out a large vacant lot in our neighborhood. It was satisfying to see the amount of constructive exercise I could get during this daily period. It also made a difference in the safety and beauty of the neighborhood.
—*Mark Cerbone*
Philadelphia, Pa.

Spiritual Renewal ● Amid busy schedules and heavy workloads, our African friends fasted regularly. They spoke highly of its value in strengthening their spiritual lives. We were attracted, but weren't quite able to discipline ourselves.

Finally the pressure of work and responsibilities seemed overwhelming. People seemed to be everywhere all the time. How could we renew our spiritual resources?

Africans rise early in the morning. We could, too. So at 5:00 A.M. we began our day with two hours of prayer and Bible study. People waited to call on us until after 7:00 o'clock. We set apart one of our two small bedrooms for a place where we could shut the door and be alone with God.

This period of renewal soon became a fixed habit. We hadn't yet set aside a time for fasting, but we had begun to fast on certain occasions for special reasons, especially during crisis experiences.

Then we came home to America to retire. Pressures were no less than in Africa. We had to make adjustment to a new way of life. More than ever we enjoyed our two-hour period alone with God early every morning. It was at this point that we began fasting regularly.

One way we try to do this is by buying and eating foods in a responsible way. On Friday, our fast day, we exclude all solid foods. Without being legalistic, we enjoy Fridays. We have more time for prayer and are convinced that for us, fasting belongs with Bible study and prayer.
—*Ed and Irene Weaver*
Hesston, Kan.

God used the Honey Locust Fellowship, a Christian community near Elkhart, Indiana, to influence us in our eating and living habits. Restructuring our diet to include more whole grains and legumes and less meat and sugar hasn't been easy, but we now leave our table feeling much more satisfied.

Fasting became another adventure for us. Having experimented with total and partial fasts, we presently fast one twenty-four hour period per week. This gives our bodies a Sabbath day of rest and brings us in touch with the suffering experienced by others. We begin our fast after an evening meal, breaking it the following evening with a light meal of lettuce salad, roasted soybeans, and sunflower seeds. We set aside the money that would have been used for food that day for global justice and food distribution programs. Our time of fasting may include prayer, meditation, and Bible reading. We prefer fasting on a day of little activity since our bodily systems are slowed down by the lack of food.

We have found this meaningful for our lives. Fasting for us is a small step in identifying with our Lord by voluntarily identifying with the poor.
—Steve and Debbie Fath
Elkhart, Ind.

●●●●●●●●●●●●●●●●●●●●●●●●●●●

How-To:
Directions for Games to Play at Home

Any number of players may be involved in these three games. Smaller children can participate by being paired with parents or older children.

Geography Game
● Materials Needed:
—scrap paper and pencil for each player
—clock or timer
● Directions:
1. One player suggests a letter of the alphabet and sets the timer for one minute.
2. At the signal to begin each player writes on the paper all the geograhical names which come to mind beginning with that letter. These may be any names found on a map: countries, states, towns, rivers, oceans, etc.
3. When time is up, each player reads his/her list in turn and records the number of times a name is duplicated by other players.
4. Scoring (optional): Each name is initially worth as many points as the number of people participating. A point is lost for each duplication. For example, if 10 are playing, the name "New York" is worth 10 points. If 6 people write "New York" on their papers, it is worth only 4 points. Each player totals his own score after each round.
—Judy Weaver
Akron, Pa.

Dictionary Game
● Materials Needed:
—one dictionary
—uniform slips of paper to avoid giving away clues
—pencils
● Directions:
1. One player finds a word in the dictionary which is unfamiliar to all the players.

2. Each player writes that word on his paper, spelled out by the leader.
3. The leader writes the dictionary definition beside the word while all other players write an imaginary definition, making it as authentic-sounding as possible.
4. The leader collects the papers, shuffles them, and reads aloud all the definitions.
5. Each player chooses the definition he believes to be the right one.
6. Scoring (optional): The player with the dictionary gets one point for each person who does not choose his/her (i.e., the correct) definition. The other players each get one point for choosing the correct definition. Each round has the same number of points. Only the leader of each round can accumulate more than one point that round.

—Diane Clemens Leland
Waynesboro, Pa.

Who Did It?

After a meal with guests, we're reluctant to break up the dining-room fellowship. We clear off the dishes and remain around the table. We sometimes play this game. It's fun and encourages people to share their history.

● Materials Needed:
—pencils
—uniform slips of paper to avoid giving away clues
● Directions:
1. Each player writes on paper a personal happening, the more unusual, the better. Examples: "I once took care of forty-nine rabbits," "I can say the alphabet backwards," or "I once won a free five-minute shopping spree and picked up two hundred dollars worth of groceries."
2. Players sign their names and hand the paper to a designated leader who numbers them and reads each happening aloud without revealing names.
3. Each person guesses to whom the incidents happened, writing names beside numbers on a second paper.
4. After the guessing list is complete, the leader rereads the papers and reveals the identity of each.

—Elda Bachman
Newton, Kan.

●●●●●●●●●●●●●●●●●●●●●●●●

How-To:
Directions for Games to Play While Traveling

These games include any number of players and few, if any, materials.

Two-Way Bible Quiz
● Directions:
  1. IT poses the problem.
     E.g., "I'm thinking of a Bible character whose name begins with A."
  2. Participants guess in the form of questions.
     E.g., "Is it Isaac's father?"
     "Is it the first man?"
  3. IT answers, using the name implied in the question.
     E.g., "No, it isn't Abraham."
     "Yes, it is Adam."
  4. The player who guesses correctly is IT. IT loses his turn to the questioner if he cannot answer correctly.
—*Amanda Toews*
   Scio, Ore.

Write a Story
We find our children's creativity beautiful. Each person gets his moment to be heard and appreciated.
● Materials:
  —paper and pencil for each player
● Directions:
  1. One player suggests five words to begin with the game.
     E.g.: shampoo, alligator, grandma, helicopter, job.
  2. Players each write a story, in a few sentences, including those words.
  3. After an agreeable interval, 2 to 4 minutes, call out another group of 3 or 4 words.
     E.g.: swim, spaghetti, China, flute. These also are incorporated into the story.
  4. All players take turns reading their stories aloud.
—*Barbara Weaver*
   New Holland, Pa.

Mental Memory Album
While traveling from one place to the next on a trip, we enjoy reinforcing memories and reliving details with this game.
● Directions:
  1. We establish a context for the guessing, such as "any place we stopped yesterday" or a particular point of interest just visited.
  2. IT thinks of an object everyone noticed and gives a clue concerning its size:

—Large (buildings, trees, mountains)
—Medium (restaurant table, picture in an art gallery, rowboat)
—Small (ice-cream cone, chipmunk, quarter found on the ground)

3. Other players ask questions which may be answered with yes or no.
"Was it inside the national park?"
"Is it something we all touched?"

4. Whoever guesses the object becomes IT.

—Author's Entry

●●●●●●●●●●●●●●●●●●●●●●●●●●●

How-To:
Make Tin Can Toys

A Walker ● Nursery school children in Swaziland love tin can walkers.

Balancing on the tin cans, the children pull on the handles as they lift their feet and take steps.

● Materials Needed:
—2 tin cans (open at bottom end)
—wire or string
—hammer
—nail

● Directions:
1. Punch 2 nail holes in top of each can, close to rim.
2. Thread with wire or string, adjusted to child's height.
3. Tie or twist inside can.

—Ardith Frey
Mbabane, Swaziland

Push Toy ● This was a favorite in Haiti. One tin can turns as it rolls along the ground acting as a toothless gear to turn the other can.

● Materials Needed:
—two tin cans with both ends (use cans from liquid, emptied by punching holes)
—wire, such as a clothes hanger
—hammer
—nail

- Directions:
  1. Punch nail holes in the center of each end of the cans.
  2. Insert wire so that one can touches the other at right angles.

wire is bent
to stay in place

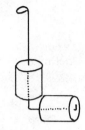

  3. Adjust handle to child's height.
  4. Optional: Decorate the top can with bright colors, decals, paper wings, etc., to make a kaleidoscopic effect as the cans rotate.

—*Susan Kenagy*
Goshen, Ind.

We make building blocks by packing crumpled balls of newspaper tightly into cardboard boxes, covering the outside with flour paste and a layer of newspaper, drying, and adding more newspaper and paste layers for strength. We decorate the blocks with crayons or paint. The children enjoy building large structures with these and no one is ever hurt when the blocks fall down.
—Ardith Frey
  Mbabane, Swaziland

An old electric sewing machine motor became my eight-year-old grandson's favorite toy.
—Amanda Toews
  Scio, Ore.

Whenever I had a painting project and my little children wanted to help, I gave them each a paintbrush and a can of water and let them paint the sidewalk to their hearts' content.
—Martha Zimmerly
  Orrville, Ohio

We made a manipulative toy box for our small daughter by covering a wooden box with parts of old blue jeans and leftover fabric scraps. Labeled drawstring and zipper bags keep smaller toys sorted inside the box. We put things like crayons, books, keys, and scissors in the pockets around the outside. Zippers, buttons, snaps, laces, and buckles are among the items a child can manipulate to learn motor skills.
—Denise Epp
  Flin Flon, Man.

Woodworking is an important part of our nursery school curriculum. I go to the lumberyard every Tuesday and Thursday nights for mill ends of white pine and plywood which have been put out on the street for the garbage pickup. The pieces are just the right size for children. The variety of shapes and sizes encourages their creativity.
—Jim King
  New York, N.Y.

Plastic detergent bottles partially filled with sand make good bowling pins.
—Ardith Frey
  Mbabane, Swaziland

Several of my friends and I exchange magazines and church papers even though they might be a couple of months old until we receive them. Most of us would not subscribe to many magazines for ourselves had we not decided to share them with each other.
I pass on extra Sunday school papers from my weekly lessons to an older friend who enjoys reading them and passing them on to children who don't get these papers from their own church.
—Carol Norr
  Akron, Pa.

Avoid expensive training wheels when teaching a child to ride a bicycle. Instead wrap a bathtowel around the child's waist and hold the two ends in back. Demonstrate to the child how you will hold him suspended and safe from a fall. Walk alongside giving the children the feel of the bike.
—Vernon R. Wiebe
Hillsboro, Kan.

A playhouse in an old granary, an attic, or other odd corner seems to delight children. A shack they put together themselves is more fun than an expensive, beautiful, or even Dad-made one.
—Martha Zimmerly
Orrville, Ohio

Candlemaking is good family fun. We keep it simple so all can participate. We use anything from tin cans to paper milk cartons for molds and use up bits of crayon and old candles.
—Delores Friesen
Accra, Ghana

A jigsaw, not very expensive if you get it secondhand, is a creative tool for both boys and girls. Large simple designs as well as small intricate puzzles can be cut out of scrap lumber. The public library is a good place to check for pattern ideas. Ambitious children might try doll furniture.
—Sue Richard
Iowa City, Iowa

While teaching and touring in Africa in 1960, I was impressed by the dearth of books in schools. When I returned home I invited friends to help collect and send books to Africa. To me an unused book is the sorriest of withholdings. If it has enriched me, it deserves to be used again. Bibles, reference books, Christian education materials, school texts, medical and nutrition books are all needed. Since its beginning in 1961, Books Abroad has sent reading materials to more than fifty countries. Volunteers collect and ship them. Other organizations similar to this one exist in North America. The coordinator of Books Abroad may be reached at Box 375, Elkhart, Indiana 46515.
—Elizabeth Showalter
Harrisonburg, Va.

With a little paint and fabric my empty thread spools become living characters to illustrate stories.
—Mary Hochstedler
Kokomo, Ind.

Our three small children bathe together in the same bath water. It's fun for them and saves water.
—Arlene Leaman
La Junta, Colo.

I use large round ice-cream cartons to store craft supplies. I label them and arrange them alphabetically on shelves so children in my classes have access to materials as quickly as possible.
—Ruth Penner
Wichita, Kan.

8.   *meetinghouses*

●●

Some of you have been through it. Others have read about it
only in the church board minutes. The setting is the Main
Street Church committee room. The scenario goes something
like this:

> Church School Superintendent: We have no place for the
> third- and fourth-grade classes to meet.
>
> Head Usher: Setting up extra chairs in the foyer every
> Sunday is distracting and tiring.
>
> Evangelism Committee Representative: I feel uncomfortable
> inviting new people to church. It's so crowded.
>
> Senior Trustee: We have several large bequests which we can
> put toward a new building.
>
> Women's Group Leader: When we build let's make it a
> sanctuary that will be a tribute to God.

This is merely Act I in a continuing drama. Several meetings
of a similar nature follow. Too often the imagination runs dry.
The only obvious recourse seems to be to build a fashionable
new facility in the suburbs. An architect is hired to decide
which way to pile the bricks.

This chapter does not call for a moratorium on new church
buildings. Rather, it asks us to look thoroughly and
courageously at alternatives before breaking ground. It also
calls us to more efficient use of existing places of worship.

Responsible living includes the amount we spend to facilitate our worship.

"A church building should not be a monument to God, to the architect, or to the congregation," says LeRoy Troyer, an architect from Mishawaka, Indiana. "It should be a tool used by the people of the church to accomplish the church's mission and purpose for being. It is nothing more or nothing less than that."

Addressing a 1979 consultation on church buildings he said, "Current cost of facilities for Mennonite churches ranges from thirty cents to one dollar for each use per person over a thirty-year period. It's like putting this much money in the offering for each time you are in the building. Mennonites are spending far too much on church buildings for no more than they are used."

Church construction in the 1970s is estimated to have cost $3.9 billion annually (1967 dollars) in the United States alone.[1] During one of these years, 1975, Protestants in both the United States and Canada gave about one tenth of this amount for overseas missions.[2]

Our church buildings
may or may not
impress God,
but they make
an indelible impression
on visitors
from underdeveloped
countries.

After visiting churches in North America in 1978, Maria Sacapano, a pastor's wife from the Philippines, commented, "If we could only have one fourth of some of the Mennonite church buildings for our use in the Philippines! I don't mean I want the *beauty* of those churches for our work—just the roof and the walls."

A missionary reported the words of a Nicaraguan pastor returning home after a visit to North America. The missionary was especially interested in hearing Pastor Palacios' first comments about his trip—an indication of what impressed him most about North America. After only a few minutes in the car, Palacios began describing his experiences to his brother-in-law. "You wouldn't believe the churches in North America. They are all luxurious. For one church there we could build fifty here. Some are three stories high [including the basement]

and have twenty classrooms. Everything is carpeted." And
then the clincher. "They are even more luxurious than the
Catholic churches here."[3]

In spite of Luke's words in Acts 17:24 that God does not live
in shrines made by humans, Scripture is used to justify the
most lavish structures. Jesus' complimentary words about the
woman who annointed his head (Mark 14:6–9) are used to
support any extravagance: "It's in God's honor. Shouldn't he
get our best?"

Another justification for elegant church structures or
furnishings is simply, "We can't have our church look poorer
than our homes." And because our homes have studies, living
rooms, or formal dining rooms that get used only twice a week,
as well as extra bedrooms and bathrooms that see duty only
two times a year, we need separate committee rooms, kitchens,
and fellowship rooms that are used only weekly or quarterly in
our churches. Our standards may be too high. Paul's Law for
kitchens, page 139, often applies to church buildings, too. The
more luxurious the building, the less activity will be allowed in
it.

Many churches can cite examples of activities prohibited by
trustees for fear of chipping paint, smudging porcelain door
knobs, or spoiling the carpet. In 1977 the Night Hospitality
program of the Sojourners Fellowship and the Community for
Creative Nonviolence wrote letters to 1,100 Washington, D.C.,
churches, synagogues, and mosques to ask for space for the
city's homeless. All food, provisions, and supervision would be
provided by the two communities. Only one church, Luther
Place Memorial, responded positively. The homeless needing a
night's lodging hardly fare better in that city today than they
did in Bethlehem 2,000 years ago.

The Bible does not give us a list of specific instructions for
building a meetinghouse. The persecution of the early church,
its close association to Judaism, and the relatively short history
of the New Testament did not give the writers opportunity to
address the subject. This may be a blessing. It forces us to
concentrate on what is important—the quality of life of the
believing community—rather than on the physical facilities. It
helps us recognize that church is wherever God's people meet,
be it a barn, a house, or a building with a steeple and a cross.

The building
    facilitates the reality
of the church,
    but it does not
determine it.

The title of this chapter—
"Meetinghouses"—
is deliberate.
Buildings are just that,
places for the
gathered
community of
believers to meet.

Following are some principles to help guide us in more responsible decisions about church facilities:

1. **Balance the ideal with the responsible.** Too long the principle has been to balance the ideal with the possible, the possible being the amount the finance committee can raise or a mortgage the congregation can afford. Responsible use of resources does not allow for large spaces that are used only one hour a week. If Jesus were in conversation with the Samaritan woman at the well today, he probably would declare fifteen-meter (fifty-foot) arched ceilings as unnecessary for worship as was a mountain location in his time.

2. **Before building seek out other alternatives.** Laying brick to brick may not be the only or best response to the need for more room. Entries that follow describe alternate ways to finding meeting space.

3. **Use space fully—double up.** Maintenance and energy costs decline on a per hour or per use basis when facilities are used more fully. Parts of the building can be rented for community use, for day care, civic meetings, nursery school, or youth clubs. Architect Troyer says, "One of the hindrances to flexible use of educational space is the janitorial work required. Another is that a strong, possessive sense of ownership often surfaces. However, it can easily be proven that it is more economical to hire a custodian to reorganize multiple-use space than it is to build additional facilities and pay owning and operating costs.

   Sharing church facilities is not new. It is believed that early Christians utilized Jewish synagogues for worship. Beginning in colonial times and continuing into the early part of the twentieth century, Lutheran and Reformed churches in the Middle Atlantic States used the same facilities on alternate Sundays.

4. **Build modestly.** Renting, doubling up, disseminating into small house church groups, or buying an old building may not meet every church's needs. If build you must, find an

architect who will work with your ideas. Then build modestly with maximum space for multiple-use purposes, using minimal land area. Use energy efficiently. Find a location requiring the least driving distance for the most members.

Small, energy-efficient meetinghouses can be beautiful. Today's varied building materials allow many esthetic expressions. Massive structures and costly materials are not necessary ingredients for beauty. Simplicity often lends elegance.

Notes

1
Ronald J. Sider, "Cautions Against Ecclesiastical Elegance," *Christianity Today* (August 17, 1979), p. 14.

2
Edward R. Dayton, ed., *Mission Handbook: North American Protestant Ministries Overseas* (Monrovia, California: Missions Advanced Research and Communications Center, 1976), p. 57.

3
Letter from Charles Musser to Editor, *Evangelical Visitor* (August 25, 1978), p. 2.

●●●●●●●●●●●●●●●●●●●●●●●●●●

f

Renting Is Flexible ● The Gathering of Believers at Silver Spring, Maryland, is a Christian community of between 300 and 400 people. We see ourselves as an expression of the body of Christ in our city.

In distributing financial resources, we sense the Lord leading us to emphasize the building of the kingdom in people rather than in brick and mortar. We support sixteen men and women in full-time pastoral capacity and have ample assets for a benevolence and widows' fund to meet other needs generously. Elders discern the validity of each need.

For us, renting a building is the most efficient and viable course of action for weekly gatherings and special seminars. As we grow we simply rent a larger building. So far we've moved from the basement of a home to the sanctuaries of two meetinghouses and finally to a hall in a civic building. We're looking at the possibility of public school cafeterias and auditoriums for future use.

We've experienced little inconvenience in renting. Church buildings have been readily available except on Sunday mornings and evenings. We've used them Saturday evenings, with some seminars on other nights of the week.

Our community has grown to the point where half gather on Sunday morning for worship and half on Sunday afternoon. For use of the civic building from 9:00 A.M. until 4:30 P.M., we pay $200, approximately $27 per hour. Once a month the entire community meets, using the building from noon until 4:30 P.M. and paying $140—about $31 per hour.

We don't have Sunday school classes. Children between ages five and ten have a special meeting for the last hour of the 2½-hour Sunday meeting. Thirty-one home groups (four to fifteen people) meet every second Thursday or Friday evening throughout the city.

Our perspective is that the church is people rather than a building, but we don't rule out the possibility of owning a building in the future if the Lord so directs.
—*Chip Ward*
  Silver Spring, Md.

ji

Trading in the Cadillac ● A suburban church in Wichita, Kansas, Eastminster Presbyterian, had launched a $525,000 building program when earthquakes hit Guatemala, destroying thousands of homes and buildings. Many communities were devastated.

At a meeting of the board of elders a layman spoke up. "How can we set out to buy an ecclesiastical Cadillac," he asked, "when our brothers and sisters in Guatemala have just lost their little Volkswagen?"

The elders agreed to modify the building program

drastically. They paid the architect and settled for a $180,000 alternative. Then they sent their pastor and two elders to Guatemala to find out just how they could help believers there.

The team reported to the board of elders. They, in turn, with the enthusiastic backing of the whole congregation, borrowed $120,000 from a local bank and used the money to rebuild twenty-six churches and twenty-eight pastors' houses in Guatemala!

Inspired by the example of Eastminster, another congregation modified building plans and sent $60,000 to Guatemala. And a church in India, hearing about the project, raised $1,200 for Guatemala relief!
—*Waldron Scott*
  Colorado Springs, Colo.

"And, apart from other things,
there is the daily pressure upon me
of my anxiety for all the churches.
Who is weak, and I am not weak?
Who is made to fall,
and I am not indignant?"
—*2 Corinthians 11:28–29*

The Two Remain One ● The Hanover-Chesley Mennonite Fellowship is one congregation meeting at two locations for worship on Sunday mornings while coordinating all other activities.

Location One: In 1967 when we were still a small group, we built a 8.5 x 16 meter (28 x 52 foot) worship building for $20,000. Secondhand pine lumber and doors, a donated ceiling job, a contribution of beautiful stones for the front exterior, and volunteer help from our own and other congregations cut costs. Careful buying and planning included no-interest loans. With movable walls, stack armchairs, and a portable lectern, the building is functional for worship services, singing groups, programs, community Bible school, communion around tables, and quilting sessions.

Location Two: When this facility became crowded, about forty people formed another group, transforming a one-room country school on a beautiful tree-shaded lot into a place of worship. We retained the brick building's character complete with a school bell in the tower. A new foyer features a stained-glass window reclaimed from a dismantled neighboring church. We complemented the original ornate ceiling and light fixtures with new walls and a new floor. Again, stacking chairs, a movable secondhand pulpit, good used piano, and tables for celebration and games furnish the building. This isolated location has become a favorite place for weekend retreats.

We believe this method of church planting recycles human

and material resources. Lay members help conduct worship services. Our pastor is responsible for sermons at both places on the first and second Sundays but only at one place on each of the following Sundays.

For us, this is an excellent alternative to building one large church structure.
—*Martha Grove*
—*Ernie Martin*
  Hanover, Ont.

From Firehall to Schoolhouse • My fondest childhood memories of church are those involving meetings in a firehall. When I was little, my parents belonged to a congregation which rented such a facility. My Sunday school class met in a back room which stored canned goods. Now I belong to a church which meets in a schoolhouse and I'm still pleased with our fellowship in this cozy setting.

Although we don't have special Sunday school rooms which we can keep ready for the next week, we do have freedom to be creative in the worship experience. We don't have pews to inhibit us, for example. In wintertime we save energy by having from twenty to forty people in one classroom.

During the week we meet in homes to discuss business matters and for small house church groups. This seems to foster a deep fellowship with others in the church.
—*Debbra Keppler*
  Ephrata, Pa.

God's Presence in the Rec Center • Surely a beautiful sanctuary is an appropriate setting for worship. Yet we sing of his presence in a grubby, stark, unpainted, graffiti-covered recreation center on deteriorating Wayne Street in Philadelphia. I know God has been worshiped in caves and sewers and under bridges just as well as in grand cathedrals, but I cringe at the ugliness surrounding me and am a little ashamed when visitors come.

Our fellowship group outgrew our living rooms where the warmth and intimacy seemed appropriate to the church model to which we were committed—brothers and sisters sharing their total lives with each other. We had explored sharing space with another church group or worshiping with residents of a nursing home, but settled for the recreation center. Unused on Sundays and almost rent-free, it also provides outdoor play equipment and contact with our neighborhood.

I feel certain God wants us to worship here in the midst of poverty and oppression. We can't be complacent about those around us, so worship prepares us for service.

We want to channel our giving into human needs rather than an expensive structure. Perhaps some colorful banners, collages, and murals could reflect our faith and depict city life,

balancing the journey inward and journey outward. Room
dividers and roll-up rugs would improve acoustics and add
intimacy. Then our surroundings would truly reflect the
awesomeness of bowing before the Lord of the universe, the joy
of our dancing, and our commitment to service in the world.
—Arbutus Sider
  Philadelphia, Pa.

A Search ● About five years ago we joined a small group of
Mennonite families who moved to Paoli, Indiana, to begin a
medical practice.

We wanted to keep our faith alive and to teach our children
what we believe. We began meeting in homes until growth
necessitated finding a larger place. Now we rent part of a local
church building, using a large room for worship and smaller
rooms for discussion and Sunday school groups. We meet on
Sunday evenings to avoid conflict with the other church's
program, and still use our homes for weekly small-group
meetings and an occasional special weekend. The rental cost is
twenty-five dollars per meeting, including parking and outdoor
play equipment.

Basically, this has been a suitable arrangement. Because of
growth, however, we again need more classroom space, space
for interest centers, worship symbols, a library, and a place to
keep teaching materials.

We feel we have four options: stay where we are, try to rent a
more suitable facility, keep the house church concept by
obtaining a large house and adapting it to our needs, or build a
facility. We've also considered dividing to maintain smaller
fellowship groups. Our search is for a tool that will truly reflect
the feeling of the congregation.
—Mary Nafziger
  Paoli, Ind.

●●●●●●●●●●●●●●●●●●●●●●●●●●

Recycled Buildings

Storefront ● In 1954 when the members of St. Ann's
Mennonite Church decided to move several blocks to a
different building, they chose a site in a row of storefronts
which had three floors of apartments above them. They created .
a worship space in the storefront, rented out the apartments,
and fixed up the basement for club and youth activities.
Church members who rent the apartments above the church
provide an invaluable presence. People know where they can
find someone if they have a need.

More recently the congregation purchased a neighboring
sandwich shop which is used as a community center for
recreation and tutoring. Rent from the apartment goes toward

the upkeep of the two buildings. If we owned a traditional
church building, we would be paying upwards of $9,000
annually just for our heating bill which, even now, is well over
our annual offering figures.

Some people who enter the sanctuary remark that this
doesn't look like a real church. We emphasize that members
make up the church.
—*John Bauman*
   Bronx, N.Y.

Factory ● Our congregation is concerned about the use of
resources. We believe church buildings are not sacred
sanctuaries, but rather places for God's people to meet and to
use in response to community and world needs. These concerns
have implications for the kind, use, and size of buildings which
become our meetinghouses.

In early years, our congregation met in a variety of places—a
lounge on a college campus, the stage of an auditorium, a
doctor's waiting room, a dance studio which stood vacant on
Sunday, and a winterized pavilion in the local park.

Eventually we wanted a building of our own to expand
congregational life and community ministries. What kind
should it be? We didn't want to invest heavily in real estate and
wanted a building that would be multipurpose.

After months of searching, we bought a one-story, 13.5 x 33
meter (44 x 110 foot) factory building. The initial cost was
$34,000, though some renovations will need to be made.

One section of the building is to be used as an apartment,
where a household will be living to supply the presence of
members in the building and community and to facilitate
ministries we hope to develop. The entire building is available
during the week for congregational and community needs. Two
good possibilities are day care for kindergarten children and
emergency housing. The larger open area of the factory will
serve nicely as a meeting place for worship and celebration.

It's an adventure in faith to recycle a factory for kingdom
use!
—*Assembly Mennonite Church*
   Goshen, Ind.

Auto Body Shop ● During the winter of 1976–77, rapid
growth of our church community, Reba Place Fellowship,
made it necessary for us to purchase a new meetinghouse. For
the first fourteen years of our life as a congregation we
worshiped in one of our fellowship houses, restructured for
that purpose. Then from 1972 until we moved into our present
meetinghouse, we used what had been a grocery store for
worship services.

The building we now occupy was chosen mainly for its size
and location in our neighborhood. It is a single story brick

structure, originally a car dealership and later an auto body shop. Our fellowship work crew did most of the remodeling.

The meetinghouse contains a large area for worship. On one side is a half circle of elevated risers on which we place chairs for about 350 people. During services and other functions the worship leader and our music group complete the circle. A space behind the music group provides more congregational seating. We've found the circular seating arrangement highly effective because it both enhances the spirit of unity as well as greatly improves visibility.

In the open area in the center of the circle we have ample space for creative movement, interpretive dance, and drama. These three are now meaningful aspects of our worship. Underneath this center area, covered by a carpeted lid, is our baptism pool, a circular concrete structure with stairs curving down one side.

Our meetinghouse is also used for Friday evening community meals when adults and their guests share dinner together. The extensive floor space and our roomy kitchen allow well over 100 people to dine together comfortably. One room is used as a food co-op while another provides space for a play group for two- and-three-year-olds. Some Sunday school classes meet in the church but most groups locate themselves in our other buildings. Among the other uses we've found for our meetinghouses are wedding ceremonies, concerts, a medieval Christmas pageant, and several conferences.

The Lord provided us with a building that not only meets our needs in a fairly inexpensive way, but also has allowed us to use our creative powers in designing and executing the final product.

—Bob Crepeau
Evanston, Ill.

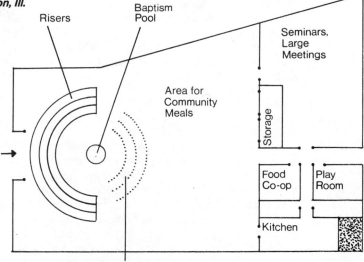

Before

After

Egg-Grading Building ● A new congregation in Wellesley, Ontario, met for worship and study on September 7, 1975, in rented facilities. After several months the congregation decided to search for a building which could be renovated into a meeting place.

The building we purchased had been used to operate an egg-grading and feed business. It is of concrete block construction with a flat roof. We now use the larger area of the building as a meeting room for worship and informal activities. A portable platform and about 175 movable chairs allow a variety of seating arrangements and settings.

We also renovated a smaller area to include children's classrooms, kitchen, lounge area, church office, and infants' room. The only new part of the structure is a public entry built onto the existing building. This includes washrooms and heating units.

Total cost of land, building, and renovations was $106,000. Of this, $60,000 is land value and $46,000 was our additional cost for building and renovations. People in the congregation did much of the inside renovation on a voluntary basis, including plumbing, painting, and carpentry. To construct a building of equal size would have cost about $121,750. Our congregation realized a saving of at least $75,000 as a result of purchasing and renovating an existing building.
—*Gerald Schwartzentruber*
  Wellesley, Ont.

Come or Be • Ecumenikos is a church in the Johnson
County suburb of Kansas City committed to exploration and   **P**
intentional living in theology, community, and mission. We
want to challenge dehumanizing and overly materialistic
values. Our definition of spirituality is "invisible form with
visible power and results." We believe people too often *come* to
church rather than *be* the church.

We feel that when not needed full time, a building leads to
increased organizational structure and diverts energy and
money from a people-oriented ministry. We use homes for
town meetings and house churches where informal contacts
foster active participation. We share rented office space with
other community service agencies. This provides the
coordinator with companionship and valuable contacts. For
monthly celebrations, which usually include a meal, we rent
apartment club houses, community centers, or church space.
Occasionally we rent church camps for retreats.

Focal points such as an office, newsletter, and phone tree,
while necessary for cohesiveness and communication, tend to
diminish a truly shared ministry. Periodically we rotate
leadership, including a salaried coordinator, to alleviate tension
between efficiency and participation.
—*Bruce R. Southard*
  Shawnee Mission, Kan.

Meetinghouse Expanded • Our building program of
1976 began with some members wondering why we should   **P**
build while others were convinced that the need was urgent.
The original structure of 1924 was a typical red brick
Mennonite meetinghouse with front doors and outside steps
facing the street. A three-level rear addition had been built in
1955.

We had several problems—congestion inside the front doors,
little room for fellowship before and after services, no provision
for handicapped people, outside steps and walks dangerously in
need of repair, washrooms in poor condition, and too few
Sunday school classrooms. We wanted the addition to be
functional, integrated with the original building, and attractive
in simplicity.

We decided to build a U around the front of the building. A
stairway leads directly to the basement and a narrow ramp into
the center of the basement. Instead of steps we built a wide
ramp to the auditorium. We added an adult library, a large
fellowship room with divider, three washrooms, a children's
worship room and library, a room for the Mennonite Central
Committee Self-Help display, a nursery, and spacious kitchen.
Our total project, including interest, cost approximately
$120,000 as we had estimated.

Our new building expresses our concern for Christian

community. The older and younger generation meet each other
as we enter and leave by a common doorway. One handicapped
person said, "With a ramp I feel included." It expresses our
faith as a Mennonite congregation through its simplicity. This
one-year process strengthened our fellowship in Christ and
renewed our vision.
—*Aden H. Bauman*
  Elmira, Ont.

A Converted Church ● The Blenheim meetinghouse was
built in 1901 in a rural community of about 100 members.
Because membership decreased substantially, our congregation
agreed to disband and join churches nearest our homes. We
gave the church property, along with a 15-year-old parsonage,
to the Ontario Mennonite Conference. When the conference
decided to convert the building into a retreat center, money
from the sale of the parsonage was used for renovations.

The building was in good repair. After removing the pulpit
and benches we installed a carpet, new basement windows, a
fridge, stove, cupboards, dishes, tables, and chairs to serve 100
people.

Since its opening in November 1976 the Blenheim Retreat
Centre is used nearly every weekend as well as for weekday
activities. Youth and women's groups, church councils, and
house churches enjoy the building. Mennonite Central
Committee alumni reunions, weddings, anniversary
celebrations, and family gatherings have been held here. Other
denominations in the community are welcome to use it and

have often done so. Our rates are low enough so many can afford the facilities.

Former members of the congregation are happy to see the building in good repair and still a house of God.

—Gladys Cressman
Plattsville, Ont.

9. *eating together*

●●●

Indonesia: island of Java, town of Kudus. A large urban
Mennonite church had just completed a new building. We
were invited to the dedication celebration.

They were holding afternoon and evening meetings spaced a
few hours apart. In between, the people would have to eat. As
one who helped feed crowds at similar events in North
America, I watched to see how it would be done.

We stood around chatting. No lines formed, but several
areas did buzz with activity as workers hovered over huge pots
of rice and something else they had carried in. Then they began
filling shallow soup plates, and suddenly everyone was handing
everyone else what proved to be the meal: much rice with a
little fragrant meat-vegetable mixture mounded on top, and a
spoon resting alongside. People deferred to each other, but
finally everyone had food.

We stood and talked and ate. The rice wasn't warm, but it
didn't matter, since the meat mixture was HOT. By
observation I learned to work around it, easing just a little of
the peppery stuff onto every spoonful of bland rice. It came out
right. When we put down our bowls, people came by with trays
holding glasses of sweet tea, then bananas. I felt satisfied, but
not overly full. As usual in Asia, virtually no one was
overweight.

Rice, the mixture, tea, bananas. A bowl and spoon and cup.

No garbage but banana peels. I remembered that at committee meetings to plan North American church suppers someone usually said, "Let's keep this simple." But never were we as successful as the Kudus Food Committee.

We do what is expected in our culture; they follow theirs. Might it be time for North American church groups to break out of a culture grown overindulgent and learn from others? Dare we even invite Christians from around the world to take a look at our church eating practices? Along with much good, they would also see:

— *Church cookbooks and potlucks* specializing in fat-and-sugar-rich salads and desserts—all gooey variations of pink and green gelatin, cake and pudding mix, sour cream, nuts, and whipped topping; overstuffed people standing in line for the selection; diet books in the church library.

— *A Food and Fellowship Committee* doing a dinner with a missionary speaker; committee members losing sight of the meal's intent and nursing inflated notions of calamity—"What if we run out of rolls?" "What if the flowers don't arrive soon for these centerpieces?" "What if *she* doesn't take more responsibility!" The next day the pastor must handle three broken relationships and counsel a missionary who fears furloughs.

— *Monday morning garbage* by the church's back door: heavy-duty plastic bags gorged with single-use styrofoam cups, trays, and plastic spoons.

— *On the bulletin board:* Poolside prayer coffee Thursday morning at the Millers'; Christian Women's Monthly Luncheon at the Hilton East Room; Men's Weekly Breakfast at the Holiday Inn; urgent fund appeals for urban, minority, and prison ministries.

— *Banquets* for this and banquets for that, five or ten dollars a meal; portion-controlled meat, powdered mashed potatoes, canned gravy and corn; a whole evening narrowed to conversation with two other guests; neckties too tight; a speaker straining at jokes to spark a static audience.

— *Conference participants* scurrying here and there trying to find light but nutritious food—if they're paying out of pocket; dutifully putting down one big meal after the next if all was paid for in the registration[1]; sitting by the hour with no exercise, hearing the plight of others, eating again.

— *Church board members* in a hotel conference room deliberating programs for the poor; no break except meals; no meals on the hotel menu except meat, french fries, and dessert; no afternoon sessions with everyone awake; no expense account turned in except big ones.

What Does the Lord's Supper Include?

Practices that
offend nutrition,
ecology, and thrift
take place regularly
at church and
church conference
meals.

More serious is our failure to comprehend the full meaning of
Christians overeating together at a time when so many go
hungry.

The Lord's Supper, the Eucharist, culminates the experience
of Christians gathered to eat. If we believe in a worldwide body
of believers, then we've got to look again at the familiar words
from 1 Corinthians 11:23 which typically introduce that
celebration: "The Lord Jesus on the night when he was
betrayed took bread. . . ."

Why did Paul write this now-treasured passage? What was
the setting? A quick reading of 1 Corinthians 11:17–34 shows
he wasn't introducing the idea of communion, he was
correcting an abuse.

The story may have direct meaning for the way we conduct
church dinners. Today we don't invest these settings with
eucharistic meaning. We limit communion symbolism to
miniscule portions of juice and crackers, partaken in pews on
specified Sundays. But Paul is talking about a practice which
included more, for in chiding the Corinthians, he says, "Each
one goes ahead with his own meal. . . ."

This is not to suggest that every setting in which Christians
eat together today should bear the whole meaning of our
Lord's death and resurrection. But taking a world-view of the
church, we can't escape the similarity between habitual
overeating at North American church dinners and the abuse
Paul roundly condemns. For the problem was that some
feasted while others were hungry.

Ronald Sider in *Rich Christians in an Age of Hunger* takes a
careful look at the Corinthian passage. Here is a segment of his
analysis:

Apparently wealthy Christians feasted at the eucharistic
celebration while poor believers went hungry. Paul angrily
denied that they were eating the Lord's Supper at all
(1 Corinthians 11:20–22). In fact they were profaning the

Lord's body and blood because they did not discern his body
(1 Corinthians 11:27–29).

But what did Paul mean when he charged that they did
not discern the Lord's body? To discern the Lord's body is
to understand and live the truth that fellowship with Christ
is inseparable from membership in his body where our
oneness in Christ far transcends differences of race or class.
. . . Discernment of that one body is totally incompatible
with feasting while other members of the body go hungry.
. . . As long as any Christian anywhere in the world is
hungry, the eucharistic celebration of all Christians
everywhere in the world is imperfect.[2]

This failure to be sensitive to those who have less is where
the problem starts. Communion, whether genuine or abused,
takes place not only when we pass little glasses and bread trays.
We say as much about how well we discern the Lord's body by
the way we conduct potlucks, dinners, and banquets, as by how
reverently we bow through the Eucharist. Even if poor
communications allowed us to ignore the rest of the world,
obedience of Jesus' suggestion within our own communities
could quickly adjust the perspective: "When you give a party,
ask the poor, the crippled, the lame, and the blind" (Luke
14:13, NEB).

The intent here
is not
to throw a wet blanket
over celebrating.

God's people should often gather to eat and be joyful, but in
view of the poor and our own society's dissipation, simplicity
must be our mark.

I want to go to more church conferences where a dollar or
two gets you through the soup and bread line. I want to meet
more church administrators like one I know who routinely
skips one meal a day when board meetings make him
dependent on high-priced restaurant meals. He takes apples
and dried fruit in his suitcase and claims this disciplined light
eating cuts costs and clears his head for the Lord's business. I
want to see women's groups specialize again in brown-bag
luncheons. I praise the congregation in which men who gather
early to pray also cook their own simple breakfast and wash
the dishes.

Keys to Freedom
Here are starting points for more-with-less feeding of groups:

1. **Relax about your reputation as planner and cook.** You won't lose your friends or your place in God's kingdom even if things go wrong with the food!
2. **For one or two meals or even a weekend, don't be tense about nutritional adequacy.** Getting the basics is simple: bread, rice, noodles, potatoes, or beans provide carbohydrates for energy; meat, eggs, milk, cheese, nuts, peanut butter, or beans add protein; fruit or vegetables give vitamins, minerals, and crunch! For one lunch, whole-wheat bread, cheese, and apples is a fine meal. In fact, such simplicity is preferable to padding the menu with sugar and fat.
3. **Help everyone become more self-sufficient.** Jesus became a servant—he took the towel and basin. The Apostle Paul made tents. Gandhi spun cloth and cleaned toilets. It's a false busyness that keeps us from saving a styrofoam cup through several coffee breaks or bringing our own mug. False values tell us that a half hour discussing "the real issues" benefits our world more than the same time at the dishpan avoiding another garbage bag of plastic waste.
4. **Devise easy ways to serve.** If you don't want long lines, place makings for a simple meal at several locations around the room. Or, if people are already seated around tables, bring each group of ten a tray containing good bread on a board, several spreads, knives, vegetable sticks or fruit, paper napkins, drink, and cups. Most of this could be arranged hours in advance. Simplify coffee and tea service like this: at one table, arrange a coffee maker heating only water, jars with hot drink mixes and tea bags, and cups with instructions to mark and reuse.
5. **Do allow extra time for large quantities of food to cook.** Choose dishes which hold well rather than those requiring last-minute fuss. Be free to co-opt help on the spot as needed.

Brown-Bag Solutions

One-day meetings: Request on invitations that participants bring their lunch. An hour before lunch, take a show of hands of any who didn't. Then send someone to the nearest grocery store for bread, cheese or meat, fruit, and paper napkins. At lunchtime make this available on a tray with a donation cup.

Miracle Meal: For a meeting at which half or more will be from the local community, ask "locals" to bring large bag lunches with extra for sharing; tell out-of-towners that lunch will be provided. At noon, divide the group into circles, with some "locals" in each circle. Reenact the miracle of loaves and fishes by free sharing. Complete the drama by sending around baskets to recirculate leftovers and make sure they aren't discarded. A bit risky, but fun. At a one-day church conference, this is a good way to mix members of a hosting congregation with out-of-town guests.

Be My Guest: When you attend a conference in your own community, pack yourself a generous lunch. During the morning, find someone with whom you'd like to talk who would otherwise need to buy his/her lunch. Ask him/her to share yours, and find a quiet spot together.

Brown-Bag Banquet: Planners for an Eastern Mennonite College Class of '64 Reunion avoided an expensive restaurant luncheon with this invitation: "A spacious room in the Administration Building has been reserved for our use from 11:30 A.M. to 2:30 P.M. Plan to bring the family and a bag with finger food for a Brown-Bag Banquet. The food will be placed on tables at the four sides of the room and will be shared by everyone." Planners later evaluated this alumni banquet as a fine success, especially in terms of group interaction and fun.

Finger Food Potluck: For many years Akron Mennonite Church, Akron, Pennsylvania, has held periodic Sunday noon fellowship meals, following a single pattern. On the Sunday before, the bulletin asks each household to bring table service and enough sandwiches for itself plus a few extra. In addition, A–K brings raw vegetable sticks, L–R fruits, and S–Z cookies or cupcakes—for twenty. Everyone takes their food to the kitchen before church. Later the meal is quickly assembled onto trays and served buffet-style with punch and coffee. For a group which eats together often, a standing arrangement for finger foods simplifies greatly.

Briefcase Lunch: Early one morning a Mennonite Central Committee staff person and I flew from Pennsylvania to Chicago for a one-day airport meeting to which we had invited about eight other people. At lunchtime, instead of steering us to a restaurant, my colleague surprised everyone by pulling sandwiches and other treats from his large briefcase. He had packed and refrigerated our lunch at home the night before, making the equivalent of a forty-dollar contribution. We continued business as we ate, getting the most from a short time together.

Grocery Store Resource

Two ideas from Marian Claassen Franz, Washington, D.C.:

Seminar Lunch for Fifty: "Groups of from thirty to fifty church members often come to Washington for seminars. Speakers and visits to government agencies make the schedule tight, and cafeteria lines are long. Usually we opt for this simple lunch: In a few minutes we spread a seminar table with loaves of bread (folded open on top so slices are easy to take), cold cuts, cheese, carrots, celery, cookies, and fruit. A staff person has to buy only groceries and clean vegetables. We do this mainly to make sure people are on time for afternoon appointments, but it also provides lunch at less than a dollar per person." Katie Funk Wiebe, after attending one of these Washington seminars, wrote about the lunch, "In the happy melee which resulted as we shared bread together, I met and talked to more people than at a formal meal."

Bread and Cheese and Fruit and Tea: "Bread-and-Cheese-and-Fruit-and-Tea has become one word when I plan office meetings. Most people I meet with here in the city are available only at lunch or after work in the evening before they travel home. My office, where we gather around this attractive meal, is a restful place compared to noisy cafeterias. Nothing has to be done ahead of time except for shopping. I keep cheese and fruit in the refrigerator for weeks, bread for days. When we meet after work, those who will have their evening meal later at home can snack to take the edge off their hunger, while others who make it their meal find it filling and tasty, especially with a good Italian bread."

Easy Hot Meals

Soup Line: Prepare in advance a quantity of hearty soup. If the weather is cold, store it outdoors in a safe spot or be sure of other adequate refrigeration. Allow plenty of time to slowly reheat. At serving time, you need only bowls, spoons, paper napkins to hold thick chunks of French bread, and a tray of apples, bananas, or pears. Have plenty of refills. A simple meal doesn't mean going hungry, but eating generously of a few good things. See recipes at the end of this chapter.

In the Stew: Proceed as above, using stew or a casserole. For a local meeting you might simmer a surprise stew while you do business. Designate someone to buy meat, and ask each person to bring a few vegetables. Brown the meat when the meeting begins, add vegetables, then simmer until mealtime. Enjoy your unique creation with bread and fruit.

On Rice: Rice must be the most versatile of hot foods— anything goes well on top. It's easier to handle in quantity than noodles or pasta. An oven simplifies preparation. Delores Friesen, missionary in several African countries, says, "Quite easily I've done groundnut stew and rice for one hundred people. I prepare rice in the oven, cook two big kettles of stew, and ask individual families in the church to bring condiments: chopped bananas, onions, green peppers, tomatoes, pineapple. Or we just leave out that part—it's a British addition to the African dish anyway. Curry, especially with potatoes or cabbage, is also a good choice."

Other possibilities for topping: thick chili, lentils, any meat and vegetable combination prepared with a sauce. The simplest casseroles are raw rice baked with raw chicken or lean ground beef, beans or lentils, vegetables, sauce, or seasonings.

Potatoes: Our habit of requiring gravy plus several other

dishes alongside potatoes makes them hard to manage as a basic food to fill a crowd. But potatoes are a highly nutritious food, readily available in North America, and cheap. Find ways to simplify!

A popular snack always sold at the Pennsylvania Farm Show held in January is a hot baked potato with a pat of butter served on a little paper tray. Would that go with cider on a cold night as well as doughnuts? You might base a meal on baked potatoes by serving them with plenty of a high-protein, low-fat sour cream substitute: blend cottage cheese until smooth, add lemon juice, salt and pepper to taste, stir in chopped chives and parsley.

Notes

1
Katie Funk Wiebe, "The More We Eat Together," *Gospel Herald* (May 1, 1979), p. 364.
2
Ronald J. Sider, *Rich Christians in an Age of Hunger* (Downers Grove, Ill.: InterVarsity Press, 1977), pp. 105–106.

●●●●●●●●●●●●●●●●●●●●●●●●●●

All My Relatives • Twenty people overnight? Four guest meals in a row? It sounded like a lot of work when I first considered inviting six families of my relatives to our farm for a summer weekend.

Several weeks in advance my sister-in-law and I planned all the details. We sent out a duplicated letter giving a schedule for the weekend, simple meal plans, and lodging information. Everyone brought some of the food, sleeping bags, and their own towels. Some slept in a camper, some in a tent, and some in the house. Because we hoped for maximum interaction, we delegated various family combinations as dishwashers for each meal. We planned time to worship and play together.

I thought I would feel like Rabbit with all his relations in the Pooh stories. But when we tried it, everyone had a good time and no one worked very hard—including me. The following summer I welcomed them all back again!
—*Ellen Longacre*
Barto, Pa.

The Dinner Group • A few years ago most of my friends were single college students living off campus. Two women shared an apartment down the street from three men. Tired of cooking for themselves only, the women invited the men to eat with them on a regular basis.

Later the women said, "Enough of this. You men pitch in on the cost of the food, or better yet, take turns preparing meals." The men agreed and the Dinner Group grew. Some of the singles consolidated themselves into couples, and more singles joined until we finally split into two groups for want of space.

Dinner is served at a different person's house each week night. Couples, if they have two incomes, cook once a week, and singles cook every other week. People may trade nights to cook to accommodate their schedules. When members have finished eating they are free to go their way, although many stick around to talk. Whoever cooks on a given night also does the clean-up.

Twice a year the group goes on a weekend campout—sometimes for pure recreation, at other times to discuss issues like "How are we growing spiritually?" or "Should we all pool our resources to buy a farm?"

The Dinner Group saves money and food, eats a good variety of foods, and is a source of spiritual and emotional support and fellowship.
—*Marti Stockdale*
Canton, Ohio

●●●●●●●●●●●●●●●●●●●●●●●●●●●

Move the Emphasis to People

We learned while living in Zaire that having guests does not
have to be fatiguing. The extended family concept taught us a
lot about living together with many people. When guests arrive
we welcome them, ask them in, and *sit down* with them.
Sharing these first moments is important in sensing their mood,
first impressions, or reactions. We get clues as to their needs.

Zaireans have a custom of "giving greetings." First the guest
tells about himself without interruption: his trip, what has
happened since we last saw each other, the purpose of the visit.
Then the host gives a response. This exchange is a good
listening exercise and important for communication.

After that, guests don't have to be entertained nor will they
run away! I ask them to join me in work that needs doing or
just excuse myself. Often they're tired and appreciate a chance
to sit quietly.

I always plan a simple meal such as a casserole and bread
which I can leave unattended. A drink or appetizer, perhaps
vegetables with dip, makes the evening special and relaxing.
Coffee or tea and fruit or cookies follow later in the living
room. This way I like to move the emphasis from the table and
food to people and relationships.
—*Sara Regier*
  North Newton, Kan.

While working in Papua New Guinea we learned from our
Australian friends that fellowship around the table can be more
relaxed and pleasant if diners aren't rushed from one course to
the next. After a course is finished, the Australian hostess
remains seated at the table and joins in the conversation. Quite
a few minutes later, when there is a natural break in the
conversation, she rises to clear the table for the next course.
This is in contrast to many American homes where the hostess
keeps shifting her eyes around to find the last guest to finish
and, as soon as the offender lays down his fork, immediately
pops up to get the next course. Conversation and friendship are
more important than clockwork.
—*John and Tina Bohn*
  Maseru, Lesotho

●●●●●●●●●●●●●●●●●●●●●●●●●

Beyond the Law of Hospitality ● We all have our own
little additions to the moral code. For me, the statement, "I
wanted to have you over but I've just been too busy," not only
reflects bad habits and bad manners, but immoral values. A
number of years ago I confronted myself with this. I
determined to find a satisfactory way of serving meals so that

they would not be so burdensome. We want to live out what we believe about the importance of hospitality.

The answer was a standard menu that is nutritious, simple almost to the point of being symbolic, and economical in both time and money. Since then, every guest who eats around our table probably has the same meal as any other—stew or hearty soup, crusty bread, and fresh fruit—and absolutely no trimmings or additions except occasionally a pot of fresh garden mint tea.

For those who have great gifts in the area of cooking, such a plan may be unsatisfactory. For me it is right. It multiplies our capacity for "having people in" or responding with joy when they drop in! I no longer wonder if someone will like this or that. I just serve it. It's equally simple for four guests or fourteen. Obviously more time and money would be necessary for forty, yet the preparation would still be basically the same.

Preparing the table is a task I thoroughly enjoy. After all, making a meal standard or simple does not preclude serving it with beauty and even elegance.
—*Miriam Lind*
Goshen, Ind.

●●●●●●●●●●●●●●●●●●●●●●●●●●

Out and In

On our last visit to Canada and the United States we were surprised and even shocked to note how often people eat out. Instead of cooking a meal and having people "in," the trend was to entertain at a restaurant. We remember looking forward to spending an evening in the home of friends. When we arrived, we all piled into their car and drove across town to eat out. We knew the hostess was a super cook, so this added to our disappointment.

Our suggestion for meals including several families is to invite each household to bring a dish to share while the hostess fixes a simple main dish. Fellowship can be just as rich when water, rather than an expensive bottled drink, is served with the meal. We also avoid reliance on disposable dishes, to us a cause for alarm. We've learned that when adults get together to help with dishes the job is soon done. Some of our best discussions are in the kitchen over the sink.
—*John and Tina Bohn*
Maseru, Lesotho

Entertaining by going to commercial eating places is costly. By inviting people to our home to share a meal and receiving return invitations, we gain three benefits:
1. The food we eat is more nutritious than many commercial meals.

2. Overall cost is considerably less.
3. Family friendships developed in this way are invaluable.
—*Bill Wiebe*
  Hillsboro, Kan.

●●●●●●●●●●●●●●●●●●●●●●●●●●

Equipping for a Hopeful Future ● Before coming to
Bolivia I was the manager of Nutrition 1985, an innovative
food service program at Whitworth College in Spokane,
Washington.

Nutrition 1985 started as a result of a world hunger
emphasis in 1976 and is an alternative to the regular food
service for boarding students.

Whitworth runs its food service through a contract with a
food service corporation. At a typical meal they provide three
meat entrées, vegetables, a salad bar, and five desserts. There
was incredible selection. You really ate a lot. You were out of
touch with what you were doing. And the waste! Every student
ought to have to spend one day behind the window where trays
are returned to understand how much comes back.

After the world hunger emphasis on campus, some of us
students no longer believed that we had a right to this
unlimited consumption nor to the obvious interest in taste and
esthetics rather than in good nutrition.

We wanted to work for ethical eating. When we learned that
our college president and other students were willing to help,
we called an open meeting of food service managers, students,
teachers, and administrators.

After many meetings, much planning, and a sample dinner
showing what we wanted to do, food service managers and the
faculty graciously cooperated and granted the use of a small
faculty dining room. Nutrition 1985 began.

There were many changes. Mainly we want students to *think*
about what they do. We provide a menu using local foods,
saving energy, using agriculturally efficient and less refined
foods. We try to correct the main problems in the American
diet: too much sugar, too many saturated fats, too little
roughage, and too many chemical additives.

To help people make choices, we provide information on
nutritive values and calorie content of foods; then students
serve themselves. Earlier it was just portion control. We did
away with trays and put silverware at the end of the line.
People are asked to take only the utensils they really need—it
takes energy to clean what we use! Students in the program
also make and care for their own cloth napkins. We find they
really like having this sense of control and responsibility.

There's a relaxed quiet in our dining room that allows true
socializing. We don't want students to get all hyped up at
lunch and have the blues in the afternoon. We provide

educational emphases with reading material and occasional
brief speakers and discussions. People in the program choose to
study one of these areas: nutrition and health, energy saving
and ecology, social and political issues, or personal Christian
responsibility.

About one fourth of the student body of 1,125 participate by
electing at the beginning of the semester to use our food
service. Many of the faculty eat lunch with us. We don't claim
to have the answer to world hunger but we think a college
dining hall is a good place to equip people to make decisions
reflecting a hopeful future for all.
—*Valerie Morrison*
  Santa Cruz, Bolivia

School Lunch ● When schools in Holland began using
plastic cups for milk, I became annoyed at the waste involved.
In the nursery school, of which I am head teacher, it meant
throwing away 70 cups every day. This made 350 cups weekly
and 14,000 cups yearly for one small nursery school.

I wrote to the administration of our school saying I didn't
think use of disposable cups was conducive to protecting the
environment. They supported me enthusiastically and we went
back to using nondisposable cups. The most important reason
to give up these plastic cups was to teach the children to take
care of their surroundings.
—*Cockie de Boer-van den Berg*
  Syob ag Tynje, Holland

Conference Food Service ● In planning for a regional
church conference last summer, we wanted to have meals
based on *More-with-Less Cookbook* suggestions. The food
services director at the college where we were to meet agreed to
serve this kind of meal at the time when the largest group was
expected. We advertised the meal as sponsored by the college
food service department and our world hunger committee.
Comments I received were positive as people responded
favorably to a lighter meal.
—*Donella Clemens*
  Souderton, Pa.

●●●●●●●●●●●●●●●●●●●●●●●●●●●

Food for Fifty

Unless otherwise indicated, recipes are adapted from the *More-with-Less Cookbook* (Herald Press, 1976).

In using metric weights and measures, some quantities were rounded off for ease in measuring without affecting the final product.

All recipes were tested at the Mennonite Central Committee Dining Hall in Akron, Pennsylvania, under the supervision of Evie Lehman Shaar.

●●●●●●●●●●●●●●●●●●●●●●●●●●●

Soups:
Yield: about 15 L (4 gal)

Lentil-Sausage Soup
Brown in a large kettle:
   2.5 kg (5½ lb) pork sausage, broken into chunks
Remove meat and pour off all but 240 mL (1 c) dripping.
Add:
   10 medium onions, chopped
   5 cloves garlic, minced
   20 medium parsnips, cut in chunks (optional)
Cook five minutes or until onions and garlic are tender.
Add:
   2 kg (4–4½ lb) lentils
   75 mL (5 T) salt
   15 mL (1 T) marjoram
   6 L (6 qt) cooked tomatoes or juice
   7 L (7 qt) water
   browned sausage
Simmer about 30 minutes

Cheese and Corn Chowder
Combine in a large kettle:
   1 L (4 c) water
   3.5 L (3½ qt) potatoes, diced
   2 L (2 qt) carrots, sliced
   2 L (2 qt) celery, chopped
   30 mL (2 T) salt
   10 mL (2 t) pepper
Cover and simmer 10 minutes. Add:
   3.5 L (3½ qt) cream-style corn
Simmer 5 minutes. Add:
   3.5 L (3½ qt) milk
   450 g (1 lb) cheese, grated
Stir until cheese melts and chowder is heated through.
Do not boil.

Ham and Green Bean Soup
Combine in a large kettle:
  4 kg (8–9 lb) meaty ham bones
  8 L (8 qt) water
Cook 1½ hours. Remove meat from bone and cut in chunks. Add to soup stock, along with:
  4 L (4 qt) green beans, cut
  3 L (3 qt) potatoes, diced
  8 medium onions, chopped
  240 mL (1 c) fresh parsley, chopped
  20 mL (4 t) salt
  5 mL (1 t) pepper
  fresh summer savory, tied in a bunch or chopped
    or 20 mL (4 t) dried savory
Bring to a boil; reduce heat and simmer, covered, 20 minutes or until vegetables are tender. Skim off excess fat. Just before serving, stir in:
  1 L (1 qt) light cream or milk

Smokestack Chili
Soak overnight:
  2 kg (4–4½ lb) kidney beans
  1 kg (2¼ lb) pinto beans
Drain. Then add:
  8 L (8 qt) tomatoes, cooked, fresh, or frozen
  6 medium green peppers, chopped
  12 medium onions, chopped
  75 mL (5 T) salt
  5 mL (1 t) pepper
  80 mL (⅓ c) chili powder
  5 mL (1 t) cayenne pepper
  10 mL (2 t) cumin
  5 mL (1 t) paprika
Brown separately, then add to above:
  1 kg (2¼ lb) ground beef
Bring mixture to a slow boil. Then simmer 2–3 hours, stirring occasionally.
Within half an hour of serving, stir in:
  720 mL (3 c) wheat germ
  1.5 L (6 c) bran
Mixture thickens considerably. Add water if desired.
—Paul J. Renn III
  Red Lion, Pa.

●●●●●●●●●●●●●●●●●●●●●●●●●●

On Rice:
Oven-cooked Rice
175C (350F)
Oven time: 1 hour
In two large roasters or other baking dishes, combine:
   3.25 L (3½ qt) rice
   6.5 L (7 qt) hot water
   35 mL (7 t) salt
   180 mL (¾ c) margarine
Bake, covered.

●●●●●●●●●●●●●●●●●●●●●●●●●●

Rice Toppings:
Creamed Tuna
Melt in a large, heavy pan:
   1.25 L (5½ c) margarine
Blend in, cooking and stirring until bubbly:
   1.25 L (5½ c) flour
   40 mL (2½ T) salt
Using a wire whisk to prevent lumps, stir in
   7 L (7 qt) milk
Add:
   2 L (2 qt) frozen peas
   2.5 L (10 c) drained, flaked tuna
Cook just until smooth and thickened.
Variations:
1. Substitute diced, cooked chicken for tuna and use chicken broth or bouillon as half the liquid. Add 30 mL (2 T) poultry seasoning.
2. Vary the vegetables, or use in combination.
3. Vary the flavor with chopped parsley, chives, hard-boiled eggs, onion, or celery salt.

Groundnut Stew
In a heavy kettle, heat:
   120 mL (½ c) oil
Add:
   4–4.5 kg (8–10 lb) beef cubes rolled in flour
While browning, add:
   25 mL (5 t) nutmeg
   150 mL (10 T) chili powder
When meat is browned, add:
   40 medium onions, sliced
   10 cloves garlic, minced
   2 L (2 qt) tomato paste
   14 L (14 qt) water
   red pepper, if desired
Simmer till meat is tender, about one hour.

At least a half hour before serving:
Add:
>   **4 L (4 qt) peas**
>   **4 L (4 qt) cooked, diced sweet potato or pumpkin**

Heat:
>   **1.5 L (6 c) chunky peanut butter**
>   **240 mL (1 c) oil**

Stir over medium heat 5 minutes.
Then add slowly to stew.
Simmer over low heat 20 minutes.
May be accompanied with small dishes of condiments, e.g.:
>   **chopped raw vegetable or fruit, chopped hard-boiled egg,
>   raisins, coconut.**

Ground-Beef Vegetable Curry
Sauté:
>   **480 mL (2 c) margarine**
>   **2.5 L (2½ qt) onion, chopped**
>   **10 cloves garlic, minced**

Add:
>   **4 kg (8–9 lb) ground beef**

Brown well. Stir in:
>   **150 mL (10 t) curry powder**
>   **75 mL (5 T) salt**
>   **10 mL each (2 t) pepper, cinnamon, ginger, turmeric**
>   **5 L (5 qt) cooked tomatoes**
>   **20 medium potatoes, diced**
>   **5 L (5 qt) peas or green beans, fresh or frozen**

Cover and simmer 25 minutes.
Variation: Squash, sweet potato, or pumpkin may be
substituted for some of the potato.

●●●●●●●●●●●●●●●●●●●●●●●●●●●

Casseroles:
175C (350F)

5 greased oven dishes, each 33 x 21 x 5 cm (13 x 9 x 2 in.) or 4 L (4 qt) capacity

Roman Rice and Beans
Oven time: 30–45 minutes
> **1 kg (2¼ lb) onions, finely chopped**
> **2 kg (4–4½ lb) carrots, finely chopped**
> **360 mL (1½ c) celery, chopped**
> **240 mL (1 c) fresh parsley, chopped**
> **60 mL (4 T) basil**
> **30 mL (2 T) oregano**
> **8 cloves garlic**
> **4 kg (8–9 lb) tomatoes, coarsely chopped**
> **1.5 kg (3 lb) kidney or pinto beans, cooked and drained**
> **or about 570 g (20 oz) raw**
> **3.5 kg (7½ lb) brown rice, cooked or 1.25 kg (2¾ lb)**
> **raw**
> **900 g (2 lb) cheese, grated**
> **60 mL (4 T) salt**
> **8 mL (1½ t) pepper**
> **Oil as needed.**

1. Sauté onions, carrots, celery, parsley, basil, oregano, and garlic in oil until onions are golden.
2. Add tomatoes, beans, rice, salt, pepper, and half the cheese. Mix gently but well.
3. Place in baking dishes. Sprinkle with remaining cheese.
4. Bake until thoroughly heated (covered).

—Whitworth College
Spokane, Wash.

Baked Lentils
Oven time: 2 hours
Combine in a large kettle and bring to a boil:
> **3.5 kg (7½ lb) lentils**
> **6 L (6 qt) water**
> **60 mL (4 T) salt**

Cover and simmer 30 minutes.
Without draining, add:
> **1.25 L (5 c) tomato ketchup**
> **480 mL (2 c) golden corn syrup**
> **60 mL (¼ c) cooking molasses**
> **45 mL (3 T) dry mustard**
> **15 mL (1 T) Worcestershire sauce**
> **240 mL (1 c) onions, chopped**
> **5 mL (1 t) garlic powder**

Combine well. Pour into baking pans.

Top with 1 kg (2 lb) nitrite-free bacon which has been cut in small pieces and sautéed slightly. (optional)

Cover and bake for 1¼ hours.

Uncover and bake another 45 minutes.

Add water if necessary.

—Joanna Lehman
  Evanston, Ill.

Meat, Cheese, and Potato Scallop

Oven time: 1 hour 15 minutes

Make a cheese sauce:

350 mL (1½ c) margarine
300 mL (1¼ c) flour
13 mL (2½ t) salt
3.5 L (3¾ qt) milk
1 kg (2 lb) cheese, grated

Combine in baking dishes:

10 medium onions, sliced
40 medium potatoes, sliced

Pour cheese sauce over vegetables.

Cover and bake for ½ hour.

Add 6 L (about 6 qt) leftover cooked ham or canned luncheon meat, diced.

Bake, covered, another ½ hour.

Remove cover and bake 15 minutes.

Baked Egg with Cheese

Oven Time: 30 minutes

50 eggs, hard-boiled
1.5 kg (3 lb) cheese, grated
9 L (9 qt) bread, cubed
30 mL (2 T) salt
8 mL (1½ t) pepper
1.5 L (6 c) milk
840 mL (3½ c) light cream or evaporated milk

Slice eggs.

Arrange alternate layers of bread cubes, egg, and cheese in baking dishes.

Season with salt and pepper.

Combine milk and cream and pour over mixture.

Sprinkle with crumbs. (optional)

Bake for 30 minutes.

—Adapted from **Mennonite**
  Community Cookbook

Chicken and Rice Bake

Oven time: 2 hours and 15 minutes

> **50 pieces of chicken**
> **5 L (5 qt) boiling water**
> **720 mL (3 c) onions, chopped**
> **3 L (3 qt) mushroom soup or medium thick white sauce**
> **3 L (3 qt) brown rice, raw**
> **180 mL (¾ c) margarine**
> **60 mL (4 T) salt**
> **30 mL (2 T) curry**

Mix together all ingredients except the chicken. Place in baking pans and bake for one hour, covered.

Place chicken on top. Bake for another 1¼ hours, uncovered, adding a little water if rice becomes too dry.

—MCC Dining Hall
  Akron, Pa.

●●●●●●●●●●●●●●●●●●●●●●●●●●●

Hot Sandwiches:
Super Tacos
(2–3 each generous servings)
Brown:
   3 kg (6–7 lb) ground beef
Add and cook together 10 minutes:
   1.5 L (6 c) onion, chopped
   6 medium green peppers, chopped
   2 L (2 qt) celery, diced
   4.5 L (4½ qt) tomato sauce or juice
   90 mL (6 T) chili powder
   60 mL (4 T) cumin
   30 mL (2 T) each garlic salt, paprika, oregano
Add and cook till tender:
   24 medium potatoes, raw, grated
To prepare taco shells (100–120):
   Fold warm tortilla in half and use as is or fry each tortilla
briefly in shallow hot fat, turning once and then folding in half
before tortilla becomes too crisp. Drain folded shells on
absorbent paper and keep warm until ready to use.
Spoon the filling into shells.
Serve with bowls of
   3 heads shredded lettuce
   2 kg (4–4½ lb) grated cheese
   24 diced tomatoes
—Rachel Gross
   Athens, Ohio

Tuna Burgers
175C (350F)
Oven time: 25–30 minutes
   50 buns, split
   3 kg (6½–7 lb) drained, flaked tuna
   3 small onions, minced
   750 mL (3 c) celery, finely chopped
   1.25 L (5 c) mayonnaise
   100 slices cheese
Combine tuna, onion, celery, and mayonnaise and spread on
split buns.
Bake on cookie sheets for 20–25 minutes, or until topping is
hot.
Top each with a slice of cheese and return to oven for another 5
minutes or until cheese melts.
—MCC Dining Hall
   Akron, Pa.

●●●●●●●●●●●●●●●●●●●●●●●●●●●●

Salad Bar Suggestions:

About 4 kg (9 lb) of salad greens will provide 50 one-cup servings. Include endive, escarole, head and leaf lettuce, spinach, watercress, chicory, cabbage, and dandelion greens in any combination for a tasty salad base.

Bowls of fresh vegetables in season could be brought by various individuals ready to serve on the greens.

Toppings might include croutons, nuts, sliced hard-boiled eggs, strips or cubes of cheese, bean and alfalfa sprouts.

●●●●●●●●●●●●●●●●●●●●●●●●●●●●

Salad Dressings:
Oil and Vinegar Dressing
Yields about 2 L (8 cups)
Combine and blend well:
   1.25 L (5 c) oil
   480 mL (2 c) vinegar
   240 mL (1 c) sugar
   1 small onion (shredded)
   25 mL (5 t) celery seed
   25 mL (5 t) salt
   25 mL (5 t) dry mustard
—*Linda Frey*
New Holland, Pa.

Thousand Island Dressing
Yields about 3 L (12 c)
Combine and blend well:
   1.5 L (6 c) mayonnaise
   360 mL (1½ c) chili sauce or ketchup
   180 mL (¾ c) green pepper, finely chopped
   180 mL (¾ c) onion, finely chopped
   180 mL (¾ c) pickle relish
   30 mL (2 T) paprika
   15 mL (1 T) salt

●●●●●●●●●●●●●●●●●●●●●●●●●●●

Our Bible study group enjoys a salad picnic. Everyone signs up to bring one of the ingredients for tossed salad. Then you go down the colorful table and put together what you want. The meal is complete with drink, rolls, watermelon, and cupcakes.
—Ruth S. Weaver
  Reading, Pa.

Inviting many people to eat with you may be a problem if you intend to seat them all at a table. Try a floor arrangement as do millions in our world. Spread a sheet in the center as the tablecloth. "Set the table" as you would according to number expected. Give only one spoon to save on dishwashing. Take off shoes when ready to eat, and sit cross-legged in front of your plate, holding it on your lap if you wish. Children especially love this arrangement.
—Marie M. Moyer
  Telford, Pa.

My sister and her husband served fresh fruit and homemade breads for their wedding reception.
—Delores Friesen
  Accra, Ghana

I belong to a group of women who much enjoy being together, but time and schedules are limiting. We discovered an easy way to meet every other week with minimum preparation for the person who is entertaining: each person brings her own lunch and the hostess provides dessert and drink. Once a special brown-bag lunch was called for on short notice to meet friends visiting from a distance.
—Elizabeth Bauman
  Goshen, Ind.

Eating together is an old and well-loved Mennonite tradition; however, we eat too much at a carry-in dinner. At a recent meal at College Mennonite Church we brought beef stew, salads, and ice cream. One main dish means less temptation to overindulge.
—Ruth Sherman
  Goshen, Ind.

If there is one outstanding discovery many Mennonite Paxmen made in the Greece experience, it was that a loaf of bread and a piece of cheese was adequate provision as they moved around the villages in their daily pursuits.
—John Wieler
  Winnipeg, Man.

At our Ann Arbor Mennonite Fellowship monthly potlucks we encourage people to bring reusable plates and cups rather than paper products.
—Ruth Guengerich
  Ann Arbor, Mich.

Asian Indians often sit in silence the first five or ten minutes with guests at mealtime. For them food is so precious that a good meal is always special and deserves full attention and appreciation.
—Marie M. Moyer
  Telford, Pa.

Our backyard farm picnics give us more pleasure than just that of eating. Even doing dishes is pleasant. While some folks remain around the picnic tables and the children scatter to play, we bring a pan of hot, sudsy water out on our return trip from taking leftover food indoors. We wash the dishes on one end of the picnic table and use whatever large containers are handy for rinsing and dripping dry. No one misses the talk, joshing, or chance to help.
—Amanda Toews
  Scio, Ore.

My daughter-in-law and I kept many overnight guests in our homes during a recent church conference. By freezing sandwiches in advance, we made it possible for everyone to pack their noon meal quickly and take it along, saving money and time. At breakfast we simply put frozen sandwiches, fresh fruit, and brown bags out on a tray and invited people to help themselves.
—Meta Juhnke
  McPherson, Kan.

strengthening each other

Mennonite Central Committee runs child sponsorship programs in various countries. The following letter was one of a batch sent by a vacation Bible school class to their adopted friend in Calcutta. Only names and places are changed:

Dear Subil,

My name is Mike Miller. I am ten years old. I am in sixth grade and go to Hilltop School. I like baseball, tennis, football, and swimming. The name of my baseball team is Bingham Mutual Insurance. I have an extremely big house; it has sixteen garages. Three of them are Travelhome trailer garages. I hope you learn the Word of God.

Sincerely,
Mike Miller

Perhaps Mike did indeed have a flight of fancy with the garage count. Still, what does his world as he perceives it say to the Indian boy who needs assistance even to attend school? What is Mike beginning to understand about following Christ in a world of rich and poor?

Likely Mike knows his Bible pretty well. Probably he was raised on lusty choruses like "The B-I-B-L-E." He stands alone on the Word of God and trusts Subil will learn to do the same. Or does he?

Clearly someone is failing Mike. Obviously it's his parents

and likely also his Bible school teacher. They aren't telling him
what's really in that Book. Yes, they related the stories about
John the Baptist and Zacchaeus and the early church of Acts,
and had him memorize the Beatitudes and other words of
Jesus. But their lives must have been like dark black editing
pencils, striking out those passages that cry good news to the
poor and warnings to the rich. Maybe they told Mike these
were just "spiritual truths."

They've done him no favor. Mike has to live in the same
world with Subil and millions like him, hopefully in peace. He
has to live with himself in the process.

Creative Deprivation

I muse on a quote by Colman McCarthy:

"To creatively deprive
a child
means to keep his
senses
and mind free
of material goods
that overwhelm
him."[1]

It takes less than sixteen garages and their contents to choke
out the qualities our children are sure to need: a gentle way of
handling the earth; versatility in the face of shortage; inner
provision for contentment; and more than all that,
commitment to live justly in the kingdom of God.

These are the new challenges.

But too many of us
are still
raising children
by the idea
that each generation
has the right
to more material
comforts
than the one before.

Minority groups excepted, contemporary parents of teens and under grew up in the forties and fifties with no real hardships. One bathroom, one car, yes. But not privation. Yet we hang onto the dream, then legitimate, which we heard from *our* parents: "I don't want you to have it so rough." Today, not having it so rough usually means luxury. A magazine ad showing a twelve-year-old with her own television says, "Of course, you were probably a lot older when you got your first Sony, but times have changed. Give her advantages you never had as a kid."

To deprive creatively is not as easy as to float with the old dream. That's why this chapter on teaching values to others is called "Strengthening Each Other." Mainly it's about nurturing and reinforcing values. We must do it for our children and with them. And we must do it for each other.

In discussions on simple living, parents often assume an air of helplessness and say, "But we want our children to feel accepted. It's so important to them to be like their peers."

True, children like to have the same kind of bikes and sneakers as their friends. They're taken in by the buzz and sparkle of gadgets. But aren't adults the same? If we take off our mature-parent masks, are we any different? Why else do grownups fiddle with eye makeup, heat-lamp suntans, or the proper width of neckties? Or expensive toys like thousand-dollar stereo systems and gas-gulping four-wheel-drive vehicles used mainly on paved suburban streets?

Parents and children, single adults, the old and young—everyone needs support from somebody. Everyone needs a hand to hold while walking upstream, a voice to challenge when one wants to turn around and drift. Testimonies in this chapter suggest ways to find and give support. Below are summarizing principles.

Helping Children Live More with Less
1. **Change comes slowly.** Be patient and see small changes as part of lifetime commitment.
2. **Give honest reasons.** Discuss, but don't preach.
3. **Living speaks more clearly than talking.** For example, an important factor in limiting children's TV watching is to curtail your own.
4. **Mix in plenty of humor and recreation.** Says John Alexander, editor of *The Other Side,* "When simple living stops being fun, you'll see my taillights!"
5. **Plan on nonconformity, but not simply for the sake of being different.** There are many harmless and even beneficial ways for children to identify with peers. Wisdom means deciding together with children when a principle is of sufficient importance to venture an alternate route.
6. **Time is the most valued gift.**

7. **Children, as they become more mature, need space** in which to choose and develop their own values. Accept that as normal.
8. **Children are strengthened by friends whose families hold values similar to their own.** Admit this need and seek out such friends. But these supporting persons need not always be of the same age and sex as the child.

Helping Adults Live More with Less

All of the above apply when adults support each other! Jot down your own additional ideas as you read the entries in this chapter.

Note

1

As quoted in *Alternative Celebrations Catalogue,*
third edition, p. 2. Alternatives, 4274 Oaklawn Drive,
Jackson, Miss. 39206.

●●●●●●●●●●●●●●●●●●●●●●●●●●●

I. **Toward Learning to Understand** ● Many people here in India eat only once a day. To understand their struggles as much as possible, I decided that for a month I would do likewise. I hoped this would help indicate whether the food-for-work and other projects which I planned were realistic in terms of the workers' resources and energy.

My schedule during the month included office work in Delhi, with occasional trips to flooded areas. Usually I ate my meal between 8:00 and 9:00 P.M. In the morning I drank a few glasses of water. Sometimes I had a cup of tea in the office.

The first week I sensed no major difference. In the second week, I began noticing where food and food smells originated. By the third week, I was especially glad for a cup of Indian tea with plenty of sugar. Drinking it was no longer a social act. I savored it slowly, feeling an immediate surge of energy that lasted an hour or two.

Now I became keenly aware of fat people and thin people, those who threw away food and those who begged for it. I began to see food in terms of survival.

By the fourth week my major concentration was on eating and feeling the strength food gave. Like the cup of tea, eating had lost its social function. I didn't want any conversation interrupting my meal.

At the end of the month, although I still had lots of mental energy, I was physically tired. Sometimes I just sat. It wasn't that I didn't want to work. I just didn't have the energy. But I still had one security poor people don't have—enough money in my pocket to purchase food.

Because of this experiment I learned that I really cannot do anything significant *for* or *with* the poor. Unless I *am* poor, I can't help. Until we eat what they eat, sleep where they sleep, experience the struggles they experience, we cannot really understand.
—Paul Kennel
Calcutta, India

For you know the grace of our Lord Jesus Christ, that though he was rich, yet for your sake he became poor, so that by his poverty you might become rich."
—2 Corinthians 8:9

●●●●●●●●●●●●●●●●●●●●●●●●●●

Cross-Cultural Wisdom

I. **Nepal** ● When my Nepali women friends came to see my newborn baby they were astonished to find him sleeping all alone. They became seriously concerned upon realizing we even had him in his own room at night. How could I hear him if he cried?

Nepali babies sleep in their mother's bed with her until three or four years of age. They aren't allowed to cry for more than a few seconds, spending nearly every waking moment in someone's arms.

When I asked one new mother how often her infant nurses in a day she laughed at the absurdity of the question. The thought that one would even consider the number of times had never entered her mind. She couldn't imagine how to answer me.

How naturally the Nepalese leave chores to love, fondle, and relate to infants! Their willingness to include them in almost every moment of their waking hours, their joy in new life, even in the midst of high infant mortality, and their hope in spite of adversity are an inspiration to us.
—*Twila Miller*
  Butwal, Nepal

Tanzania • During our three years in Tanzania I rarely heard infants crying except in cases of illness. The constant closeness of being carried on the mother's back, tied snugly against her, provided complete security. To satisfy any hunger and sucking needs, the mother casually swung her baby forward for nursing.

When her baby became fussy, a Tanzanian mother swayed her body from side to side in a rocking motion. I couldn't help contrasting this womb-like movement with that of the metal and plastic swings we hang in doorways to keep our babies content or the closeness of body contact with the cold infant seats in which we Americans carry our babies.

When a Tanzanian child needed to be in the hospital, the mother stayed with the child. She shared the bed, did the feeding, and with her presence reassured the child that he/she was not abandoned. In our sterile, sanitary, North American pediatrics wards, this concept of family involvement in the care and treatment of children is only now beginning to be considered.
—*Flo Harnish*
  Ephrata, Pa.

Vietnam • While living in Vietnam, I occupied a small room with three young Vietnamese men. One day one of them announced that he would be moving out. He planned to rent a small house in order to take care of his aging mother.

In American society we think of all the problems living with the aged creates. Vietnamese look at the positive side. Elderly parents help take care of small children. This frees parents and gives grandparents a continued value. Grandparents spend hours with children teaching them customs and manners, telling them folk stories, or relating the history of their country

and people. The children not only gain knowledge, but watch grandparents growing old. They don't find old age a frightening and secretive thing. They learn to connect age and wisdom and can look forward to the time when they too will be respected for their years of experience and accumulated knowledge.
—*Max Ediger*
Bangkok, Thailand

C **Backward Look at Parenting** ● In my family, Dad was always consistent in his values and Mom was the most thrifty person in the county. Anything related to ecology and saving they were doing before it ever became popular. We were constantly nagging Pop because he had only two pairs of pants and both of them looked as if they were ready to fall apart.

As we got older we began to understand. Their priorities were to provide food for the family and a good education. They encouraged us to go to college and gave us some money to make it possible. They managed on the salary they had because they were committed to Christian principles.

We used to think the old people were oddballs. Now we find out that we're the oddballs!
—*Paul Kennel*
Calcutta, India

●●●●●●●●●●●●●●●●●●●●●●●●●●
Stewardship and Family Planning

I come from a family of seven children. Years ago I wanted to have four of my own. But because ours is a different world from that of our parents, my wife and I decided to stop at two. We want to use the world's limited resources wisely.

What does the size of our families have to do with this? Plenty. When God told Adam and Eve to be fruitful and multiply, he also commanded them to be stewards of the earth.

Some people argue that they can have as many children as they want as long as they can support them. They advocate controlling population in countries like India.

But, in fact, every North American baby born claims 25 percent more of the world's resources than a baby born in India. Since our Christian ideals call us to share equally, our decisions concerning the size of our families are important.
—*Ray Martin*
Accra, Ghana

Barb and I decided to adopt children rather than have a biological family. In our world of limited resources, many children already exist who are receiving inadequate care. Because of my experiences at a school for homeless and

emotionally disturbed boys, we believe that having our own
biological children would betray homeless children worldwide
who are experiencing physical, psychological, and spiritual
problems.

This decision was not easy for us, nor was it made until after
more than six years of marriage. We do not feel all should
agree with us.

Both of us love children and want to share our home with
them. In June 1978 Jonathan David, a 2½-year-old from
Korea, became our son—a truly thrilling experience!
—*H. A. Penner*
  Guatemala City, Guatemala

●●●●●●●●●●●●●●●●●●●●●●●●●●●●

Breast-feeding

Breast-feeding is not all instinctive, but information and   C
preparation help things go smoothly. I'm glad I tried it. The
emotional benefits were certainly a plus. My babies never
needed a pacifier and our family could go anywhere together
without much fuss.

Unfortunately, bottle-feeding has spread to poor countries
where the result is often disastrous. On a trip to Asia last year I
was glad to see North American church workers nursing their
babies. It's a good example to set. Our toddler benefited from
nursing on that trip when food was strange, milk rare, and the
water suspect.
—*Jill Miller Frey*
  Seneca, S.C.

When children were orphaned a century ago, relatives or other   P
families in the community raised them as their own. Another
emergency situation where caring means life involves sharing
human milk with sick babies or those who have lost their
mothers. Here are some facts:
1. A nursing mother can nurse two babies. Sucking stimulates
   milk production so a mother's milk supply can be doubled.
2. It's possible to collect and freeze excess human milk which
   can be shared with babies in need. Hand-express the milk,
   cool it, and freeze it in a clean glass jar. Milk can be
   collected at various times, cooled, and added to already
   frozen milk.
3. An adopted baby can be breastfed. I did this with
   reasonable success.
—*Mary Jane Hershey*
  Harleysville, Pa.

For information concerning all aspects of breast-feeding,
contact La Leche League International which has branches in
major North American cities.
—*Connie Buller*
Blair, Neb.

●●●●●●●●●●●●●●●●●●●●●●●●●●

Creative Deprivation

We've often needed to ask by whose standards we measure our
needs. Conforming just to establish our identity with those
about us doesn't seem right. By purchasing their every desire,
we might be depriving our children of the opportunity to be
creative.

Our daughter entered first grade in Japan. It was customary
there for a family to buy a desk for each new student. Everyone
seemed to be buying the well-advertised accessory-laden desk.
We knew a homemade one would be more sturdy. What should
we do? No one else in the class would have a homemade desk.
We discussed the pros and cons together and agreed to build.
Father, son, and daughter sat down to design it on paper. Later
everyone who saw it exclaimed over the craftsmanship. It even
prodded other fathers to try their hand at woodworking.

At this same time we had to decide what kind of backpack
our new elementary student would tote to school. Thirty to
fifty dollars seemed an exorbitant amount to pay for a child's
leather bag. Few children used hand-me-downs. Usually
grandparents bought the backpack, but ours in Iowa certainly
didn't know this. After hearing our daughter tell her feelings,
we realized that being different on this special occasion might
color the rest of her school experience. We bought the bag she
chose without flinching at the price.
—*Sue Richard*
Iowa City, Iowa

For several years we coaxed each of our children to take piano
lessons without much enthusiasm on their part. Then we
realized that for the cost of a year's lessons we could pay for
one of the refugee houses Mennonite Central Committee was
building in Bangladesh. Friends were going to Bangladesh to
help in the resettlement program. It seemed more meaningful
to be part of that effort than to be forced to practice the piano.
We decided to use the money for a refugee house.

Piano lessons are still a possibility in the future. They will be
more worthwhile when the children are interested in learning
to play.
—*LaVonne Platt*
Newton, Kan.

I had just returned from an overseas trip. Briefing me on
developments during my absence, Gladys concluded with a
reminder of Kristine's upcoming birthday. Unmistakably, our
youngest child wanted a new bicycle.

Still preoccupied with the poverty I had seen, I asked,
"What about all the bikes we already have rusting away in the
garage? For us to buy another bike would be a sin."

"I know what you mean," Gladys responded, "but each of
the other children got a new bike. She has her heart set on it."

It isn't right to ask an eight-year-old girl to bear the
responsibility for world poverty. How could I deny her what
she wanted when I was gone so often? I decided to talk to her
to see if she could enter into a decision with us.

Choosing the occasion and my words carefully, I explained
that we knew she needed a different bike, that the other
children had each owned a new one, and that on that basis of
equality she could demand one too. Then I told her the reasons
why we didn't want to buy another new bicycle just now.

I made a suggestion: "Let's get a can of paint and refinish
Susan's old twenty-six-incher. We can buy some decals and
make it look good. And then let's send a check for seventy-five
dollars to our mission board."

I could tell immediately this was a winner. We did the work
together: sanding, painting, adjusting, and straightening the
old wheel. We called it her "recycle bycle." When we wrote out
the check, Kristine prepared the cover letter, asking that the
money be used to buy food for the hungry—not cars or other
things!

She never regretted it. Every time she rode it she seemed to
have a private, inner satisfaction. Today she cherishes the
memory of a beautiful experience which helped teach her self-
denial and concern for others.

—Edgar Stoesz
  Akron, Pa.

I remember when our children asked for something that we
preferred not to purchase, often I told them we couldn't afford
it. But then I realized I wasn't telling the truth. I began to tell
them the real reason for not buying certain items so they could
learn to be selective themselves.

—Loretta M. Leatherman
  Akron, Pa.

●●●●●●●●●●●●●●●●●●●●●●●●●

Building Convictions

P   We involve our children, two of whom are teenagers, in
decision-making. Daily Bible reading and discussion of current
problems and issues are part of this process, giving them
reasons for their faith.

We encourage our children to participate in activities that
express their Christian concerns, including demonstrations and
letter-writing. We want them to know that they can do things
that aren't popular if backed by Christian convictions. Our
own example is most important. We don't make derogatory
remarks about their decisions.

Many friends visit us from all over the world.
Nonjudgmental listening gives us new ways of seeing ourselves.
We're glad our children can enjoy the enthusiasm and
expression of these visitors.
—*Sara Regier*
North Newton, Kan.

C   As a member of a citizens' group called Garbage Probe, I try to
educate people about the problems of waste. This includes
writing to all levels of government as well as to school boards
and churches. I've also spoken to many restaurant owners and
industrial executives about overpackaging.

In my talks with dozens of groups I find children most
receptive. The idea that every soda pop can takes ten cents of
their allowance, or that Dad pays enough in taxes for disposal
to buy a new bike each year or that it takes 400 trees a day to
print our newspaper is really mind-boggling for them. Children
can be taught not to abuse natural resources. Adult example is
required.
—*Carol Unruh*
Waterloo, Ont.

I.   I capitalize on the children's interests and incorporate them
into useful work. Their urge for adventure motivates Marta
and Ken, our ten- and eight-year-olds, to set out on a hike with
friends to look for firewood. They also feel good about panning
for shrimp and minnows on hot afternoons when the most
comfortable spot is in the river.
—*Dorothy Beidler*
Kalimantan, Indonesia

C   We allow or gently pressure our children to have small
businesses or otherwise use their talents and opportunities to
earn money in lieu of allowances.

The best project, passed on from child to child, has been the
watercress bed dug according to Department of Agriculture
bulletin directions. Cress is a healthful product in great

demand by farm markets, organic food distributors, and
others. It requires little care, and earnings per hour can double
minimum wage.
—*Ruth Eitzen*
  Barto, Pa.

●●●●●●●●●●●●●●●●●●●●●●●●●●●●

Weekly Poverty Meals

Meal I ● We lived in Samaru, Nigeria, for eleven years. Two
years ago when we moved to Kansas we were concerned that
our children—then ages ten, eight, and two—be brought up
feeling close to the problems faced by people in other countries.
As an agricultural economist with a major interest in
international agriculture, David was especially eager that we
do something together weekly about world hunger. As a result,
once a week our family has one supper which excludes meat,
fish, milk, and dessert. Our meal may be a starch and a
vegetable, rice with a little egg, or broth with bread. After
about two hours we may have a cup of coffee or tea. We each
put forty cents into a globe bank, accumulating this for a
nutrition project to alleviate malnourishment among the
world's poor.
—*Linda and David Norman*
  Manhattan, Kan.

Meal II ● We calculate one dollar per person each week as
money saved by having one simple meal and give it to a famine
relief program in addition to regular tithes and offerings.
   In this way a family of four can contribute $208 per year.
This would amount to $6,500 for a congregation of 125.
—*Joe and Constance Longacher*
  Richmond, Va.

●●●●●●●●●●●●●●●●●●●●●●●●●●●

Closing the Generation Gap ● My wife and I lived for
twenty-eight years in an apartment owned by Mennonite
Publishing House. When this space was needed for offices and
book storage, our daughter, Winifred, invited us to move in
with them. She and her husband had raised their children and
were living alone in a house we had helped them build on the
edge of town.
   After giving away extra furniture to grandchildren and
families who needed it, the four of us began integrated living.
We eat together, sharing the cost of groceries and utilities.
Shared housekeeping duties gives each person more free time.
We have more opportunity for meeting relatives, including
grandchildren and great-grandchildren. The older couple stays

younger by meeting the younger couple's friends. We can play
games together because there are more players.

This plan, often used by our forebears, has economic
advantages, too. It conserves energy by requiring less space to
heat or cool, less cooking, less electricity, and fewer appliances.
Rent and taxes are cut in half. Savings result from sharing a
telephone, a yard, a garden, transportation, newspapers, and
magazines. One couple is a tax deduction for the other. One
family looks after the home while the other goes on vacation.

As we share or sacrifice for each other, we get training in
unselfishness. This is the fuel for love. Each needs to give and
take.

—*Paul and Alta Erb*
   Scottdale, Pa.

Gifts from Grampop • My grandfather, John S. Longacre,
lived with us in our home while I was growing up. In a day of
searching for roots, I'm grateful for memories of Grampop
reminiscing about his teaching career, chuckling over antics of
his dating days, telling tales of my father's childhood years,
and describing the struggles of the church at the turn of the
century.

Whether we were washing dishes, podding peas, or peeling
peaches, his stories made every work project less tedious. A
close bond grew between us.

Perhaps the greatest gift I received from him was
undemanding companionship. Maybe because the
responsibility of discipline wasn't his, he listened
unjudgmentally to my girlish tales.

Grampop knew how to live in an intergenerational family;
he was useful without interfering. He expressed his opinions,
but didn't try to force his way on us. He was independent,
financially and otherwise, until his last years, driving his own
car till he was ninety. He enjoyed the privacy of his own room,
and the family respected one corner of our large living room as
his: a place for his chair, magazine rack, radio, and a
windowsill bookshelf.

Our life together wasn't always smooth. Grampop didn't do
the best job as dish drier. He didn't like pizza or other spicy
foods cooked to please teenagers. Loud religious radio
broadcasts and an extra-warm house temperature annoyed us
at times.

But the adjustments went both ways. Grampop's room
became his escape hatch when sibling rivalry was too intense or
teenagers' parties too loud and late. In later years when ill
health affected his good spirits, he sometimes criticized or
compared our ways with the ways of the past.

Life with a grandparent gave me an awareness of the
rhythms of life. I learned about the aging process through

Grampop's frequent catnaps in his chair and his bouts with
illness. He spent many hours reading his Bible. His many
conversations about heaven gave me a perspective of life as
eternal, beyond the immediate.
—*Anna Mary Brubacher*
  Kitchener, Ont.

Status or Sharing • What does one do with a lovely
fourteen-room Lancaster County farmhouse that has been in
the family for almost 100 years? In its prime, Herrbrook
housed Grandpa and Grandma Herr, daughter Susan and
husband Harry with their three children, Aunt Anna, and
Uncle Jake. Traveling relatives often relied on its spare
bedrooms.

The status and responsibility of owning this small farm with
its renovated three-apartment house have made Rod and me
increasingly uncomfortable. We could continue the apartment/
landlord arrangement but our search is for a better solution.
We wanted a way of life to symbolize our Christian pilgrimage.

The extended family which originally lived here inspired us.
Why not return to a shared community by renting the
apartments to intentional neighbors who would challenge and
reinforce our discipleship?

During the past six years we've loved and learned from the
numerous tenants who've been a part of our Herrbrook
community. Our children's bedtime prayers reveal their love
for our family as they ask God to bless Bob, Phil, or Kirsten.
At the same time we've felt the need for more permanency than
renting permits. A long-term commitment of joint ownership
seems a better way to share this bit of acreage that is ours only
to use, not to possess.

Letting siblings double-up in bedrooms, using certain rooms
and possessions in common, and offering garden space to city
dwellers are just a few of the ways we can be stewards. We
know our ancestors who built Herrbrook for sharing with
others would approve.
—*Mary Lou Houser*
  Lancaster, Pa.

One House, Two Families • For our two families, living
together began with a deep commitment to Jesus as Lord of
our lives. We had all lived among the poor and needy of other
cultures and wanted to simplify. We wanted to grow spiritually
and recognized the need for daily involvement, interaction, and
discipline. We also wanted our children to have other adults
who would know, love, and share responsibility for them.

After buying a large house we used all the rooms on the
main floor and basement in common. Upstairs each family had
its own bedroom area and bathroom. We put incomes, debts,
and assets in a common treasury from which each family

received an allowance to cover individual needs. The adults
took turns planning a weekly evening meeting for the five
children including puppet shows, stories, slides, hikes, baking,
and art activities. We ate our meals together, shared household
chores, and rotated leadership responsibilities. Together we
prayed and sang, worshiped and studied the Bible, laughed and
cried. We saved economically and environmentally and had
more free time to become involved in projects outside the home
because of shared chores.

Living together this way for three years we couldn't
maintain the illusion of being nice people. We had to learn to
resolve conflicts, to confess, and to challenge each other.
Decision-making was deliberate but time-consuming.

Our decision to separate was difficult. It seemed like an
admission of failure, a denial of a call, a step backwards from
the community we all wanted. To our surprise, decisions
concerning finances and possessions were not the most difficult.
We weren't sure if we could resolve interpersonal conflicts in
order to separate with respect for each other. As we counseled
we found healing for hurts and affirmed a time of separation.

Living under the same roof, we grew as individuals and in
our love for each other. Although we don't plan to live
together in the immediate future, we want to continue
challenging each other in spiritual life and awareness of world
needs.
—*Ken and Libby Nissley*
  Mt. Joy, Pa.
—*Herb and Sarah Myers*
  Rheems, Pa.

Keeping Up with the Sojourners ● Sojourners

Fellowship, a Christian community of about fifty people,
constantly calls me back to the biblical model of simplicity: I
am held accountable as a good steward of God's earth. In
supportive community we learn to trust each other and to trust
God whose love truly surpasses all *things*.

Two years ago even the pacifist in me might have preferred
to go to war if some nation appeared ready to cut off United
States oil supplies, threatening my "right" to unlimited use of
such "necessities" as a personal car and central heating. I've
come to realize that captivity to oil makes me captive to much
more, including support for dictators in countries that help
supply the American marketplace.

At Sojourners Fellowship we worship and minister together,
living quite well but rather simply by sharing all of our
resources. The cost of living in Washington, D.C., especially
for housing, is high. After subsistence costs that come to about
$200 per person per month, all else is freed for various
ministries in our neighborhood, our city, and, mostly through
Sojourners magazine, the larger world.

My lifestyle transformation is not complete nor has it been
without momentary pain. The important thing is that little
transformation could have been possible without the help of
brothers and sisters in a Christ-centered community. It's easier
to keep up with the Joneses when the Joneses live with you and
praise the God of compassion, not the God of consumption.
—Jim Stentzel
Washington, D.C.

A Change of Pace ● Recently our family decided that I
would leave a church agency administrative job. In the past
I've always had meaningful work in which the position or role
explained my identity. Then I read the following:

It is important to choose a profession not where we can do
the most good or find the most meaning, but where we can
live according to our humanity.—Jean Vanier

They [certain leaders] have learned to achieve far beyond the
average, but often for the wrong reasons. They may, in fact,
be achieving because of immaturity. They may be
performing in order to resolve a basic identity problem, or to
gain a sense of acceptance or security.—Virgil Vogt

I began to realize that meaning should come from being
whole within, focusing on my relationship with God rather
than a professional role.

Traveling was a major part of my job. It was interesting,
exciting, and growth-producing. But it took me away from our
family. We have two young children, and I want to experience
the coming years of their lives together with them. Someday I
can do this type of work again but I can never repeat these
years of their lives.

Finally, I feel called to a deep commitment to a local body of
believers. I need to be present to live out my conviction. This
can't be done when traveling.
—Lynn Roth
Lancaster, Pa.

Example Teaches ● In July 1976 our congregation invited
Samuel and Ollie Setianto, an experienced pastor couple from
Indonesia, to join us as pastor associates of Pleasant View for
approximately ten months. Before they came we were much
concerned about the practical aspects of their stay—housing,
financing, clothing, furniture, and transportation. Upon their
arrival, however, we soon realized that their contentment and
happiness were derived from personal and spiritual realities
rather than from the physical or material.

Sam and Ollie clearly understood God's call and direction
for them. In telling us of their courtship, their schooling, of
their preaching trips around Indonesia, and the birth of their
daughter, they spoke first of all of God's miraculous direction

and provision. They lived selflessly, sharing their concern for and experience in personal evangelism.

Both were tactfully sensitive to our materialism but some of our customs seemed shocking to them. "Think how many of our people would be living in a house this size," I heard Sam remark while visiting in our home. The amount of meat we eat and the disposables we take for granted were other cases in point.

Sam and Ollie must surely have had to struggle with the tension between the simplicity they knew in Indonesia and the complexities they found in middle-class America. Happily they were able to resist the tendency to be assimilated. Perhaps the test of the value of our experience with them is whether any of us at Pleasant View were able to adopt their Christlikeness of material detachment.
—*David Sommers*
  Goshen, Ind.

Caring for the Terminally Ill • In more than thirty years of nursing I have often witnessed death. Just as often I've wondered why we pay strangers to care for our loved ones at times like these. When death comes to someone you love, be a part of it.

My sister's thirteen-year-old son died of cancer at home in an attractive front room where he was part of the daily happenings. He could see his family at the dinner table and who drove up the lane. He enjoyed a pet spider outside his window and visits from the dog and cat. Although folding doors provided privacy when he wanted it, he loved being among his family. My sister took him on a fishing trip, something that he wanted to do. It was a joyous occasion— watching the sun rise and set and giggling over the milk carton urinal. His death was a treasured experience for the whole family because they were with him all the time.
—*Doris Hamman*
  Harrod, Ohio

He has given you the whole world to use, and life and even death are your servants.
—*1 Corinthians 3:22, LB*

●●●●●●●●●●●●●●●●●●●●●●●●●●

Sin and Healing

As Daniel purposed in his heart not to eat the king's meat, I purposed in my heart to obey God with all my being. With prayer and support, obedience was realized. I lost eighty pounds in five months.

I feel obesity is a sin. Scripture compares gluttony with

drunkenness; we've translated it into less abrasive terms such
as obesity and overweight. When I realized my tendency to
feed my frustrations with physically gratifying things instead of
looking to God for answers and satisfaction, change could
occur.

God lets us live overweight, if we want to live that way. But
he offers freedom through choice: "I have set before you life
and death, blessing and curse; therefore choose life"
(Deuteronomy 30:19). He strengthens us for the task.

Very few of us have inherent physiological defects that
predispose us to gain weight. Doctors can guide in weight
control. I didn't need to be told about being fat. I needed
brothers and sisters who loved me enough to care and pray
with me. This was the most important help I had.
—*Marc Waddell*
  Akron, Pa.

No doubt weight-watchers clubs have done people a lot of
good. But in a caring Christian community we should be able
to say to each other: "Hey, listen, I'm too fat, too; let's get
together and watch it." We could help each other and use the
money we'd ordinarily spend at a commercial club for more
worthwhile causes.
—*Katie Myers*
  Dacca, Bangladesh

●●●●●●●●●●●●●●●●●●●●●●●●●

I remember a little old man who gave me a peach seed he had carved into a basket. I don't remember his name, where he lived, or the occasion. I do remember the kindness.
—Carolyn Urich
  Bluffton, Ohio

We could all learn a great deal more about living a simpler life and enjoying it more if we listened to our elderly people. Saving time, money, and materials has always been part of their life.
—Dee Nussbaum
  Kidron, Ohio

The realm of international justice often seems so intangible and overwhelming. What can one person do? As I make an effort to become friends with foreigners who live around me I learn to appreciate their roots. As I gain friends I become concerned about the well-being of those in their homeland.
—Joan Barkman
  Akron, Pa.

Everything in our society is centrifugal to the family, or tears it apart. What can we do that is centripetal?
—William T. Snyder
  Akron, Pa.

We find it difficult to change our style of living drastically in one step. We often lack the imagination to do so. As we continually strive to eliminate the unnecessary, alternatives gradually become natural.
—Cathy Bowman
  Sumatra, Indonesia

In our church we had a whole Sunday evening service on obesity. A doctor spoke on obesity and disease, four people who lost a total of 200 pounds gave testimonies on how they lost weight and kept it off, and the pastor preached about it.
—Andrew Shelly
  Newton, Kan.

The exclusiveness of the nuclear family in America always strikes me. I think therein lies its death knell. One husband and wife can't be all that children need. Somalis seem to understand this better than we do.

Friends and relatives are more essential to family life than an abundance of time spent alone. The life of the family flows into the extended family.
—Bertha Beachy
  Salunga, Pa.

We were challenged to live simply during our three years among the rural poor in Africa. When we moved back to Pennsylvania, we decided to live in a community with poor people so that tension between rich and poor could still check us.
—Rich and Martha Sider
  Lancaster, Pa.

Sidewalk Lullaby

Tonight the children of no one
Will say their prayers on the street;
They will kneel to hollow god Hunger;
The shadows around tuck them in.
—Shari Miller
  Tegucigalpa, Honduras

Lord, I know not why I eat
And millions die of hunger.
What doth it profit thee to give me food?
What give I in return?
Crumbs, just crumbs.
Lord, here is thy bread.
—M. T. Brackbill
  from "Bread for Bread"
  published in Gospel Herald

He who knows one culture,
knows no culture.
—Source unknown

Kindness does not go rotten.
—Swahili proverb

Hope makes a good breakfast,
but a poor supper.
—Botswana proverb

Being well dressed
does not prevent one from being poor.
—proverb from Zaire

The garment of righteousness
never wears out.
—Oriental proverb

Index

Biblical Index